TOP
10
OF EVERYTHING
2010

TOP
10
OF EVERYTHING
2010

Russell Ash

hamlyn

Contents

Produced for Hamlyn by
Palazzo Editions Ltd
2 Wood Street, Bath, BA1 2JQ

Publishing director: Colin Webb
Art director: Bernard Higton
Managing editor: Sonya Newland
Picture researcher: Sophie Hartley

An Hachette UK Company
www.hachette.co.uk

First published in Great Britain in 2009 by
Hamlyn, a division of
Octopus Publishing Group Ltd
2–4 Heron Quays, London E14 4JP
www.octopusbooks.co.uk

ISBN 978-0-600-61742-6

A CIP catalogue record for this book is
available from the British Library.

Printed and bound in China.

10 9 8 7 6 5 4 3 2 1

Introduction

AGE OF MAJORITY

Twenty-one was once a significant number – the 'age of majority' at which one legally became an adult, traditionally and symbolically given the keys of the door and allowed to vote. There were 21 shillings in a guinea, the 21st Amendment to the US Constitution repealed Prohibition and leaders are honoured by 21-gun salutes. And a decade into the 21st century, this is the 21st annual edition of *Top 10 of Everything*.

BIG NUMBERS

One of the aims of *Top 10 of Everything* is to offer a snapshot of a wide range of topics – some people buy it as a sort of time capsule or memento of what was happening in the year in which a child was born. Work on this latest edition began as the world economic crisis struck and few escaped: the number of billionaires quickly declined, car makers cut output and airline traffic dwindled. As the world's debt mountain grew to unprecedented heights, figures in billions and trillions, once a feature of certain major Top 10 lists, became part of our everyday language. Its effects will endure for many years and will increasingly be reflected in future editions of *Top 10*. Yet alongside economic shrinkage, many lists demonstrate the opposite: there are still plenty of companies making vast profits, and as the Burj Dubai, the tallest structure ever built, nears completion we see though a series of Top 10 lists how the world's skyscraper skyline has altered over the past 100 years. We also consider the most common first names across the past 100 years, surnames around the world and the highest-earning films of each decade, with *Mamma Mia!* becoming highest-earning musical film ever. Four films have now earned more than £1 billion worldwide.

SURPRISE, SURPRISE...

While the world's largest countries and richest economies inevitably make a strong showing in many Top 10 lists, not every entry is a foregone conclusion: I continue to be surprised when the facts and figures reveal the unexpected – that Ireland out-eats the USA in chips and out-drinks the UK in tea; that Britain has the largest Sikh population outside India, while the biggest-selling English newspaper is not published in the USA or UK; that Barack Obama is some way off being the youngest US president. Alongside such facts as these, you will discover the fattest, the oldest and the tallest people, the world's strongest man, the country with the most letter boxes and the leading teams in the extreme sport of elephant polo, the album that stayed at No. 1 in the charts for over two years, the most venomous reptiles, the worst forest fires, the most corrupt countries, the countries with the fastest-shrinking populations, the year when London was overtaken as the world's largest city, the most northerly capital cities, the largest cities that are not capitals and the tallest buildings with holes in them.

MORE THAN JUST THE NO. 1

All these lists follow a rule that has been true since the first edition of *Top 10 of Everything*, which is that every list has to be quantifiable – measurable in some way or other: the biggest, smallest, first, last, tallest, deepest, sunniest, dullest, or worst, or chronologically the first or last. All the lists thus offer more than just the No. 1, and provide

a perspective in which to compare the subjects of the list. There are no 'bests', other than bestsellers, and 'worsts' are of disasters, military losses and murders, where they are measured by numbers of victims. Unless otherwise stated, film lists are based on cumulative global earnings, irrespective of production or marketing budgets and – as is standard in the movie industry – inflation is not taken into account, which means that recent releases tend to feature disproportionately prominently. Countries are independent countries, not dependencies or overseas territories. All the lists are all-time and global unless a specific year or territory is noted. If the UK does not figure in a country-based list, it is generally added as an extra entry.

SOURCES

My sources encompass international organizations, commercial companies and research bodies, specialized publications and a network of experts around the world who have generously shared their knowledge. As always, I happily acknowledge their important contribution (see page 255 for a full list of credits), along with that of everyone who has been involved with the book at all stages of its development on this and the previous 20 annual editions.

OVER TO YOU

I hope you enjoy the book. Your comments, corrections and suggestions for new lists are always welcome. Please contact me via the publishers or visit the *Top 10 of Everything* website www.top10ofeverything.com or my own www.RussellAsh.com

Russell Ash

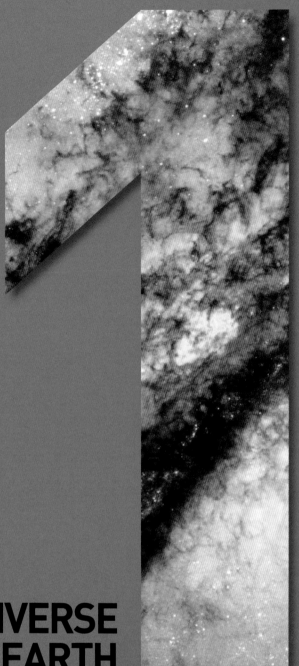

THE UNIVERSE & THE EARTH

Stars

TOP 10 **LARGEST STARS**

STAR / SOLAR DIAMETER*

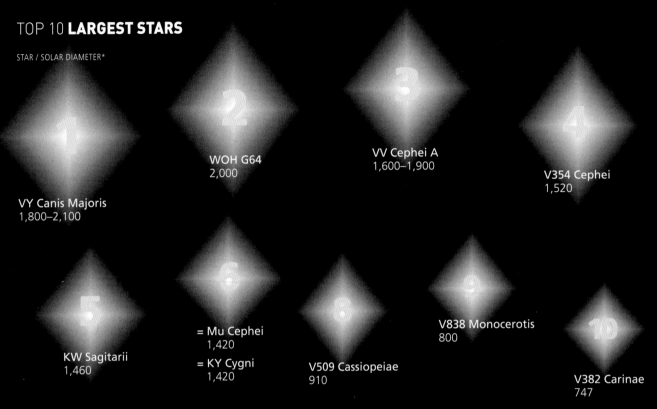

VY Canis Majoris
1,800–2,100

WOH G64
2,000

VV Cephei A
1,600–1,900

V354 Cephei
1,520

KW Sagitarii
1,460

= **Mu Cephei**
1,420
= **KY Cygni**
1,420

V509 Cassiopeiae
910

V838 Monocerotis
800

V382 Carinae
747

* Compared with the Sun = 1 (1,392,000 km/864,950 miles)

TOP 10 **BRIGHTEST STARS***

STAR	CONSTELLATION	DISTANCE#	APPARENT MAGNITUDE
1 Sirius	Canis Major	8.61	-1.44
2 Canopus	Carina	312.73	-0.62
3 Arcturus	Boötes	36.39	-0.05†
4 Alpha Centauri A	Centaurus	4.40	-0.01
5 Vega	Lyra	25.31	+0.03
6 Capella	Auriga	42.21	+0.08
7 Rigel	Orion	772.91	+0.18
8 Procyon	Canis Minor	11.42	+0.40
9 Achernar	Eridanus	143.81	+0.45
10 Beta Centauri	Centaurus	525.22	+0.61

* Excluding the Sun
# From the Earth in light years
† Variable

This Top 10 is based on apparent visual magnitude as viewed from Earth – the lower the number, the brighter the star. On this scale, the Sun would be -26.73 and the full Moon -12.6.

TOP 10 **STARS NEAREST TO EARTH***

		DISTANCE	
STAR	LIGHT YEARS	KM (MILLIONS)	MILES (MILLIONS)
1 Proxima Centauri	4.22	39,923,310	24,792,500
2 Alpha Centauri	4.39	41,531,595	25,791,250
3 Barnard's Star	5.94	56,195,370	34,897,500
4 Wolf 359	7.78	73,602,690	45,707,500
5 Lalande 21185	8.31	78,616,755	48,821,250
6 Sirius	8.60	81,360,300	50,525,000
7 Luyten 726-8	8.72	82,495,560	51,230,000
8 Ross 154	9.69	91,672,245	56,928,750
9 Ross 248	10.32	97,632,360	60,630,000
10 Epsilon Eridani	10.49	99,240,645	61,628,750

* Excluding the Sun

Source: Peter Bond, Royal Astronomical Society

Although the nearest stars are just over four light years from Earth, a spaceship travelling at 40,237 km/h (25,000 mph) – faster than any human has yet reached in space – would take more than 113,200 years to reach Earth's closest star, Proxima Centauri.

Starlight
*Easily observed from Earth's southern hemisphere, the unusually shaped
lenticular (between elliptical and spiral) Centaurus Galaxy is the fifth brightest.*

TOP 10 **BRIGHTEST GALAXIES**

GALAXY/NO.	DISTANCE FROM EARTH (MILLIONS OF LIGHT YEARS)	APPARENT MAGNITUDE
1 Large Magellanic Cloud	0.17	0.91
2 Small Magellanic Cloud	0.21	2.70
3 Andromeda Galaxy/NGC 224 M31	2.6	4.36
4 Triangulum Galaxy/NGC 598 M33	2.8	6.27
5 Centaurus Galaxy/NGC 5128	12.0	7.84
6 Bode's Galaxy/NGC 3031 M81	12.0	7.89
7 Silver Coin Galaxy/NGC 253	8.5	8.04
8 Southern Pinwheel Galaxy/NGC 5236 M83	15.0	8.20
9 Pinwheel Galaxy/NGC 5457 M101	24.0	8.31
10 Cigar Galaxy/NGC 55	4.9	8.42

Messier (M) numbers are named after French astronomer
Charles Messier (1730–1817), who compiled the first catalogue
of galaxies, nebulae and star clusters.

TOP 10 **GALAXIES NEAREST TO EARTH**

GALAXY	DISCOVERED	DIAMETER	APPROX. DISTANCE (1,000 LIGHT YEARS)
1 Sagittarius Dwarf	1994	10	82
2 Large Magellanic Cloud	Prehist.	30	160
3 Small Magellanic Cloud	Prehist.	16	190
4 = Draco Dwarf	1954	3	205
= Ursa Minor Dwarf	1954	2	205
6 Sculptor Dwarf	1937	3	254
7 Sextans Dwarf	1990	4	258
8 Carina Dwarf	1977	2	330
9 Fornax Dwarf	1938	6	450
10 Leo II	1950	3	660

Source: Peter Bond, Royal Astronomical Society

These, and other galaxies, are members of the so-called Local
Group. As the Solar System and Earth are at the outer edge of the
Milky Way, this is excluded. Over the next 100 million years, the
Sagittarius Dwarf Elliptical Galaxy, our nearest neighbouring galaxy,
will be progressively absorbed into the Milky Way.

The Solar System

Comet hunter
Caltech's Palomar Observatory, with its 200-inch Hale telescope,
a leading member of the Near-Earth Asteroid Tracking programme.

TOP 10 LONGEST YEARS IN THE SOLAR SYSTEM

	BODY*	LENGTH OF YEAR# YEARS	DAYS
1	Eris	557	295
2	Makemake	310	33
3	Pluto	247	256
4	Neptune	164	298
5	Uranus	84	4
6	Saturn	29	168
7	Jupiter	11	314
8	Ceres	4	220
9	Mars	1	322
10	Earth	0	365

* Planets and dwarf planets, excluding satellites
\# Period of orbit round the Sun, in Earth years/days

Venus and Mercury are the only planets in the Solar System with years of shorter duration than Earth-years – 225 and 88 days respectively.

TOP 10 ASTEROID-DISCOVERY OBSERVATORIES

	OBSERVATORY / PERIOD	ASTEROIDS* DISCOVERED
1	Lincoln Laboratory ETS, New Mexico, USA 1980–2008	96,589
2	Steward Observatory, Kitt Peak-Spacewatch, Arizona, USA 1981–2008	16,594
3	Palomar Mountain/NEAT, California, USA 1988–2007	11,925
4	Lowell Observatory-LONEOS, Arizona, USA 1998–2008	11,721
5	Palomar Mountain, California, USA 1949–2007	6,446
6	European Southern Observatory, La Silla, Chile 1976–2005	5,392
7	Catalina Sky Survey, Arizona, USA 1998–2008	4,859
8	Haleakala-AMOS, Hawaii, USA 1995–2005	4,804
9	Oizumi, Japan 1991–2002	2,422
10	Siding Spring Observatory, New South Wales, Australia 1975–2007	1,714

* Including other Near Earth Objects

TOP 10 LARGEST METEORITES EVER FOUND

	LOCATION / DISCOVERY / PRESENT LOCATION (IF DIFFERENT FROM IMPACT SITE)	ESTIMATED WEIGHT (TONNES)
1	Hoba West, Grootfontein, Namibia, 1920	60.00
2	Campo del Cielo ('El Chaco'), Argentina, 1969	37.00
3	Ahnighito ('The Tent'), Cape York, West Greenland, 1894, American Museum of Natural History New York	30.88
4	Armanty, Xinjiang, China, 1895, Xinjiang Geology and Mineral Museum, Urumqi City, Xinjiang	28.00
5	Bacuberito, Sinaloa, Mexico, 1863, Centro de Ciencias, Culiacán, Sinaloa, Mexico	22.00
6	Agpalilik ('The Man'), Cape York, 1963, West Greenland, University of Copenhagen, Denmark	20.10
7	Mbosi, Rungwe, Tanzania, 1930	16.00
8	Campo del Cielo, Argentina, 2005	14.85
9	Williamette, Oregon, USA, 1902, American Museum of Natural History, New York	14.14
10	Chupaderos, Chihuahua, Mexico, 1852, Palacio de Mineria, Mexico City	14.11

This lists only the largest meteorites or parts of meteorites, not the total weight of fragments. The Hoba West was found on a farm of that name in 1920. A 2.73 x 2.43 m (9 x 8 ft) slab, it consists of 82 per cent iron and 16 per cent nickel.

TOP 10 **COMETS COMING CLOSEST TO EARTH**

COMET	DATE*	AU#	DISTANCE KM	DISTANCE MILES
1 Comet of 1491	20 Feb 1491	0.0094	1,406,220	873,784
2 Lexell	1 Jul 1770	0.0151	2,258,928	1,403,633
3 Tempel-Tuttle	26 Oct 1366	0.0229	3,425,791	2,128,688
4 IRAS-Araki-Alcock	11 May 1983	0.0313	4,682,413	2,909,516
5 Halley	10 Apr 837	0.0334	4,996,569	3,104,724
6 Biela	9 Dec 1805	0.0366	5,475,282	3,402,182
7 Grischow	8 Feb 1743	0.0390	5,834,317	3,625,276
8 Pons-Winnecke	26 Jun 1927	0.0394	5,894,156	3,662,458
9 Comet of 1014	24 Feb 1014	0.0407	6,088,633	3,783,301
10 La Hire	20 Apr 1702	0.0437	6,537,427	4,062,168

* Of closest approach to Earth
# Astronomical Units: 1AU = mean distance from the
Earth to the Sun (149,597,870 km/92,955,793 miles)

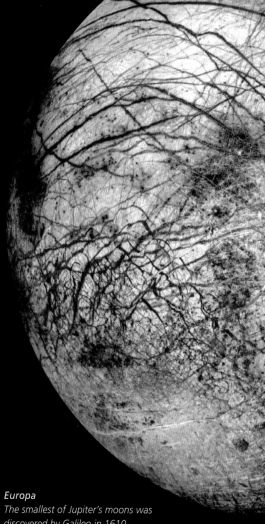

Europa
The smallest of Jupiter's moons was discovered by Galileo in 1610.

HALLEY'S COMET

Before Astronomer Royal Edmond Halley (1656–1742) studied and predicted the return of the famous comet that now bears his name, no one had succeeded in proving that comets travel in predictable orbits. Halley computed the orbits of some 24 comets, but the return in 1759 – as he had calculated – of the comet he had observed in 1682 established the science of cometary observation. Because it is a bright 'naked-eye' comet, numerous sightings were noted during preceding centuries, and by comparing them with calculations of the comet's orbit, these can now be identified as having been Halley's Comet. There have been about 30 recorded appearances, including that of 1066, believed to presage the victory of William the Conqueror, and the most recent in 1986 when it was examined by the *Giotto* probe.

Above: Halley's Comet on the Bayeux Tapestry, seen as a portent of William's 1066 victory.

Right: Westminster Abbey's 1986 memorial plaque to Halley depicts his comet and the Giotto spacecraft.

TOP 10 **LARGEST PLANETARY MOONS**

MOON / PLANET	DIAMETER KM	DIAMETER MILES
1 Ganymede Jupiter	5,262.4	3,269.9
2 Titan Saturn	5,150.0	3,200.1
3 Callisto Jupiter	4,820.6	2,995.4
4 Io Jupiter	3,642.6	2,263.4
5 Moon Earth	3,476.2	2,160.0
6 Europa Jupiter	3,121.6	1,939.7
7 Triton Neptune	2,706.8	1,681.9
8 Titania Uranus	1,577.8	980.4
9 Rhea Saturn	1,528.0	947.6
10 Oberon Uranus	1,522.8	946.2

Spaceflight

THE 10 FIRST MOONWALKERS

ASTRONAUT	SPACECRAFT	HRS:MINS	TOTAL EVA* MISSION DATES
1 Neil Armstrong	Apollo 11	2:32	16–24 Jul 1969
2 Edwin 'Buzz' Aldrin	Apollo 11	2:15	16–24 Jul 1969
3 Charles Conrad Jr	Apollo 12	7:45	14–24 Nov 1969
4 Alan Bean	Apollo 12	7:45	14–24 Nov 1969
5 Alan Shepard	Apollo 14	9:23	31 Jan–9 Feb 1971
6 Edgar Mitchell	Apollo 14	9:23	31 Jan–9 Feb 1971
7 David Scott	Apollo 15	19:08	26 Jul–7 Aug 1971
8 James Irwin	Apollo 15	18:35	26 Jul–7 Aug 1971
9 John Young	Apollo 16	20:14	16–27 Apr 1972
10 Charles Duke Jr	Apollo 16	20:14	16–27 Apr 1972

* Extra Vehicular Activity – time spent out of the lunar module on the Moon's surface

Second step
On 21 July 1969, Edwin 'Buzz' Aldrin followed Neil Armstrong to become the second man to set foot on the Moon.

THE 10 FIRST ANIMALS IN SPACE

NAME / ANIMAL / STATUS	COUNTRY	DATE
1 Laika (name used by Western press – actually the name of the breed to which the dog named Kudryavka, a female Samoyed husky, belonged) Died in space	USSR	3 Nov 1957
2 = Laska and Benjy (mice) Re-entered Earth's atmosphere, but not recovered	USA	13 Dec 1958
4 = Able (female rhesus monkey) **and Baker** (female squirrel monkey) Successfully returned to Earth	USA	28 May 1959
6 = Otvazhnaya (female Samoyed husky) **and an unnamed rabbit** Recovered	USSR	2 Jul 1959
8 Sam (male rhesus monkey) Recovered	USA	4 Dec 1959
9 Miss Sam (female rhesus monkey) Recovered	USA	21 Jan 1960
10 = Belka and Strelka (female Samoyed huskies) **plus 40 mice and two rats** First to orbit and return safely	USSR	19 Aug 1960

Top dog
A stray called Laika was the first animal to orbit the Earth aboard the Soviet Sputnik 2.

TOP 10 **LONGEST SINGLE SPACEFLIGHTS**

PERSONNEL* / SPACECRAFT / DATES	DURATION DAYS	HRS	MINS
1 Valeriy V. Polyakov Soyuz TM-18 / Mir / Soyuz TM-20 8 Jan 1994–22 Mar 1995	437	17	58
2 Sergei V. Avdeyev Soyuz TM-28 / Mir/ Soyuz TM-29 13 Aug 1998–28 Aug 1999	379	14	51
3 Musa K. Manarov, Vladimir G. Titov Soyuz TM-4 / Mir / Soyuz TM-6 21 Dec 1987–21 Dec 1988	365	22	38
4 Yuri V. Romanenko Soyuz TM-2 / Mir / Soyuz TM-3 5 Feb 1987–29 Dec 1987	326	11	38
5 Sergei K. Krikalyov Soyuz TM-12 / Mir / Soyuz TM-13 18 May 1991–25 Mar 1992	311	20	1
6 Valeriy V. Polyakov Soyuz TM-6 / Mir / Soyuz TM-7 29 Aug 1988–27 Apr 1989	240	22	34
7 Oleg Y. Atkov, Leonid D. Kizim, Vladimir A. Solovyov Soyuz T-10 / Salyut 7 / Soyuz T-11 8 Feb–2 Oct 1984	236	22	49
8 Michael E. Lopez-Alegria (USA), Mikhail V. Tyurin Soyuz TMA-9 / ISS / Soyuz TMA-9 18 Sep 2006–21 Apr 2007	215	8	22
9 Anatoli N. Berezovoi, Valentin V. Lebedev Soyuz T-5 / Salyut / Soyuz T-7 13 May–10 Dec 1982	211	9	4
10 Nikolai M. Budarin, Talgat A. Musabayev Soyuz TM-27 / Mir / Soyuz TM-27 29 Jan–25 Aug 1998	207	12	51

* All USSR/Russian unless otherwise stated

The longest single spaceflight by a woman was that of Sunita Williams (USA), who travelled to the ISS (International Space Station) on 10 December 2006, returning to Earth on 22 June 2007, a total of 194 days, 18 hours and 2 minutes.

Time traveller
Her long-duration missions aboard the ISS have placed Peggy Whitson at the top of the US astronauts table and in 20th place worldwide.

TOP 10 **MOST EXPERIENCED US ASTRONAUTS***

ASTRONAUT	MISSIONS	TOTAL DURATION OF MISSIONS DAYS	HRS	MINS
1 Peggy Whitson	2	376	17	22
2 C. Michael Foale	6	373	18	18
3 Edward M. Fincke	2	365	21	32
4 Michael López-Alegria	4	257	22	46
5 Carl E. Walz	4	230	13	4
6 Leroy Chiao	4	229	8	41
7 Daniel W. Bursch	4	226	22	16
8 William S. McArthur	4	224	22	19
9 Shannon Lucid	5	223	2	50
10 Kenneth Bowersox	5	211	14	12

* To 8 April 2009

The six missions of British-born NASA astronaut Colin Michael Foale, including extended stays on the Mir and International Space Station, established a US duration record, but was overtaken in 2008.

Oceans & Seas

THE 10 DEEPEST OCEANS AND SEAS

		AVERAGE DEPTH	
	OCEAN/SEA	M	FT
10	Mediterranean Sea	1,429	4,688
9	Gulf of Mexico	1,486	4,875
8	Bering Sea	1,547	5,075
7	Red Sea	1,611	5,285
6	South China Sea	1,652	4,150
5	Caribbean Sea	2,647	8,684
4	Atlantic Ocean	3,926	12,999
3	Indian Ocean	3,963	13,002
2	Pacific Ocean	4,028	13,215
1	Southern Ocean	4,496	14,750
	World ocean average	*3,730*	*12,237*

THE 10 DEEPEST DEEP-SEA TRENCHES

		DEEPEST POINT	
	TRENCH*	M	FT
10	Yap	8,527	27,976
9	Puerto Rico	8,605	28,232
8	Izu	9,780	32,087
7	New Britain	9,940	32,612
6	Bonin	9,994	32,789
5	Kermadec	10,047	32,963
4	Philippine	10,540	34,580
3	Kuril-Kamchatka	10,542	34,587
2	Tonga	10,882	35,702
1	Marianas	10,911	35,798

* With the exception of the Puerto Rico (Atlantic), all the trenches are in the Pacific

Each of the eight deepest ocean trenches would be deep enough to submerge Mount Everest.

TOP 10 HIGHEST TIDES

		AVERAGE*	
	LOCATION	M	FT
1	Burncoat Head (Bay of Fundy), Nova Scotia, Canada#	14.5	47.5
2	La Rance Estuary, France	13.5	44.3
3	Avonmouth, Bristol Channel, UK	12.3	40.4
4	Anchorage, Alaska, USA	9.0	29.6
5	Liverpool, UK	8.3	27.1
6	St John, New Brunswick, Canada	7.2	23.6
7	Dover, UK	5.7	18.6
8	Cherbourg, France	5.5	18.0
9	Antwerp, Belgium	5.4	17.8
10	Yangôn, Myanmar	5.2	17.0

1 man = approx. 1.8 m (6 ft)

* Average spring tidal range is the average difference between high and low waters during spring tides
# 16.27 m (53.38 ft) maximum

Endangered environment
Among the richest of the world's ecosystems, coral reefs are vulnerable
to over-fishing, pollution and the consequences of global warming.

THE 10 **SMALLEST SEAS**

SEA* / OCEAN	APPROX. AREA SQ KM	SQ MILES
1 Gulf of California, Pacific Ocean	153,070	59,100
2 Persian Gulf, Indian Ocean	230,000	88,800
3 Yellow Sea, Pacific Ocean	293,960	113,500
4 Baltic Sea, Atlantic Ocean	382,000	147,500
5 North Sea, Atlantic Ocean	427,090	164,900
6 Red Sea, Indian Ocean	452,990	174,900
7 Black Sea, Atlantic Ocean	507,900	196,100
8 Andaman Sea, Indian Ocean	564,880	218,100
9 East China Sea, Pacific Ocean	664,590	256,600
10 Hudson Bay, Atlantic Ocean	730,120	281,900

* Excludes landlocked seas

The two smallest seas are both gulfs – long bays extending far inland. The Gulf of California stretches south-east from the mouth of the Colorado River, separating the Baja California Peninsula from the Mexican mainland. The Persian Gulf is an arm of the Arabian Sea between Iran and Saudi Arabia.

TOP 10 **COUNTRIES WITH THE LARGEST AREAS OF CORAL REEF**

COUNTRY	REEF AREA (SQ KM)	% OF WORLD TOTAL
1 Indonesia	51,020	17.95
2 Australia	48,960	17.22
3 The Philippines	25,060	8.81
4 France – overseas territories (Clipperton, French Polynesia, Guadeloupe, Martinique, Mayotte, New Caledonia, Réunion, Wallis and Futuna islands)	14,280	5.02
5 Papua New Guinea	13,840	4.87
6 Fiji	10,020	3.52
7 Maldives	8,920	3.14
8 Saudi Arabia	6,660	2.34
9 Marshall Islands	6,110	2.15
10 India	5,790	2.04
World total (including those not in Top 10)	*284,300*	*100.00*

Source: UNEP World Conservation Monitoring Centre, *World Atlas of Coral Reefs*

Waterways

TOP 10 **LONGEST RIVERS**

RIVER / LOCATION	APPROX. LENGTH	
	KM	MILES
1 **Nile** Burundi, Dem. Rep. of Congo, Egypt, Eritrea, Ethiopia, Kenya, Rwanda, Sudan, Tanzania, Uganda	6,650	4,132
2 **Amazon** Bolivia, Brazil, Colombia, Ecuador, Peru, Venezuela	6,400	3,976
3 **Yangtze (Chang Jiang)** China	6,300	3,915
4 **Mississippi-Missouri** USA	6,275	3,899
5 **Yenisei-Angara-Selenga** Mongolia, Russia	5,539	3,441
6 **Yellow (Huang He)** China	5,464	3,395
7 **Ob-Irtysh** China, Kazakhstan, Russia	5,410	3,362
8 **Congo-Chambeshi** Angola, Burundi Cameroon, Dem. Rep. of Congo, Rep. of Congo, Central African Republic, Rwanda, Tanzania, Zambia	4,700	2,920
9 **Amur-Argun** China, Mongolia, Russia	4,444	2,761
10 **Lena** Russia	4,400	2,734

The source of the Nile was discovered in 1858, when British explorer John Hanning Speke reached lake Victoria Nyanza. By following the Amazon from its source up the Rio Pará, it is possible to sail for some 6,750 km (4,195 miles) – longer than the Nile – but because this entire route is not regarded as part of the Amazon basin, the Nile is still considered the world's longest river.

Major river
The Nile and its tributaries flow though nine countries in East Africa.

TOP 10 **LONGEST RIVERS IN THE UK**

RIVER	LENGTH	
	KM	MILES
1 Severn	354	220
2 Thames	346	215
3 Trent	297	185
4 Great Ouse	230	143
5 Wye	215	135
6 Ure/Ouse (Yorkshire)	208	129
7 Tay	188	117
8 Clyde	176	109
9 Spey	172	107
10 Tweed	156	97

TOP 10 **HIGHEST WATERFALLS**

WATERFALL / RIVER	LOCATION	TOTAL DROP M	TOTAL DROP FT
1 Angel Carrao	Venezuela	979	3,212*
2 Tugela Tugela	South Africa	948	3,110
3 Ramnefjellsfossen Jostedal Glacier	Nesdale, Norway	800	2,625
4 Mongefossen Monge	Mongebekk, Norway	774	2,540
5 Gocta Cataracta Cocahuayco	Peru	771	2,531
6 Mutarazi Mutarazi River	Zimbabwe	762	2,499
7 Yosemite Yosemite Creek	California, USA	739	2,425
8 Østre Mardøla Foss Mardals	Eikisdal, Norway	656	2,152
9 Tyssestrengane Tysso	Hardanger, Norway	646	2,120
10 Cuquenán Arabopo	Venezuela	610	2,000

* Longest single drop 807 m (2,648 ft)

Angel Falls
American adventurer James Angel (1899–1956) first sighted the world's tallest falls from his aircraft in 1933. When his discovery was confirmed, they were named Salto Angel, or Angel Falls, in his honour.

TOP 10 **GREATEST*** RIVER SYSTEMS

RIVER SYSTEM	CONTINENT	AVERAGE DISCHARGE AT MOUTH CU M/SEC	AVERAGE DISCHARGE AT MOUTH CU FT/SEC
1 Amazon	South America	219,000	7,733,912
2 Congo (Zaïre)	Africa	41,800	1,476,153
3 Yangtze (Chang Jiang)	Asia	31,900	1,126,538
4 Orinoco	South America	30,000	1,059,440
5 Paraná	South America	25,700	907,587
6 Yenisei-Angara	Asia	19,600	692,168
7 Brahmaputra (Tsangpo)	Asia	19,200	678,042
8 Lena	Asia	17,100	603,881
9 Madeira-Mamoré	South America	17,000	600,349
10 Mississippi-Missouri	North America	16,200	572,098

* Based on rate of discharge at mouth

Lakes

THE 10 DEEPEST LAKES

	LAKE / LOCATION	GREATEST DEPTH M	FT
10	Buenos Aires/General Carrera Argentina/Chile	586	1,923
9	Matano Sulawesi, Indonesia	590	1,936
8	Crater Oregon, USA	594	1,949
7	Great Slave Canada	614	2,015
6	Issyk-kul Kyrgyzstan	668	2,191
5	Malawi Malawi/Mozambique/Tanzania	706	2,316
4	O'Higgins/San Martín Chile/Argentina	836	2,743
3	Caspian Sea Azerbaijan/Iran Kazakhstan/Russia/Turkmenistan	1,025	3,363
2	Tanganyika Burundi/Tanzania/ Dem. Rep. of Congo/Zambia	1,471	4,8256
1	Baikal Russia	1,741	5,712

In 1990, Russian explorer Anatoly Sagalevitch set the record for the deepest freshwater dive (1,637 m/5,371 ft) in Lake Baikal in a *Pisces* submersible. On 29 July 2008, *MIR I*, a Russian mini-submarine, claimed it had set a new record in Baikal, but subsequently reported that it had attained only 1,592 m (5,223 ft). Lake Vostok, Antarctica, may be up to 1,000 m (3,281 ft) deep in parts, but it lies beneath the ice.

TOP 10 LARGEST LAKES

	LAKE / LOCATION	APPROX. AREA SQ KM	SQ MILES
1	Caspian Sea Azerbaijan/Iran/Kazakhstan/ Russia/Turkmenistan	371,000	143,244
2	Michigan/Huron* Canada/USA	117,436	45,342
3	Superior Canada/USA	82,103	31,700
4	Victoria Kenya/Tanzania/Uganda	69,485	26,828
5	Tanganyika Burundi/Tanzania/ Dem. Rep. of Congo/Zambia	32,893	12,700
6	Baikal Russia	31,494	12,160
7	Great Bear Canada	31,153	12,028
8	Malawi (Nyasa) Tanzania/ Malawi/Mozambique	29,600	11,429
9	Great Slave Canada	28,568	11,030
10	Erie Canada/USA	25,745	9,940

* Now considered two lobes of the same lake

TOP 10 LARGEST LAKES IN THE UK

	LAKE	COUNTRY	AREA SQ KM	SQ MILES
1	Lough Neagh	Northern Ireland	381.74	147.39
2	Lower Lough Erne	Northern Ireland	105.08	40.57
3	Loch Lomond	Scotland	71.12	27.46
4	Loch Ness	Scotland	56.64	21.87
5	Upper Lough Erne	Northern Ireland	42.99	16.60
6	Loch Awe	Scotland	38.72	14.95
7	Loch Maree	Scotland	28.49	11.00
8	Loch Morar	Scotland	26.68	10.30
9	Loch Tay	Scotland	26.39	10.19
10	Loch Shin	Scotland	22.53	8.70

The largest lake in England is Windermere at 14.74 sq km (5.69 sq miles), and the largest in Wales is Lake Vyrnwy at 8.03 sq km (3.10 sq miles).

TOP 10 **LAKES WITH THE GREATEST VOLUME OF WATER**

LAKE / LOCATION / VOLUME (CU KM/CU MILES)

Caspian Sea
Azerbaijan/Iran/Kazakhstan/
Russia/Turkmenistan
78,200 / 18,760

The Caspian Sea is the world's largest inland sea or lake. It contains some 40 per cent of all the planet's surface water and receives more water than any other landlocked body of water – an average of 340 cu km (82 cu miles) per annum, which is causing a steady rise in sea level.

Baikal
Russia
22,995 / 5,517

Tanganyika
Burundi/Tanzania/
Dem. Rep. of
Congo/Zambia
17,800 / 4,270

Superior
Canada/USA
12,100 / 2,903

Malawi (Nyasa)
Malawi/
Mozambique/
Tanzania
8,400 / 2,015

Michigan/Huron
USA/Canada
8,260 / 1,982

Victoria
Kenya/Tanzania/
Uganda
2,750 / 597

Great Bear
Canada
2,236 / 536

Great Slave
Canada
2,090 / 501

Issyk-Kul
Kyrgyzstan
1,738 / 417

TOP 10 **LARGEST RESERVOIRS IN THE UK**

LAKE / LOCATION	AREA	
	SQ KM	SQ MILES
1 Rutland Water England	12.59	4.86
2 Kielder Water England	11.01	4.25
3 = Grafham Water England	7.38	2.85
= Pitsford Water England	7.38	2.85
5 Chew Valley Lake England	4.87	1.88
6 Trawsfynydd Wales	4.77	1.84
7 Carron Valley Scotland	3.91	1.51
8 = Derwent Reservoir England	3.73	1.44
= Llyn Brenig Anglesey, Wales	3.73	1.44
10 Llyn Alaw Anglesey, Wales	3.13	1.21

Although Rutland Water is the UK's largest manmade lake or reservoir by area, Kielder Water is greater by volume.

Great lake
Hydrologically regarded as one entity, Lakes Michigan and Huron are together one of the largest by volume, and the largest freshwater lake by surface area.

Islands

TOP 10 **LARGEST LAKE ISLANDS**

ISLAND	LAKE / LOCATION	AREA SQ KM	SQ MILES
1 Manitoulin	Huron, Ontario, Canada	2,766	1,068
2 René-Lavasseur	Manicouagan Reservoir, Quebec, Canada	2,020	780
3 Sääminginsalo	Saimaa, Finland	1,069	413
4 Olkhon	Baikal, Russia	730	282
5 Samosir	Toba, Sumatra, Indonesia	630	243
6 Isle Royale	Superior, Michigan, USA	535	207
7 Ukerewe	Victoria, Tanzania	530	205
8 St Joseph	Huron, Ontario, Canada	365	141
9 Drummond	Huron, Michigan, USA	347	134
10 Idjwi	Kivu, Dem. Rep. of Congo	285	110

Not all islands are surrounded by sea: many sizeable islands are situated in lakes. Vozrozhdeniya Island, Uzbekistan, previously second in this list with an area of approximately 2,300 sq km (900 sq miles), has grown as the Aral Sea contracts, and has now linked up with the surrounding land to become a peninsula. There are even larger islands in freshwater river outlets, including Marajó, in the mouth of the Amazon, Brazil (48,000 sq km/18,533 sq miles), and Bananal, in the River Araguaia, Brazil (20,000 sq km/7,722 sq miles).

Largest Island in a Lake on an Island
Measuring 630 sq km (243 sq miles), Samosir, or Pulau Samosir, an uninhabited volcanic island in Lake Toba on Sumatra (the world's sixth largest island) is the third largest lake island in the world, but the largest island in a lake on an island. The largest island on an island on an island is an unnamed 0.016 sq km (0.006 sq mile) outcrop on Victoria Island, Canada.

Island nation
Honshu is the main island of Japan, the fourth-largest island country.

TOP 10 **LARGEST ISLAND COUNTRIES**

COUNTRY	AREA SQ KM	SQ MILES
1 Indonesia	1,904,569	735,358
2 Madagascar	587,713	226,917
3 Papua New Guinea	462,840	178,703
4 Japan	377,873	145,897
5 Malaysia	329,847	127,354
6 Philippines	300,000	115,830
7 New Zealand	270,534	104,453
8 Cuba	110,861	42,803
9 Iceland	103,000	39,768
10 Sri Lanka	65,610	25,332

All the countries on this list are self-contained island countries.

THE 10 **SMALLEST ISLAND COUNTRIES**

COUNTRY / LOCATION / AREA (SQ KM/SQ MILES)

1 **Nauru**
Pacific Ocean
21.2 / 8.2

2 **Tuvalu**
Pacific Ocean
26.0 / 10.0

3 **Marshall Islands**
Pacific Ocean
181.3 / 70.0

4 **St Kitts and Nevis**
Caribbean Sea
261.0 / 100.8

5 **Maldives**
Indian Ocean
298.0 / 115.1

TOP 10 **LARGEST ISLANDS**

ISLAND / LOCATION	AREA*	
	SQ KM	SQ MILES
1 Greenland (Kalaatdlit Nunaat)	2,175,600	840,004
2 New Guinea, Papua New Guinea/ Indonesia	785,753	303,381
3 Borneo, Indonesia/Malaysia/Brunei	748,168	288,869
4 Madagascar	587,713	226,917
5 Baffin Island, Canada	503,944	194,574
6 Sumatra, Indonesia	443,065	171,068
7 Honshu, Japan	227,413	87,805
8 Great Britain	218,077	84,200
9 Victoria Island, Canada	217,292	83,897
10 Ellesmere Island, Canada	196,236	75,767

* Mainlands, including areas of inland water, but excluding offshore islands

TOP 10 **LARGEST ISLANDS IN THE UK**

ISLAND / LOCATION	AREA	
	SQ KM	SQ MILES
1 Lewis and Harris, Outer Hebrides, Scotland	2,225.30	859.19
2 Skye, Hebrides, Scotland	1,666.08	643.27
3 Mainland, Shetland, Scotland	967.00	373.36
4 Mull, Inner Hebrides, Scotland	899.25	347.20
5 Ynys Môn (Anglesey), Wales	713.80	275.60
6 Islay, Inner Hebrides, Scotland	638.79	246.64
7 Isle of Man, England	571.66	220.72
8 Mainland, Orkney, Scotland	536.10	206.99
9 Arran, Inner Hebrides, Scotland	435.32	168.08
10 Isle of Wight, England	380.99	147.10

6 Malta
Mediterranean Sea
316.0 / 122.0

7 Grenada
Caribbean Sea
344.0 / 132.8

8 St Vincent and the Grenadines
Caribbean Sea
389.0 / 150.2

9 Barbados
Caribbean Sea
431.0 / 166.4

10 Antigua and Barbuda
Caribbean Sea
442.6 / 170.9

Mountains

TOP 10 HIGHEST MOUNTAINS IN EUROPE

	MOUNTAIN	COUNTRY	HEIGHT* M	FT
1	Mont Blanc	France/Italy	4,807	15,771
2	Monte Rosa	Switzerland	4,634	15,203
3	Zumsteinspitze	Italy/Switzerland	4,564	14,970
4	Signalkuppe	Italy/Switzerland	4,555	14,941
5	Dom	Switzerland	4,545	14,911
6	Liskamm	Italy/Switzerland	4,527	14,853
7	Weisshorn	Switzerland	4,505	14,780
8	Täschorn	Switzerland	4,491	14,733
9	Matterhorn	Italy/Switzerland	4,477	14,688
10	Mont Maudit	France/Italy	4,466	14,649

* Height of principal peak; lower peaks of the same mountain are excluded

All 10 of Europe's highest mountains are in the Alps; there are, however, at least 15 mountains in the Caucasus (the mountain range that straddles Europe and Asia) that are taller than Mont Blanc. The highest of them, the west peak of Mount Elbrus, measures 5,642 m (18,510 ft).

Height of Luxury

Europe's highest mountain, Mont Blanc, also has Europe's highest toilets: in 2007 two WCs were carried by helicopter to a height of 4,260 m (13,976 ft). During peak climbing season they are regularly emptied – also by helicopter.

TOP 10 LONGEST MOUNTAIN RANGES

	RANGE / LOCATION	LENGTH KM	MILES
1	Andes, South America	7,242	4,500
2	Rocky Mountains, North America	6,035	3,750
3	Himalayas/Karakoram/Hundu Kush, Asia	3,862	2,400
4	Great Dividing Range, Australia	3,621	2,250
5	Trans-Antarctic Mountains, Antarctica	3,541	2,200
6	Brazilian East Coast Range, Brazil	3,058	1,900
7	Sumatran/Javan Range, Sumatra, Java	2,897	1,800
8	Tien Shan, China	2,253	1,400
9	Eastern Ghats, India	2,092	1,300
10 =	Altai, Asia	2,012	1,250
=	Central New Guinean Range, Papua New Guinea	2,012	1,250
=	Urals, Russia	2,012	1,250

This Top 10 includes only ranges that are continuous. The Aleutian Range extends for 2,655 km (1,650 miles), but is fragmented across numerous islands of the north-west Pacific.

TOP 10 HIGHEST MOUNTAINS

	MOUNTAIN / LOCATION	FIRST ASCENT	TEAM NATIONALITY	HEIGHT* M	FT
1	Everest, Nepal/China	29 May 1953	British/New Zealand	8,850	29,035
2	K2 (Chogori), Pakistan/China	31 Jul 1954	Italian	8,611	28,251
3	Kangchenjunga, Nepal/India	25 May 1955	British	8,586	28,169
4	Lhotse, Nepal/China	18 May 1956	Swiss	8,516	27,940
5	Makalu I, Nepal/China	15 May 1955	French	8,485	27,838
6	Cho Oyu, Nepal/China	19 Oct 1954	Austrian	8,188	26,864
7	Dhaulagiri I, Nepal	13 May 1960	Swiss/Austrian	8,167	26,795
8	Manaslu I (Kutang I), Nepal	9 May 1956	Japanese	8,163	26,781
9	Nanga Parbat (Diamir), Pakistan	3 Jul 1953	German/Austrian	8,125	26,657
10	Anapurna I, Nepal	3 Jun 1950	French	8,091	26,545

* Height of principal peak; lower peaks of the same mountain are excluded

TOP 10 HIGHEST MOUNTAINS IN AUSTRALIA

	MOUNTAIN	HEIGHT* M	FT
1	Mount Kosciuszko	2,228	7,309
2	Mount Townsend	2,209	7,249
3	Mount Twynham	2,195	7,203
4	Rams Head	2,190	7,185
5	Unnamed peak, Etheridge Ridge	2,180	7,152
6	Rams Head North	2,177	7,142
7	Alice Rawson Peak	2,160	7,086
8	Unnamed peak, south-west of Abbott Peak	2,159	7,083
9 =	Abbott Peak	2,145	7,039
=	Carruthers Peak	2,145	7,039

* Height of principal peak; lower peaks of the same mountain are excluded

TOP 10 **HIGHEST MOUNTAINS IN NORTH AMERICA**

	MOUNTAIN	COUNTRY	HEIGHT* M	HEIGHT* FT
1	McKinley	Alaska, USA	6,194	20,320
2	Logan	Canada	5,959	19,545
3	Citlaltépetl (Orizaba)	Mexico	5,611	18,409
4	St Elias	Alaska, USA/ Canada	5,489	18,008
5	Popocatépetl	Mexico	5,452	17,887
6	Foraker	Alaska, USA	5,304	17,400
7	Ixtaccihuatl	Mexico	5,286	17,343
8	Lucania	Canada	5,226	17,147
9	King	Canada	5,173	16,971
10	Steele	Canada	5,073	16,644

* Height of principal peak; lower peaks of the same mountain are excluded

Mount McKinley was spotted in 1794 by Captain James Vancouver and in 1896 named after the then-US president. It was first climbed on 7 June 1913 by a party of four, led by London-born Reverend Hudson Stuck, archdeacon of the Yukon.

Far-ranging
The Cordillera del Paine, Chile, is part of the Andes, the world's longest mountain range.

TOP 10 **HIGHEST MOUNTAINS IN SOUTH AMERICA**

	MOUNTAIN	COUNTRY	HEIGHT* M	HEIGHT* FT
1	Cerro Aconcagua	Argentina	6,959	22,841
2	Ojos del Salado	Argentina/Chile	6,893	22,615
3	Monte Pissis	Argentina/Chile	6,795	22,244
4	Cerro Bonete	Argentina	6,759	22,175
5	Huascarán	Peru	6,746	22,133
6	Llullaillaco	Argentina/Chile	6,739	22,109
7	= Cerro Mercadario	Argentina/Chile	6,720	22,047
	= El Libertador	Argentina	6,720	22,047
9	Tres Cruces	Argentina/Chile	6,629	21,748
10	Incahuasi	Argentina/Chile	6,621	21,722

* Height of principal peak; lower peaks of the same mountain are excluded

Land Features

TOP 10 **LARGEST DESERTS**

DESERT / LOCATION	APPROX. AREA SQ KM	SQ MILES
1 Sahara, northern Africa	9,100,000	3,513,530
2 Arabian, south-west Asia	2,330,000	899,618
3 Gobi, central Asia	1,295,000	500,002
4 Patagonian, Argentina/Chile	673,000	259,847
5 Great Basin, USA	492,000	189,962
6 Great Victoria, Australia	424,000	163,707
7 Chihuahuan, Mexico/USA	362,600	140,000
8 Great Sandy, Australia	360,000	138,997
9 Karakum, Turkmenistan	350,000	135,136
10 Sonoran, Mexico/USA	311,000	120,078

This Top 10 presents the approximate areas and ranking of the world's great deserts, which are often either broken down into smaller desert regions or merged. The world deserts cover some 35,264,000 sq km (13,615,508 sq miles), or about one-quarter of the total land area.

Just desert
The Sahara, the world's largest desert, extends into 10 countries in North Africa, its southern border demarcated by the semi-arid Sahel.

TOP 10 **LARGEST METEORITE CRATERS**

CRATER / LOCATION	DIAMETER KM	MILES
1 Vredefort, South Africa	300	186
2 Sudbury, Ontario, Canada	250	155
3 Chicxulub, Yucatan, Mexico	170	107
4 = Manicougan, Quebec, Canada	100	62
= Popigai, Russia	100	62
6 = Acraman, Australia	90	56
= Chesapeake Bay, Virginia, USA	90	56
8 Puchezh-Katunki, Russia	80	50
9 Morokweng, South Africa	70	43
10 Kara, Russia	65	40

Source: Earth Impact Database, Planetary and Space Science Centre, University of New Brunswick

Unlike on the Solar System's other planets and moons, many astroblemes (collision sites) on Earth have been weathered over time and obscured, and one of the ongoing debates in geology is whether or not certain crater-like structures are of meteoric origin or the remnants of long-extinct volcanoes.

Maldives
Most of the Maldives has an average elevation of 1.5 m (5 ft) above sea level. Risk of sea-level rises may compel the entire population to move.

THE 10 **COUNTRIES WITH THE LOWEST ELEVATIONS**

COUNTRY*	HIGHEST POINT	ELEVATION M	FT
1 Maldives	Unnamed on Wilingili island in the Addu Atoll	2.4	7.8
2 Tuvalu	Unnamed	5.0	16.4
3 Marshall Islands	Unnamed on Likiep	10.0	32.8
4 The Gambia	Unnamed	53.0	173.9
5 Nauru	Unnamed on plateau rim	61.0	200.1
6 The Bahamas	Mount Alvernia on Cat Island	63.0	206.7
7 Vatican City	Unnamed	75.0	246.1
8 Kiribati	Unnamed on Banaba	81.0	265.7
9 Qatar	Qurayn Abu al Bawl	103.0	337.9
10 Singapore	Bukit Timah	166.0	544.6

* Excludes overseas possessions, territories and dependencies

Source: CIA, *The World Factbook 2008*

These 10 countries are definitely off the agenda if you are planning a climbing holiday, none of them possessing a single elevation taller than a medium-sized skyscraper. Compared with these, even The Netherlands' 321-m (1,050-ft) Vaalserberg hill makes the country's appellation as one of the 'Low Countries' sound somewhat unfair.

THE 10 **DEEPEST CAVES**

CAVE SYSTEM / LOCATION / DEPTH (M/FT)

1 Krubera (Voronja), Georgia
2,191 / 7,188

2 Sniezhnaja-Mezhonnogo (Snezhaya), Georgia
1,753 / 5,751

3 Lamprechtsofen Vogelschacht Weg Schacht, Austria
1,632 / 5,354

4 Gouffre Mirolda, France
1,626 / 5,335

5 Réseau Jean Bernard, France
1,602 / 5,256

6 Torca del Cerro del Cuevon/Torca de las Saxifragas, Spain
1,589 / 5,213

7 Sarma, Georgia
1,543 / 5,062

8 Shakta Vjacheslav Pantjukhina, Georgia
1,508 / 4,948

9 Sima de la Conisa/Torca Magali, Spain
1,507 / 4,944

10 Cehi 2, Slovenia
1,502 / 4,928

Deeper and Deeper
Discovered in 1960, subsequent exploration has progressively extended the known depth of the Voronja Cave, with 2,000 m (6,562 ft) first exceeded by an international expedition in 2004.

World Weather

TOP 10 **SUNNIEST PLACES***

LOCATION# / % OF MAX. POSSIBLE /
AVERAGE ANNUAL HOURS SUNSHINE

 Yuma,
Arizona, USA
91 / 4,127

 Phoenix,
Arizona, USA
90 / 4,041

 Wadi Halfa,
Sudan
89 / 3,964

 Bordj Omar Driss,
Algeria
88 / 3,899

 Keetmanshoop,
Namibia
88 / 3,876

 Aoulef,
Algeria
86 / 3,784

 Upington,
South Africa
86 / 3,766

 Atbara,
Sudan
85 / 3,739

 Mariental,
Namibia
84 / 3,707

 Bilma,
Niger
84 / 3,699

* Highest yearly sunshine total, averaged over a
long period of years
Maximum of two places per country listed

Source: Philip Eden

TOP 10 **DULLEST PLACES***

LOCATION# / % OF MAX. POSSIBLE /
AVERAGE ANNUAL HOURS SUNSHINE

 Ben Nevis,
Scotland
16 / 736

 Hoyvik, Faeroes,
Denmark
19 / 902

 Maam,
Ireland
19 / 929

 Prince Rupert, British
Columbia, Canada
20 / 955

 Riksgransen,
Sweden
20 / 965

 Akureyri,
Iceland
20 / 973

 Raufarhöfn,
Iceland
21 / 995

 Nanortalik,
Greenland
22 / 1,000

 Dalwhinnie,
Scotland
22 / 1,032

 Karasjok,
Norway
23 / 1,090

* Lowest yearly sunshine total, averaged over a
long period of years
Maximum of two places per country listed

Source: Philip Eden

TOP 10 **WETTEST INHABITED PLACES**

LOCATION / HIGHEST TOTAL ANNUAL RAINFALL (MM/IN)

 Lloro,
Colombia
13,299.4 / 523.6

 **Mawsynram,**
India
11,872.0 / 467.4

 Mt Waialeale,
Kauai, Hawaii
11,684.0 / 460.0

 Cherrapuni,
India
10,795.0 / 425.0

 Debundscha,
Cameroon
10,287.0 / 405.0

 Quibdo,
Colombia
8,991.6 / 354.0

 Bellenden Ker,
Queensland, Australia
8,636.0 / 340.0

 Andagoya,
Colombia
7,137.4 / 281.0

 Henderson Lake,
British Colombia, Canada
6,502.4 / 256.0

 Crkvica,
Bosnia-Herzegovina
4,648.2 / 183.0

For purposes of comparison, Manchester,
which is (incorrectly) reputed to be the
wettest city in the UK, has an annual
rainfall of 800 mm (31 in).

TOP 10 **HOTTEST PLACES**

	LOCATION*	HIGHEST TEMPERATURE °C	°F
1	Al'Azīzīyah, Libya	58.0	136.4
2	Greenland Ranch, Death Valley, USA	56.7	134.0
3 =	Ghudamis, Libya	55.0	131.0
=	Kebili, Tunisia	55.0	131.0
5	Tombouctou, Mali	54.5	130.1
6 =	Araouane, Mali	54.4	130.0
=	Mammoth Tank#, California, USA	54.4	130.0
8	Tirat Tavi, Israel	54.0	129.0
9	Ahwāz, Iran	53.5	128.3
10	Agha Jārī, Iran	53.3	128.0

* Maximum of two places per country listed
\# Former weather station

Source: Philip Eden/Roland Bert

Polar opposites
Earth's climatic range, from arid desert to arctic waste, is represented in miniature by some locations that experience remarkable temperature extremes, their hot summers contrasting with sub-zero winters.

TOP 10 **PLACES WITH THE MOST CONTRASTING SEASONS***

	LOCATION#	WINTER °C	°F	SUMMER °C	°F	DIFFERENCE °C	°F
1	Verkhoyansk, Russia	-50.3	-58.5	13.6	56.5	63.9	115.0
2	Yakutsk, Russia	-45.0	-49.0	17.5	63.5	62.5	112.5
3	Manzhouli, China	-26.1	-15.0	20.6	69.0	46.7	84.0
4	Fort Yukon, Alaska, USA	-29.0	-20.2	16.3	61.4	45.3	81.6
5	Fort Good Hope, North West Territory, Canada	-29.9	-21.8	15.3	59.5	45.2	81.3
6	Brochet, Manitoba, Canada	-29.2	-20.5	15.4	59.7	44.6	80.2
7	Tunka, Mongolia	-26.7	-16.0	16.1	61.0	42.8	77.0
8	Fairbanks, Alaska, USA	-24.0	-11.2	15.6	60.1	39.6	71.3
9	Semipalatinsk, Kazakhstan	-17.7	0.5	20.6	69.0	38.3	68.5
10	Jorgen Bronlund Fjørd, Greenland	-30.9	-23.6	6.4	43.5	37.3	67.1

* Biggest differences between mean monthly temperatures in summer and winter
\# Maximum of two places per country listed

Source: Philip Eden

TOP 10 **PLACES WITH THE LEAST CONTRASTING SEASONS***

	LOCATION#	COOLEST °C	°F	WARMEST °C	°F	DIFFERENCE °C	°F
1 =	Lorengau, New Guinea	26.7	80.0	27.2	81.0	0.5	1.0
=	Malacca, Malaysia	26.7	80.0	27.2	81.0	0.5	1.0
=	Malden Island, Kiribati	27.8	82.0	28.3	83.0	0.5	1.0
=	Ocean Island, Kiribati	27.8	82.0	28.3	83.0	0.5	1.0
5 =	Kavieng, New Guinea	27.2	81.0	27.8	82.0	0.6	1.0
=	Quito, Ecuador	14.4	58.0	15.0	59.0	0.6	1.0
7 =	Andagoya, Colombia	27.2	81.0	28.0	82.4	0.8	1.4
=	Labuhan, Indonesia	27.2	81.0	28.0	82.4	0.8	1.4
=	Mwanza, Tanzania	22.6	72.7	23.4	74.1	0.8	1.4
10	Belém, Brazil	26.1	79.0	26.9	80.5	0.8	1.5

* Smallest differences between mean monthly temperatures between warmest and coolest months
\# Maximum of two places per country listed

Source: Philip Eden

Natural Disasters

Near East/Mediterranean
20 May 1202
1,100,000

Shenshi, China
2 Feb 1556
820,000

Calcutta, India
11 Oct 1737
300,000

Antioch, Syria
20 May AD 526
250,000

Tangshan, China
28 Jul 1976
242,419

Nanshan, China
22 May 1927
200,000

Yeddo, Japan
30 Dec 1703
190,000

Kansu, China
16 Dec 1920
180,000

Messina, Italy
28 Dec 1908
160,000

Tokyo/Yokohama,
Japan
1 Sep 1923
142,807

There are some discrepancies between the 'official' death tolls in many of the world's worst earthquakes and the estimates of other authorities: a figure as high as 750,000 is sometimes quoted for the Tangshan earthquake of 1976.

Black Death, Europe/Asia
1347–80s
75,000,000

Influenza, Worldwide
1918–20
20–40,000,000

AIDS, Worldwide
1981–
>25,000,000

Plague of Justinian
Europe/Asia
AD 541–90
<25,000,000

Bubonic plague, India
1896–1948
12,000,000

= Antonine Plague
  (probably smallpox)
Roman Empire
AD 165–180
5,000,000

= Plague, India
1896–1907
5,000,000

Typhus, Eastern Europe
1918–22
3,000,000

= Smallpox, Mexico
1530–45
>1,000,000

= Cholera, Russia
1852–60
>1,000,000

Precise figures for deaths during the disruptions of epidemics are inevitably unreliable, but the Black Death, or bubonic plague, is believed to have killed over half the inhabitants of London, some 25 million in Europe and 50 million in Asia.

Yellow River
(Huang He), China
Aug 1931
3,700,000

Yellow River, China
Spring 1887
1,500,000

Holland
1 Nov 1530
400,000

Kaifeng, China
1642
300,000

Henan, China
Sep–Nov 1939
>200,000

Bengal, India
1876
200,000

Yangtze River
(Chang Jiang), China
Aug–Sep 1931
140,000

Holland
1646
110,000

North Vietnam
30 Aug 1971
>100,000

= Friesland, Holland
1228
100,000

= Dort, Holland
16 Apr 1421
100,000

= Canton, China
12 Jun 1915
100,000

= Yangtze River, China
Sep 1911
100,000

THE 10 **WORST TSUNAMIS**

LOCATIONS AFFECTED / DATE / ESTIMATED NO. KILLED

Southeast Asia
26 Dec 2004
>186,983

Krakatoa, Sumatra/Java*
27 Aug 1883
36,380

Sanriku, Japan
15 Jun 1896
28,000

Agadir, Morocco#
29 Feb 1960
12,000

Lisbon, Portugal
1 Nov 1755
10,000

Papua New Guinea
18 Jul 1998
8,000

Chile/Pacific islands/Japan
22 May 1960
5,700

Philippines
17 Aug 1976
5,000

Hyuga to Izu, Japan
28 Oct 1707
4,900

Sanriku, Japan
3 Mar 1933
3,000

* Combined effect of volcanic eruption
and tsunamis
\# Combined effect of earthquake and tsunamis

Often mistakenly called tidal waves,
tsunamis (from the Japanese *tsu*, 'port'
and *nami*, 'wave'), are powerful waves
caused by undersea disturbances.

THE 10 **WORST HURRICANES, TYPHOONS AND CYCLONES**

LOCATION / DATE / ESTIMATED NO. KILLED

Ganges Delta, Bangladesh
13 Nov 1970
500,000–1,000,000

Bengal, India
7 Oct 1737
>300,000

= Coringa, India
25 Nov 1839
300,000

= Haiphong, Vietnam
8 Oct 1881
300,000

Bengal, India
31 Oct 1876
200,000

Ganges Delta, Bangladesh
29 Apr 1991
138,000

Bombay, India
6 Jun 1882
>100,000

Southern Japan
23 Aug 1281
68,000

North-east China
2–3 Aug 1922
60,000

Calcutta, India
5 Oct 1864
50,000–70,000

The cyclone of 1970 hit the Bay of Bengal
with winds of over 190 km/h (120 mph).
Loss of life was worst in the Bhola region,
as a result of which it is often known as
the Bhola Cyclone.

THE 10 **WORST FOREST FIRES**

INCIDENT / LOCATION / OUTBREAK / ESTIMATED NO. KILLED

Peshtigo, Wisconsin, USA
8 Oct 1871
1,500

Cloquet, Minnesota, USA
12 Oct 1918
551

Hinckley, Minnesota, USA
1 Sep 1894
418

Thumb, Michigan, USA
5 Sep 1881
282

Sumatra,
Kalimantan, Indonesia
Aug 1997
240

Landes, France
Aug 1949
230

Matheson,
Ontario, Canada
29 Jul 1916
223

Greater Hinggan,
Heilongjiang, China
6 May 1987
213

Victoria,
Australia
7 Feb–14 March 2009
210

Miramichi,
New Brunswick, Canada
7 Oct 1825
160

Background: Devastation at Aceh
Aceh, Sumatra, was at the epicentre of the
2004 Indian Ocean tsunami that left an
estimated 186,983 dead and 42,883 missing.

LIFE ON EARTH

Extinct & Endangered

Scaled down
*Not all dinosaurs were earth-shaking monsters:
Saltopus, discovered in 1910 and known only
from fragmentary remains, is believed to have
been the size of a domestic cat.*

THE 10 **SMALLEST DINOSAURS**

	DINOSAUR	MAX. SIZE CM	IN
1	Micropachycephalosaurus	50	20
2	= Saltopus	60	23
	= Yandangornis	60	23
4	Microraptor	77	30
5	= Lesothosaurus	90	35
	= Nanosaurus	90	35
7	= Bambiraptor	91	36
	= Sinosauropteryx	91	36
9	Wannanosaurus	99	39
10	Procompsognathus	120	47

Discovered in Argentina, Mussaurus
('mouse lizard') is, at just 18–37 cm
(7–15 in), the smallest dinosaur skeleton
found, but all known specimens are those
of infants.

TOP 10 **CHIMPANZEE COUNTRIES**

	COUNTRY	ESTIMATED CHIMPANZEE POPULATION*
1	Dem. Rep. of Congo	70,000–110,000
2	Gabon	27,000–64,000
3	Cameroon	34,000–44,000
4	Guinea	8,100–29,000
5	Côte d'Ivoire	8,000–12,000
6	Congo	10,000
7	Uganda	4,000–5,700
8	Mali	1,600–5,200
9	Liberia	1,000–5,000
10	Nigeria	2,000–3,000

* Ranked on estimated maximum

Source: Julian Caldecott and Lera Miles, *World
Atlas of Great Apes and Their Conservation*,
University of California Press, 2005

All chimpanzees of both species,
Pan troglodytes and *Pan paniscus*
are found in 20 African countries.
Estimates of their total population
range from 172,200 to 299,200.

THE 10 **FIRST DINOSAURS TO BE NAMED**

	NAME	MEANING	NAMED BY	YEAR
1	Megalosaurus	Great lizard	William Buckland	1824
2	Iguanodon	Iguana tooth	Gideon Mantell	1825
3	Hylaeosaurus	Woodland lizard	Gideon Mantell	1833
4	Macrodontophion	Long tooth snake	A. Zborzewski	1834
5	Palaeosaurus	Ancient lizard	Samuel Stutchbury and Henry Riley	1836
6	Thecodontosaurus	Socket-toothed lizard	Henry Riley and Samuel Stutchbury	1836
7	Plateosaurus	Flat lizard	Hermann von Meyer	1837
8	Poekilopleuron	Varying side	Jacques Armand Eudes-Deslongchamps	1838
9	Cetiosaurus	Whale lizard	Richard Owen	1841
10	Cladeiodon	Branch tooth	Richard Owen	1841

The name Megalosaurus, the first to be given to a dinosaur, was proposed by William
Buckland (1784–1856), the Dean of Westminster, an English eccentric who out of scientific
curiosity ate the mummified heart of the French King Louis XIV.

TOP 10 **COUNTRIES WITH THE LARGEST PROTECTED AREAS**

COUNTRY	% OF TOTAL AREA	DESIGNATED AREA SQ KM	DESIGNATED AREA SQ MILES
1 USA	24.9	2,336,406	902,091
2 Australia	13.4	1,025,405	395,911
3 Greenland	45.2	982,500	379,345
4 Canada	9.3	925,226	357,231
5 Saudi Arabia	34.4	825,717	318,811
6 China	7.1	682,410	263,480
7 Venezuela	61.7	563,056	217,397
8 Brazil	6.6	557,656	215,312
9 Russia	3.1	529,067	204,273
10 Indonesia	18.6	357,425	138,002

Protected areas encompass national parks, nature reserves, natural monuments and other sites. There are over 100,000 such designated areas around the world, covering more than 10 per cent of the total land area. In the case of some islands, such as Easter Island, almost 100 per cent is designated a protected area.

Monkey Business

The series of British television advertisements for PG Tips tea that featured chimpanzees was launched on Christmas day 1956 and ran until 10 January 2002, making it the longest-running series in the world.

Reaching the limit
Elephants are found in 22 per cent of the African continent, an estimated total of fewer than 500,000.

THE 10 **COUNTRIES WITH THE MOST AFRICAN ELEPHANTS**

COUNTRY	ELEPHANTS*
1 Botswana	133,829
2 Tanzania	108,816
3 Zimbabwe	84,416
4 Kenya	23,353
5 South Africa	17,847
6 Zambia	16,562
7 Mozambique	14,079
8 Namibia	12,531
9 Burkina Faso	4,154
10 Chad	3,885

* Definite population

Source: International Union for the Conservation of Nature, *African Elephant Status Report 2007*

Amazing Animals

Above: Sumo seals
Elephant seals can weigh as much as three tonnes and include penguins and sharks in their diets.

Left: Lion king
Although tigers are typically longer, lions are often heavier, at up to 313 kg (690 lb).

TOP 10 **BIGGEST BIG CATS**

	SPECIES / SCIENTIFIC NAME	MAX. LENGTH M	FT
1	Tiger (*Panthera tigris*)	3.30	10.8
2	Lion (*Panthera leo*)	2.80	9.2
3	Cougar (*Puma concolor*)	2.00	6.6
4	Leopard (*Panthera pardus*)	1.90	6.2
5	Jaguar (*Panthera onca*)	1.80	5.9
6	Cheetah (*Acinonyx jubatus*)	1.50	4.9
7 =	Lynx (*Lynx lynx*, etc.)	1.30	4.3
=	Snow leopard (*Uncia uncia*)	1.30	4.3
9	Asian golden cat (*Pardofelis temminckii*)	1.10	3.6
10 =	Bobcat (*Lynx rufus*)	1.00	3.3
=	Clouded leopard (*Neofelis nebulosa*)	1.00	3.3
=	Ocelot (*Leopardus pardalis*)	1.00	3.3
=	Serval (*Leptailurus serval*)	1.00	3.3

TOP 10 **LARGEST CARNIVORES**

	CARNIVORE	LENGTH M	FT	IN	WEIGHT KG	LB
1	Southern elephant seal	6.5	21	4	3,500	7,716
2	Walrus	3.8	12	6	1,200	2,646
3	Steller sea lion	3	9	8	1,100	2,425
4	Grizzly bear	3	9	8	780	1,720
5	Polar bear	2.6	8	6	600	1,323
6	Siberian tiger	3.3	10	7	360	793
7	Lion	1.9	6	3	250	551
8	American black bear	1.8	6	0	227	500
9	Giant panda	1.5	5	0	160	353
10	Spectacled bear	1.8	6	0	140	309

Of more than 260 mammal species in the order *Carnivora*, or meat-eaters, many are in fact omnivorous, with some 40 specializing in eating fish or insects, including seals and bears – the order's largest terrestrial representatives

TOP 10 **HEAVIEST TERRESTRIAL MAMMALS**

MAMMAL* / SCIENTIFIC NAME / LENGTH (M/FT)	WEIGHT	
	KG	LB
African elephant (*Loxodonta africana*) 7.5 / 24.6	7,500	16,534
Hippopotamus (*Hippopotamus amphibius*) 5.0 / 16.4	4,500	9,920
White rhinoceros (*Ceratotherium simum*) 4.2 / 13.7	3,600	7,937
Giraffe (*Giraffa camelopardalis*) 4.7 / 15.4	1,930	4,255
American buffalo (*Bison bison*) 3.5 / 11.4	1,000	2,205
Moose (*Alces alces*) 3.1 / 10.1	825	1,820
Grizzly bear (*Ursus arctos*) 3.0 / 9.8	780	1,720
Arabian camel (dromedary) (*Camelus dromedarius*) 3.45 / 11.3	690	1,521
Siberian tiger (*Panthera tigris altaica*) 3.3 / 10.8	360	793
Gorilla (*Gorilla gorilla gorilla*) 2.0 / 6.5	275	606

* Heaviest species per genus; exclusively terrestrial, excluding seals, etc.

The list excludes domesticated cattle and horses, and highlights the extreme heavyweights within distinctive large mammal groups such as bears, deer, big cats, primates and bovines (ox-like mammals).

Prime primate
The largest of all primates, gorillas can attain weights that exceed those of even the heaviest humans.

TOP 10 **HEAVIEST PRIMATES**

PRIMATE* / SCIENTIFIC NAME	AVERAGE WEIGHT RANGE#	
	KG	LB
1 Gorilla (*Gorilla gorilla gorilla*)	135–275	297–606
2 Man (*Homo sapiens*)	45–91	100–200
3 Orangutan (*Pongo pygmaeus*)	30–90	66–198
4 Chimpanzee (*Pan troglodytes*)	40–50	90–110
5 Hamadryas baboon (*Papio hamadryas*)	20–45	44–99
6 Japanese (snow) monkey (*Macaca fuscata*)	10–30	22–66
7 Mandrill (*Mandrillus sphinx*)	11–25	24–55
8 Proboscis monkey (*Nasalis lavatus*)	8–23	17–50
9 Gelada baboon (*Theropithecus gelada*)	12–21	26–46
10 Hanuman langur (*Semnopithecus entellus*)	9–20	20–44

* Heaviest species per genus
\# Average weights range across male and female, ranked by maximum

Aquatic Creatures

THE 10 **PLACES WHERE MOST PEOPLE ARE ATTACKED BY SHARKS**

LOCATION	FATAL ATTACKS	LAST FATAL ATTACK	TOTAL ATTACKS*
1 USA (excluding Hawaii)	38	2005	881
2 Australia	135	2006	345
3 South Africa	42	2004	214
4 Hawaii	23	2004	113
5 Brazil	21	2006	89
6 Papua New Guinea	25	2000	49
7 New Zealand	9	1968	47
8 Mexico	20	1997	37
9 The Bahamas	1	1968	26
10 Iran	8	1985	23

1 fin = 10 attacks

Red fin = 10 fatal attacks

* Confirmed unprovoked attacks, including non-fatal, 1580–2007

Source: International Shark Attack File/ American Elasmobranch Society/ Florida Museum of Natural History

The International Shark Attack File monitors worldwide incidents, a total of 1,969 of which have been recorded since the sixteenth century. The 1990s had the highest attack total (514) of any decade, while 71 unprovoked attacks were recorded in 2007 alone.

TOP 10 **HEAVIEST SHARKS**

SHARK / SCIENTIFIC NAME	MAX. WEIGHT KG	LB
1 Whale shark (*Rhincodon typus*)	30,500	67,240
2 Basking shark (*Cetorhinus maximus*)	9,258	20,410
3 Great white shark (*Carcharodon carcharias*)	3,507	7,731
4 Megamouth shark (*Megachasma pelagios*)	1,215	2,679
5 Greenland shark (*Somniosus microcephalus*)	1,009	2,224
6 Tiger shark (*Galeocerdo cuvieri*)	927	2,043
7 Great hammerhead shark (*Sphyrna mokarran*)	857	1,889
8 Six-gill shark (*Hexanchus griseus*)	602	1,327
9 Grey nurse shark (*Carcharias taurus*)	564	1,243
10 Mako shark (*Isurus oxyrinchus*)	554	1,221

Source: Lucy T. Verma

Freshwater Record

The heaviest freshwater fish ever caught was a 2.7-m (9-ft) white sturgeon weighing 212.28 kg (468 lb), landed after a seven-hour battle by Joey Pallotta III at Benicia, California, USA, on 9 July 1983.

White sturgeon
A fisherman's prize catch, but a relative tiddler compared with the record-holder.

Green sea turtle
Once hunted as food and for their shells, the large green sea turtle is now protected as an endangered species.

TOP 10 **HEAVIEST TURTLES**

TURTLE / SCIENTIFIC NAME	MAX. WEIGHT	
	KG	LB
1 Pacific leatherback turtle (*Dermochelys coriacea*)*	704.4	1,552
2 Atlantic leatherback turtle (*Dermochelys coriacea*)*	463.0	1,018
3 Green sea turtle (*Chelonia mydas*)	391.5	871
4 Loggerhead turtle (*Caretta caretta*)	257.8	568
5 Alligator snapping turtle (*Macroclemys temmincki*)#	100.0	220
6 Flatback (sea) turtle (*Natator depressus*)	78.2	171
7 Hawksbill (sea) turtle (*Eretmochelys imbricata*)	62.7	138
8 Kemps Ridley turtle (*Lepidochelys kempi*)	60.5	133
9 Olive Ridley turtle (*Lepidochelys olivacea*)	49.9	110
10 Common snapping turtle (*Chelydra serpentina*)#	38.5	85

* One species, differing in size according to where they live
# Freshwater species

Source: Lucy T. Verma

The largest of the 265 species of *Chelonia* (turtles and tortoises) are marine turtles, with the Aldabra giant tortoises the largest of the land-dwellers.

TOP 10 **HEAVIEST MARINE MAMMALS**

MAMMAL / SCIENTIFIC NAME	LENGTH		WEIGHT
	M	FT	(TONNES)
1 Blue whale (*Balaenoptera musculus*)	33.5	110.0	137.0
2 Bowhead whale (Greenland right) (*Balaena mysticetus*)	20.0	65.0	86.0
3 Northern right whale (black right) (*Balaena glacialis*)	18.6	60.0	77.7
4 Fin whale (common rorqual) (*Balaenoptera physalus*)	25.0	82.0	63.4
5 Sperm whale (*Physeter catodon*)	18.0	59.0	43.7
6 Grey whale (*Eschrichtius robustus*)	14.0	46.0	34.9
7 Humpback whale (*Megaptera novaeangliae*)	15.0	49.2	34.6
8 Sei whale (*Balaenoptera borealis*)	18.5	60.0	29.4
9 Bryde's whale (*Balaenoptera edeni*)	14.6	47.9	20.0
10 Baird's whale (*Berardius bairdii*)	5.5	18.0	12.1

Source: Lucy T. Verma

Probably the largest animal that ever lived, the blue whale dwarfs even the other whales listed here, all but one of which far outweigh the biggest land animal, the elephant. The elephant seal, with a weight of 3.5 tonnes, is the largest marine mammal that is not a whale.

Airlife

TOP 10 HEAVIEST FLIGHTLESS BIRDS

BIRD / SCIENTIFIC NAME*	HEIGHT CM	HEIGHT IN	WEIGHT KG	WEIGHT LB	OZ
1 Ostrich (male) (*Struthio camelus*)	255.0	100.4	156.0	343	9
2 Northern cassowary (*Casuarius unappendiculatus*)	150.0	59.1	58.0	127	9
3 Emu (female) (*Dromaius novaehollandiae*)	155.0	61.0	55.0	121	6
4 Emperor penguin (female) (*Aptenodytes forsteri*)	115.0	45.3	46.0	101	4
5 Greater rhea (*Rhea americana*)	140.0	55.1	25.0	55	2
6 Flightless steamer# (duck) (*Tachyeres brachypterus*)	84.0	33.1	6.2	13	7
7 Flightless cormorant (*Nannopterum harrisi*)	100.0	39.4	4.5	9	15
8 Kiwi (female) (*Apteryx haastii*)	65.0	25.6	3.8	8	4
9 Takahe (rail) (*Porphyrio mantelli*)	50.0	19.7	3.2	7	2
10 Kakapo (parrot) (*Strigops habroptilus*)	64.0	25.2	3.2	7	1

* By species
# The flightless steamer is 84 cm (33 in) long, but does not stand upright

Source: Chris Mead

The flightless great auk, extinct since 1844, weighed about 8 kg (17 lb 6 oz) and stood about 90 cm (35.4 in) high. Other flightless birds were much bigger. The two heaviest, at almost 500 kg (1,102 lb 5 oz) were the elephant bird (*Aepyornis maximus*) that became extinct from Madagascar 350 years ago, and the emu-like *Dromornis stirtoni* from Australia. The tallest, but more lightly built, was the biggest of the moas of New Zealand, *Dinornis maximus*, that became extinct when the Maoris colonized the country, but prior to European settlement; there is thus no account of any living moa, and all evidence is based on discoveries of bones.

March of the penguins
The emperor penguin, the tallest and heaviest penguin species, is noted for the mass land trek of entire colonies during the breeding season.

TOP 10 LONGEST BIRD MIGRATIONS

SPECIES / SCIENTIFIC NAME	APPROX. DISTANCE KM	MILES
1 Pectoral sandpiper (*Calidris melanotos*)	19,000*	11,806
2 Wheatear (*Oenanthe oenanthe*)	18,000	11,184
3 Slender-billed shearwater (*Puffinus tenuirostris*)	17,500*	10,874
4 Ruff (*Philomachus pugnax*)	16,600	10,314
5 Willow warbler (*Phylloscopus trochilus*)	16,300	10,128
6 Arctic tern (*Sterna paradisaea*)	16,200	10,066
7 Arctic skua (*Stercorarius parasiticus*)	15,600	9,693
8 Swainson's hawk (*Buteo swainsoni*)	15,200	9,445
9 Knot (*Calidris canutus*)	15,000	9,320
10 Swallow (*Hirundo rustica*)	14,900	9,258

* Thought to be only half of the path taken during a whole year

Source: Chris Mead

This list is of the likely extremes for a normal migrant, not one that has become lost and wandered into new territory. Many species fly all year, except when they come to land to breed or, in the case of seabirds, to rest on the sea; such species include some types of swift and house martin, the albatross, petrel and tern.

TOP 10 COUNTRIES WITH THE MOST BIRD SPECIES

COUNTRY / BIRD SPECIES

1 Colombia 1,897		**6** Bolivia 1,449
2 Peru 1,881		**7** Venezuela 1,417
3 Brazil 1,772		**8** China 1,319
4 Ecuador 1,670		**9** India 1,302
5 Indonesia 1,632		**10** Dem. Rep. of Congo 1,174
UK 598		

Source: Avibase

Andean condor
The Andean condor is the largest flighted bird in the western hemisphere.

Above right: Great horned owl
Found across the Americas, the great horned is one of the largest owls.

TOP 10 **LARGEST BIRDS OF PREY***

	BIRD / SCIENTIFIC NAME	MAX. LENGTH CM	IN
1	Himalayan Griffon vulture (*Gyps himalayensis*)	150	59
2	Californian condor (*Gymnogyps californianus*)	134	53
3	Andean condor (*Vultur gryphus*)	130	51
4 =	Lammergeier (*Gypaetus barbatus*)	115	45
=	Lappet-faced vulture (*Torgos tracheliotus*)	115	45
6	Eurasian Griffon vulture (*Gyps fulvus*)	110	43
7	European black vulture (*Aegypus monachus*)	107	42
8	Harpy eagle (*Harpia harpyja*)	105	41
9	Wedge-tailed eagle (*Aquila audax*)	104	41
10	Ruppell's griffon (*Gyps rueppellii*)	101	40

* By length, diurnal only – hence excluding owls

TOP 10 **LARGEST OWLS**

	OWL / SCIENTIFIC NAME*	WINGSPAN CM	IN	WEIGHT KG	LB	OZ
1	Eurasian eagle-owl (*Bubo bubo*)	75	29	4.20	9	4
2	Verraux's eagle-owl (*Bubo lacteus*)	65	26	3.11	6	14
3	Snowy owl (*Bubo scandiacus*)	70	28	2.95	6	8
4	Great horned owl (*Bubo virginianus*)	60	24	2.50	5	8
5	Pel's fishing-owl (*Scotopelia peli*)	63	25	2.32	5	2
6	Pharaoh eagle-owl (*Bubo ascalaphus*)	50	20	2.30	5	1
7	Cape eagle-owl (*Bubo capensis*)	58	23	1.80	3	15
8	Great grey owl (*Strix nebulosa*)	69	27	1.70	3	12
9	Powerful owl (*Ninox strenua*)	60	24	1.50	3	5
10	Ural owl (*Strix uralensis*)	62	24	1.30	2	14

* Some owls closely related to these species may be of similar size; most measurements are from female owls as they are usually larger

Source: Chris Mead

Pets

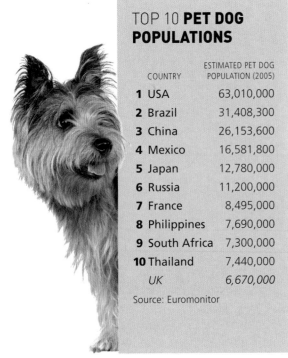

TOP 10 PET DOG POPULATIONS

	COUNTRY	ESTIMATED PET DOG POPULATION (2005)
1	USA	63,010,000
2	Brazil	31,408,300
3	China	26,153,600
4	Mexico	16,581,800
5	Japan	12,780,000
6	Russia	11,200,000
7	France	8,495,000
8	Philippines	7,690,000
9	South Africa	7,300,000
10	Thailand	7,440,000
	UK	*6,670,000*

Source: Euromonitor

TOP 10 PET CAT POPULATIONS

	COUNTRY	ESTIMATED PET CAT POPULATION (2005)
1	USA	81,420,000
2	China	58,180,100
3	Russia	17,100,000
4	Brazil	12,234,000
5	Japan	11,500,000
6	France	9,960,000
7	UK	9,200,000
8	Germany	7,600,000
9	Ukraine	7,470,000
10	Italy	7,430,000

Source: Euromonitor

TOP 10 CELEBRITY PET NAMES IN THE UK

NAME / CELEBRITY

1 Tyson (Mike)

2 Harry (Potter or Prince)

3 Ozzy (Osbourne)

4 Robbie (Williams)

5 Rooney (Wayne)

6 Beckham (David)

7 Paris (Hilton)

8 Elvis (Presley)

9 Jessie (Wallace – Kat Slater in EastEnders)

10 Britney (Spears)

Based on a survey of dogs and cats treated at the PDSA's 47 PetAid hospitals.

TOP 10 PET BIRD POPULATIONS

COUNTRY / ESTIMATED PET BIRD POPULATION (2005)

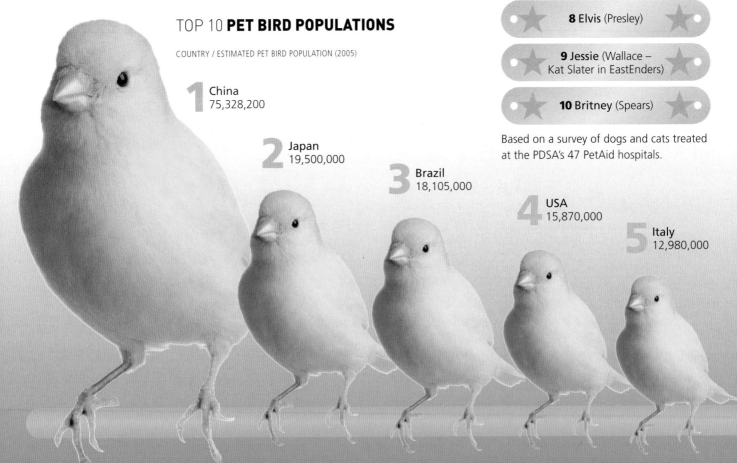

1 China
75,328,200

2 Japan
19,500,000

3 Brazil
18,105,000

4 USA
15,870,000

5 Italy
12,980,000

TOP 10 **PET FISH POPULATIONS**

	COUNTRY	ESTIMATED PET FISH POPULATION (2005)
1	USA	147,290,000
2	China	140,778,200
3	Germany	53,500,000
4	France	35,910,000
5	Japan	34,550,000
6	Italy	29,400,000
7	UK	21,800,000
8	Russia	20,600,000
9	Philippines	19,552,300
10	Australia	13,600,000

Punk pet
The ownership of certain rare or dangerous reptile species is restricted by law, but some 30 million are kept as pets in the Top 10 countries alone.

Source: Euromonitor

TOP 10 **PET REPTILE POPULATIONS**

	COUNTRY	ESTIMATED PET REPTILE POPULATION (2005)			
1	USA	18,371,000	6	Russia	600,000
2	China	4,682,100	7	Spain	234,000
3	UK	2,010,000	8	Australia	215,000
4	France	1,500,000	9	Canada	196,000
5	Italy	1,400,000	10	Thailand	195,000

Source: Euromonitor

6 Turkey 10,437,000	7 Spain 7,900,000	8 Australia 7,850,000	9 France 6,590,000	10 Germany 4,100,000

UK 2,870,000
Source: Euromonitor

Snakes & Reptiles

TOP 10 **LARGEST REPTILE FAMILIES**

FAMILY	KNOWN SPECIES
1 Colubridae (snakes)	1,827
2 Scincidae (skinks)	1,305
3 Gekkonidae (geckos)	1,076
4 Polychrotidae (anole lizards)	393
5 Agamidae (lizards)	381
6 Tropiduridae (lizards)	309
7 Lacertidae (true lizards)	279
8 Viperidae (viperid snakes)	259
9 Typhlopidae (blind snakes)	233
10 Gymnophthalmidae (spectacled lizards)	193

The *Colubridae* family encompasses approximately half of all known snake species, from grass snakes to garter snakes, with examples found on every continent except Antarctica.

Tokay gecko
The nocturnal tree-dwelling gecko is found throughout Southeast Asia and is an invasive species in several US states.

TOP 10 **FROGS AND TOADS WITH THE LARGEST CLUTCH SIZES***

	SPECIES / SCIENTIFIC NAME	EGG SIZE (MM)	AVERAGE NO. OF EGGS IN CLUTCH
1	River frog (*Rana fuscigula*)	1.50	15,000
2	Crawfish frog (*Rana areolata*)	1.84	6,000
3	Gulf Coast toad (*Bufo valliceps*)	1.23	4,100
4	Bahia Forest frog (*Macrogenioglottus alipioi*)	1.50	3,650
5	Giant African bullfrog (*Pyxicephalus adspersus*)	2.00	3,500
6	Marbled or veined tree frog (*Phrynohyas venulosa*)	1.60	2,920
7	Mangrove or crab-eating frog (*Rana cancrivora*)	1.25	2,527
8	Cape sand frog (*Tomopterna delalandii*)	1.50	2,500
9	Gladiator frog (*Hyla rosenbergi*)	1.95	2,350
10 =	Wood frog (*Rana sylvatica*)	1.90	1,750
=	Yosemite toad (*Bufo canorus*)	2.00	1,750

* For which data are available; all eggs and larvae aquatic

TOP 10 **LIZARDS WITH THE LARGEST CLUTCH SIZES**

	SPECIES* / SCIENTIFIC NAME	AVERAGE NO. OF EGGS IN CLUTCH
1	Nile monitor (*Varanus niloticus*)	40–60
2	Senegal chameleon (*Chamaeleo senegalensis*)	7–60
3	Flap-necked chameleon (*Chamaeleo dilepis*)	23–50
4	Mexican spiny-tailed iguana (*Ctenosaura pectinata*)	49
5	Green iguana (*Iguana iguana*)	24–45
6	Texas horned lizard (*Phrynosoma cornutum*)	14–37
7	Common tegu (*Tupinambis teguixin*)	6–32
8	Short-horned lizard (*Phrynosoma douglassi*)	5–31
9	Spiny-tailed iguana (*Ctenosaura similis*)	20–30
10	Spiny-tailed or black iguana (*Ctenosaura acanthura*)	17–28

* For which data available, ranked by maxima

Green mamba
The dendrotoxin in the venom of the green mamba is less deadly than that of the black mamba, but still potentially lethal.

TOP 10 **COUNTRIES WITH THE MOST REPTILE SPECIES**

	COUNTRY	REPTILE SPECIES
1	Australia	880
2	Mexico	837
3	Indonesia	749
4	Brazil	651
5	India	521
6	Colombia	518
7	China	424
8	Ecuador	419
9	Malaysia	388
10	Madagascar	383
	UK	*16*

Source: World Conservation Monitoring Centre of the United Nations Environment Programme (UNEP-WCMC)

The world total of reptile species is 8,240. This includes lizards (4,765 species), snakes (2,978), turtles (307), crocodiles (23) and tuataras (2). Although found on every continent except Antarctica, the number of species in each country ranges from the Top 10 down to those with few representatives, such as Ireland, famously having no snakes and just six reptiles.

THE 10 **MOST VENOMOUS REPTILES AND AMPHIBIANS**

CREATURE* / TOXIN / FATAL AMOUNT(MG)#

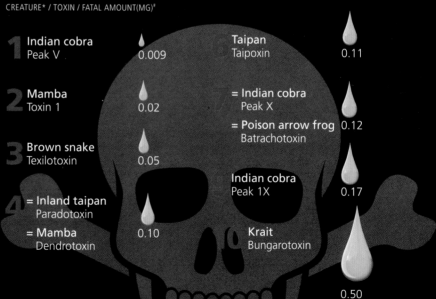

1 Indian cobra
Peak V — 0.009

2 Mamba
Toxin 1 — 0.02

3 Brown snake
Texilotoxin — 0.05

4 = Inland taipan
Paradotoxin

= Mamba
Dendrotoxin — 0.10

Taipan
Taipoxin — 0.11

= Indian cobra
Peak X

= Poison arrow frog 0.12
Batrachotoxin

Indian cobra
Peak 1X — 0.17

Krait
Bungarotoxin — 0.50

* Excluding bacteria
\# Quantity required to kill an average-sized human adult

The venom of these creatures is almost unbelievably powerful: 1 mg (the approximate weight of a banknote) of Mamba Toxin 1 would be sufficient to kill 50 people. Other than reptiles, such creatures as scorpions (0.5 mg) and black widow spiders (1.0 mg) fall just outside the Top 10. Were bacteria included, 12 kg of the deadly Botulinus Toxin A (fatal dose just 0.000002 mg) would easily kill the entire population of the world. Even deadly poisons such as strychnine (35 mg) and cyanide (700 mg) seem relatively innocuous in comparison.

Insects & Spiders

TOP 10 DEADLIEST SPIDERS

SPIDER / SCIENTIFIC NAME / RANGE

 1 Banana spider (*Phonenutria nigriventer*)
Central and South America

 2 Sydney funnelweb (*Atrax robustus*)
Australia

 3 Wolf spider (*Lycosa raptoria/erythrognatha*)
Central and South America

 4 Black widow (*Latrodectus sp.*)
Widespread

 5 Violin spider/Recluse spider (*Loxesceles reclusa*)
Widespread

 6 Sac spider (*Cheiracanthium punctorium*)
Central Europe

 7 Tarantula (*Eurypelma rubropilosum*)
Neotropics

8 Tarantula (*Acanthoscurria atrox*)
Neotropics

9 Tarantula (*Lasiodora klugi*)
Neotropics

10 Tarantula (*Pamphobeteus sp.*)
Neotropics

This list ranks spiders according to their 'lethal potential' –
their venom yield divided by their venom potency.

Sydney funnelweb spider
Australia's deadliest spider can kill in minutes.

TOP 10 LARGEST SPIDERS

	SPECIES / SCIENTIFIC NAME	LEG SPAN MM	IN
1	Huntsman spider (*Heteropoda maxima*)	300	11.8
2	Brazilian salmon pink (*Lasiodora parahybana*)	270	10.6
3	Brazilian ginat tawny red (*Grammostola mollicoma*)	260	10.2
4 =	Goliath tarantula or bird-eating spider (*Theraphosa blondi*)	254	10.0
=	Wolf spider (*Cupiennius sallei*)	254	10.0
6 =	Purple bloom bird-eating (*Xenesthis immanis*)	230	9.1
=	Xenesthis monstrosa	230	9.1
8	Hercules baboon (*Hysterocrates hercules*)	203	8.0
9	Hysterocrates sp.	178	7.0
10	Tegenaria parietin	140	5.5

TOP 10 **LARGEST BUTTERFLIES**

BUTTERFLY / SCIENTIFIC NAME	APPROX. WINGSPAN MM	IN
1 Queen Alexandra's birdwing (*Ornithoptera alexandrae*)	280	11.0
2 African giant swallowtail (*Papilio antimachus*)	230	9.1
3 Goliath birdwing (*Ornithoptera goliath*)	210	8.3
4 = Buru opalescent birdwing (*Troides prattorum*)	200	7.9
= Birdwing (*Trogonoptera trojana*)	200	7.9
= Birdwing (*Troides hypolitus*)	200	7.9
7 = Chimaera birdwing (*Ornithoptera chimaera*)	190	7.5
= *Ornithoptera lydius*	190	7.5
= *Troides magellanus*	190	7.5
= *Troides miranda*	190	7.5

ACTUAL SIZE

TOP 10 **LARGEST MOTHS**

MOTH / SCIENTIFIC NAME	WINGSPAN MM	IN
1 Atlas moth (*Attacus atlas*)	300	11.8
2 Owlet moth (*Thysania agrippina*)*	290	11.4
3 *Haematopis grataria*	260	10.2
4 Hercules emperor moth (*Coscinocera hercules*)	210	8.3
5 Malagasy silk moth (*Argema mitraei*)	180	7.1
6 *Eacles imperialis*	175	6.9
7 = Common emperor moth (*Bunaea alcinoe*)	160	6.3
= Giant peacock moth (*Saturnia pyri*)	160	6.3
9 Gray moth (*Brahmaea wallichii*)	155	6.1
10 = Black witch (*Ascalapha odorata*)	150	5.9
= Regal moth (*Citheronia regalis*)	150	5.9
= Polyphemus moth (*Antheraea polyphemus*)	150	5.9

* Exceptional specimen measured at 308 mm (12.2 in)

Top: Atlas moth
The Southeast Asian atlas moth is the largest of all members of the Lepidoptera order.

Left: Queen Alexandra's birdwing
The Papua New Guinean Queen Alexandra's birdwing has the greatest wingspan of any butterfly species.

ACTUAL SIZE

TOP 10 **MOST COMMON INSECTS***

SPECIES / SCIENTIFIC NAME	APPROX. NO. OF KNOWN SPECIES
1 Beetles (*Coleoptera*)	400,000
2 Ants, bees and wasps (*Hymenoptera*)	250,000
3 Butterflies and moths (*Lepidoptera*)	190,000
4 True flies (*Diptera*)	120,000
5 True bugs (*Hemiptera*)	100,000
6 Crickets, grasshoppers and locusts (*Orthoptera*)	20,000
7 Caddisflies (*Trichoptera*)	12,627
8 Dragonflies and damselflies (*Odonata*)	5,600
9 Lice (*Phthiraptera/Psocoptera*)	5,000
10 Lacewings (*Neuroptera*)	4,700

* By number of known species

Farm Animals

TOP 10 **SHEEP COUNTRIES**

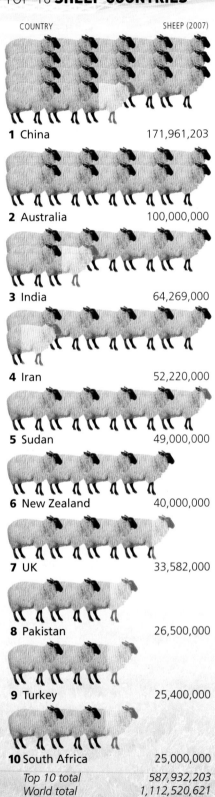

COUNTRY	SHEEP (2007)
1 China	171,961,203
2 Australia	100,000,000
3 India	64,269,000
4 Iran	52,220,000
5 Sudan	49,000,000
6 New Zealand	40,000,000
7 UK	33,582,000
8 Pakistan	26,500,000
9 Turkey	25,400,000
10 South Africa	25,000,000
Top 10 total	*587,932,203*
World total	*1,112,520,621*

Source (all lists): Food and Agriculture
Organization of the United Nations

TOP 10 **CATTLE COUNTRIES**

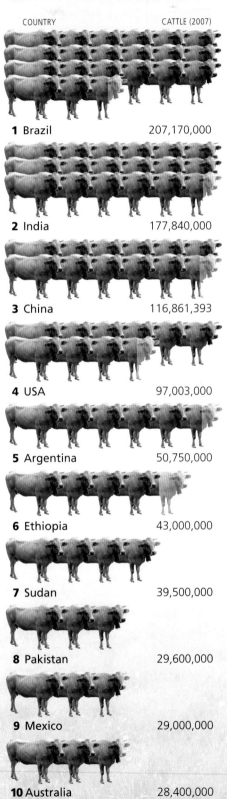

COUNTRY	CATTLE (2007)
1 Brazil	207,170,000
2 India	177,840,000
3 China	116,861,393
4 USA	97,003,000
5 Argentina	50,750,000
6 Ethiopia	43,000,000
7 Sudan	39,500,000
8 Pakistan	29,600,000
9 Mexico	29,000,000
10 Australia	28,400,000
UK	*9,987,570*
Top 10 total	*819,124,393*
World total	*1,389,590,364*

TOP 10 **HORSE COUNTRIES**

COUNTRY	HORSES (2007)
1 USA	9,500,000
2 China	7,197,465
3 Mexico	6,350,000
4 Brazil	5,800,000
5 Argentina	3,680,000
6 Colombia	2,500,000
7 Mongolia	2,114,800
8 Ethiopia	1,600,000
9 Russia	1,303,837
10 Kazakhstan	1,235,600
UK	*190,000*
Top 10 total	*41,281,702*
World total	*58,408,987*

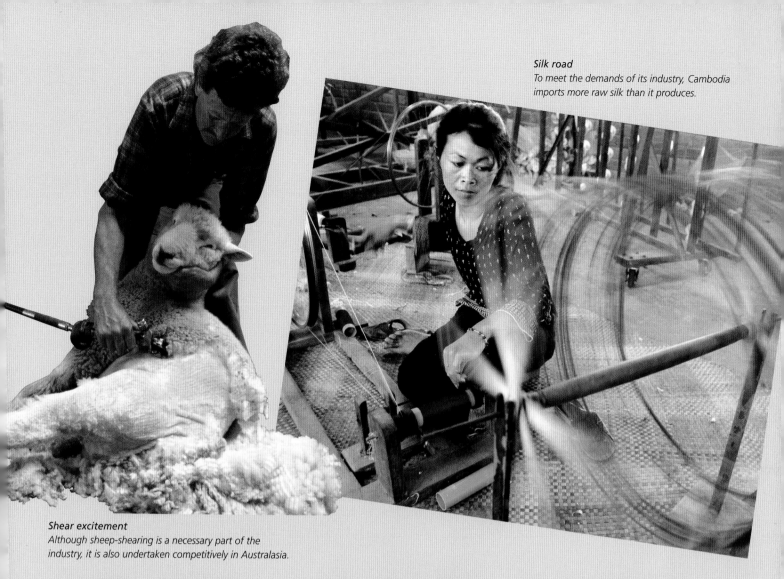

Silk road
To meet the demands of its industry, Cambodia imports more raw silk than it produces.

Shear excitement
Although sheep-shearing is a necessary part of the industry, it is also undertaken competitively in Australasia.

TOP 10 **WOOL-PRODUCTION** COUNTRIES

	COUNTRY	PRODUCTION 2007 (TONNES)
1	Australia	437,000
2	China	395,000
3	New Zealand	217,900
4	Iran	75,000
5	UK	62,000
6	Russia	52,000
7	Uruguay	50,000
8 =	Sudan	46,000
=	Turkey	46,000
10	India	45,500
	Top 10 total	*1,426,400*
	World total	*2,034,277*

Australia and New Zealand, two relative newcomers to the wool-production industry, today supply one-third of the world market.

TOP 10 **BEEHIVE COUNTRIES**

	COUNTRY	BEEHIVES (2007)
1	India	9,800,000
2	China	7,407,000
3	Turkey	5,120,000
4	Ethiopia	4,400,000
5	Iran	3,500,000
6	Russia	3,155,007
7	Argentina	2,970,000
8	Tanzania	2,700,000
9 =	Kenya	2,500,000
=	Spain	2,500,000
	Top 10 total	*44,052,007*
	World total	*72,642,755*

In 2007, world honey production stood at 1,073,017 tonnes – about a third of the total in China – and that of beeswax 61,134 tonnes.

TOP 10 **SILKWORM** COUNTRIES

	COUNTRY	PRODUCTION* 2007 (TONNES)
1	India	77,000
2	Uzbekistan	18,000
3	Brazil	8,000
4	Iran	6,000
5	Thailand	5,000
6	Vietnam	3,000
7	North Korea	1,400
8 =	Afghanistan	500
=	Japan	500
10	Cambodia	300
	Top 10 total	*119,700*
	World total	*120,626*

* Reelable cocoons

Fruit & Nuts

TOP 10 **FRUIT-PRODUCING COUNTRIES**

COUNTRY / PRODUCTION* 2007 (TONNES)

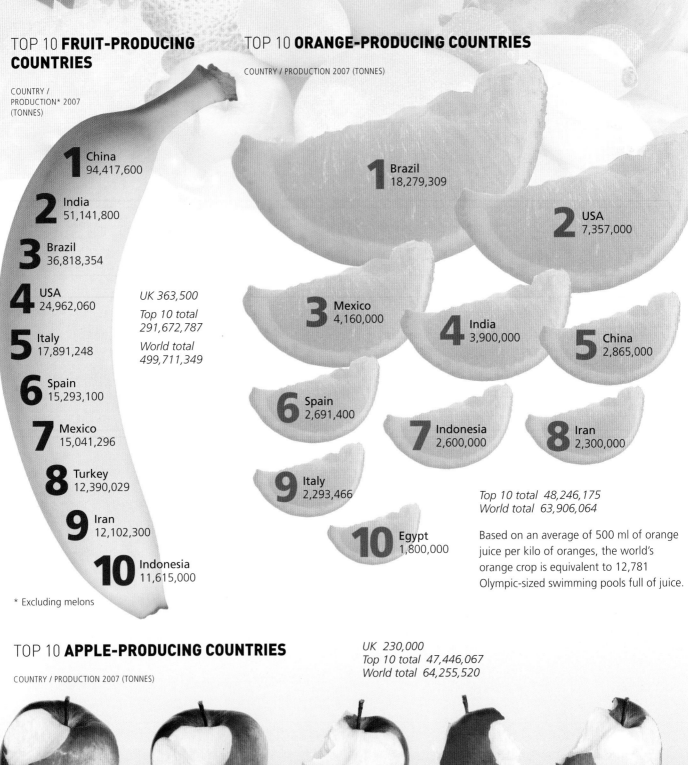

1 China 94,417,600

2 India 51,141,800

3 Brazil 36,818,354

4 USA 24,962,060

5 Italy 17,891,248

6 Spain 15,293,100

7 Mexico 15,041,296

8 Turkey 12,390,029

9 Iran 12,102,300

10 Indonesia 11,615,000

UK 363,500

Top 10 total 291,672,787

World total 499,711,349

* Excluding melons

TOP 10 **ORANGE-PRODUCING COUNTRIES**

COUNTRY / PRODUCTION 2007 (TONNES)

1 Brazil 18,279,309

2 USA 7,357,000

3 Mexico 4,160,000

4 India 3,900,000

5 China 2,865,000

6 Spain 2,691,400

7 Indonesia 2,600,000

8 Iran 2,300,000

9 Italy 2,293,466

10 Egypt 1,800,000

Top 10 total 48,246,175
World total 63,906,064

Based on an average of 500 ml of orange juice per kilo of oranges, the world's orange crop is equivalent to 12,781 Olympic-sized swimming pools full of juice.

TOP 10 **APPLE-PRODUCING COUNTRIES**

COUNTRY / PRODUCTION 2007 (TONNES)

UK 230,000
Top 10 total 47,446,067
World total 64,255,520

1 China 27,507,000

2 USA 4,237,730

3 Iran 2,660,000

4 Turkey 2,266,437

5 Russia 2,211,000

TOP 10 **COCONUT-PRODUCING COUNTRIES**

COUNTRY / PRODUCTION 2007 (TONNES)

1 Indonesia
17,000,000

2 Philippines
15,580,000

3 India
9,400,000

7
Sri Lanka
954,000

6
Vietnam
962,000

5
Thailand
1,705,446

4
Brazil
2,770,554

Top 10 total
50,357,000

World total
54,716,444

8 Papua New Guinea
677,000

9 Malaysia
568,000

10 = Myanmar
370,000

= Tanzania
370,000

TOP 10 **NUT-PRODUCING COUNTRIES**

COUNTRY / PRODUCTION 2007 (TONNES)

1 USA
118,000

2 Indonesia
104,000

3 Mexico
96,000

4 Ethiopia
75,000

5 China
50,000

6 Australia
38,000

7 Guatemala
27,000

8 Portugal
24,000

9 Thailand
23,000

10 Philippines
14,000

Top 10 total 569,000
World total 725,057

Source (all lists): Food and Agriculture
Organization of the United Nations

6 Italy
2,072,500

7 India
2,001,400

8 France
1,800,000

9 Chile
1,390,000

10 Argentina
1,300,000

Trees & Forests

TOP 10 **COUNTRIES WITH THE LARGEST AREAS OF FOREST**

COUNTRY / SQ KM/SQ MILES / % OF TOTAL

1 Russia
8,087,900 / 3,122,756
47.9%

2 Brazil
4,776,980 / 1,844,402
57.2%

3 Canada
3,101,340 / 1,197,434
33.6%

4 USA
3,030,890 / 1,170,233
33.1%

5 China
1,972,900 / 761,741
21.2%

6 Australia
1,636,780 / 631,964
21.3%

7 Dem. Rep. of Congo
1,336,100 / 515,871
58.9%

8 Indonesia
884,950 / 341,681
48.8%

9 Peru
687,420 / 265,414
53.7%

10 India
677,010 / 261,395
22.8%

UK
28,450 / 10,985
11.8%

World total
39,520,250 / 15,258,855
30.3%

Source: Food and Agriculture Organization of the United Nations, *Global Forest Resources Assessment 2005*

Mangroves
Large areas of the world's mangroves have been cleared for coconut growing, chopped down for fuel or destroyed by shrimp farming.

Tall tree
Species of North American sequoia are the tallest trees in the world.

TOP 10 COUNTRIES WITH THE LARGEST AREAS OF MANGROVE

COUNTRY	MANGROVE AREA (HECTARES)
1 Indonesia	3,062,300
2 Australia	1,451,411
3 Brazil	1,012,376
4 Nigeria	997,700
5 Mexico	882,032
6 Malaysia	564,971
7 Cuba	545,805
8 Myanmar	518,646
9 Bangladesh	476,215
10 India	446,100
Top 10 total	*9,957,556*
World total	*15,705,000*

Source: Food and Agriculture Organization of the United Nations, *The World's Mangroves 1980–2005, 2007*

A total of 124 countries have been identified as having mangroves – species of trees and shrubs that are specially adapted to growing in saline coasts of tropical and subtropical regions. A survey conducted in 1980 put the global total mangrove area at 18.8 million hectares, so over three million hectares have been lost in the past 30 years.

TOP 10 TALLEST NATIVE TREES IN THE UK*

		HEIGHT	
	TREE / LOCATION	M	FT
1	Beech Lydney Park, Gloucestershire	43	141
2 =	Common oak Belvoir Castle, Leicestershire	42	138
=	Wych elm Rossie Priory, Perth & Kinross	42	138
4	Sessile oak Knole Park, Kent	40	131
5	Black poplar Leighton Hall, Welshpool, Powys/ Longnor Hall, Shropshire	38	125
6 =	Ash Bainton, Driffield, Yorkshire	37	121
=	Scots pine Ballogie, Aberdeenshire	37	121
=	Small-leafed lime Bell Beck, Rusland, Cumbria	37	121
9 =	Alder Luton Hoo, Bedfordshire	31	102
=	Aspen Cerney House Gardens, Gloucestershire	31	102
=	Hornbeam Norwood Park, Southwell, Nottinghamshire/Priory Park, Reigate, Surrey#	31	102

* The tallest known example of each of the 10 tallest species
\# Identical height examples of species

Source: The Tree Register of the British Isles

TOP 10 MOST COMMON TREES IN THE UK

	TREE / SCIENTIFIC NAME	% OF TOTAL FOREST AREA
1	Sitka spruce (*Picea sitchensis*)	29
2	Scots pine (*Pinus sylvestris*)	10
3	Oak (*Quercus robur*)	9
4	Birch (*Betula pubescens*)	7
5	Lodgepole pine (*Pinus contorta latifolia*)	6
6 =	Ash (*Fraxinus excelsior*)	5
=	Japanese/hybrid larch (*Larix kempferi/Larix × eurolepis*)	5
8	Beech (*Fagus sylvatica*)	4
9 =	Norway spruce (*Picea abies*)	3
=	Sycamore (*Acer pseudoplatanus*)	3

Source: Forestry Commission

Seven per cent of the UK's forested areas is classified as mixed broadleaves and one per cent as mixed conifers, a large proportion of which grows in forests managed by the Forestry Commission. This body came into existence as a result of the Forestry Act of 1919, planting its first trees at Eggesford Forest, Devon, on 8 December 1919.

THE HUMAN WORLD

Human Extremes

TOP 10 **TALLEST PEOPLE**

NAME / DATES / COUNTRY	CM	HEIGHT FT	IN
1 Robert Pershing Wadlow (1918–40) USA	274	8	11.2
2 John William Rogan (1868–1905) USA	268	8	9.8
3 John Aasen (1887–1938) USA	267	8	9.7
4 John F. Carroll (1932–69) USA	264	8	7.6
5 Al Tomaini (1918–62) USA	255	8	4.4
6 Trijntje Keever* (1616-33) Netherlands	254	8	3.3
7 Edouard Beaupré (1881–1904) Canada	250	8	2.5
8 = Bernard Coyne (1897–1921) USA	249	8	1.2
= Don Koehler (1925–81) USA	249	8	1.2
10 = Jeng Jinlian* (1964–82) China	248	8	1.1
= Väinö Myllyrinne (1909–63) Finland	248	8	1.1

* Female; all others male

Robert Wadlow
Photographed in 1938, actress Maureen O'Sullivan (1.6 m/5 ft 3 in) is dwarfed by world's tallest man Robert Wadlow.

Manuel Uribe Garza
Once the world's heaviest living man, Garza has dieted to lose some 227 kg (500 lb) from his former peak weight.

TOP 10 **HEAVIEST PEOPLE**

NAME / DATES*	MAX. WEIGHT KG	LB
1 Carol Yager (1960–94)	726	1,600
2 Jon Brower Minnoch (1941–83)	635	1,400
3 Manuel Uribe Garza (b. 1965), Mexico	597	1,320
4 Rosalie Bradford (1943–2006)	544	1,200
5 Walter Hudson (1944–91)	543	1,197
6 Francis John Lang aka Michael Walker (b. 1934)	538	1,187
7 Johnny Alee (1853–87)	513	1,132
8 Michael Hebranko (b. 1953)	499	1,100
9 Patrick Deuel (b. 1962)	486	1,072
10 Robert Earl Hughes (1926–58)	485	1,069

* All USA unless otherwise stated

Precise weights of certain people were exaggerated for commercial reasons or never verified, while some were so huge that they could not be moved, or broke the scales, but these are the main contenders for the list of 'world's heaviest', based on records of their peak weights. Some later dieted and reduced their weights – in the case of Rosalie Bradford, down from her 1987 peak to 128 kg (283 lb) in 1994.

THE 10 **MOST OBESE COUNTRIES – ADULTS**

	COUNTRY	% OF OBESE ADULTS*	
		MEN	WOMEN
1	Tonga	46.6	70.3
2	Samoa	32.9	63.0
3	Nauru	55.7	60.5
4	Qatar	34.6	45.3
5	Saudi Arabia	26.4	44.0
6	Lebanon	36.3	38.3
7	Paraguay	22.9	35.7
8	Albania#	22.8	35.6
9	Mexico	24.4	34.5
10	Seychelles	14.7	34.2
	England	*23.6*	*24.4*
	Scotland	*22.4*	*26.0*
	Wales	*20.0*	*21.0*

* Ranked by percentage of obese women (those with a BMI greater than 30) in those countries and latest year for which data available
# Urban population

Source: International Obesity Task Force (IOTF)

THE 10 **OLDEST WOMEN IN THE WORLD***

	NAME / COUNTRY	BORN	DIED	YRS	AGE MTHS	DAYS
1	Jeanne Calment, France	21 Feb 1875	4 Aug 1997	122	5	14
2	Sarah Knauss, USA	24 Sep 1880	30 Dec 1999	119	3	6
3	Lucy Hannah, USA	16 Jul 1875	21 Mar 1993	117	8	5
4	Marie-Louise Meilleur, Canada	29 Aug 1880	16 Apr 1998	117	7	19
5	María Capovilla, Ecuador	14 Sep 1889	27 Aug 2006	116	11	13
6	Tane Ikai, Japan	18 Jan 1879	12 Jul 1995	116	5	24
7	Elizabeth Bolden, USA	15 Aug 1890	11 Dec 2006	116	3	26
8	Maggie Barnes, USA	6 Mar 1882	19 Jan 1998	115	10	13
9	Charlotte Hughes, UK	1 Aug 1877	17 Mar 1993	115	7	16
10	Edna Parker, USA	20 Apr 1893	26 Nov 2008	115	7	6

* Includes only women whose birth and death dates are undisputed

THE 10 **OLDEST MEN IN THE WORLD***

	NAME / COUNTRY	BORN	DIED	YRS	AGE MTHS	DAYS
1	Christian Mortensen, Denmark/USA	16 Aug 1882	25 Apr 1998	115	8	9
2	Emiliano Mercado Del Toro, Puerto Rico	21 Aug 1891	24 Jan 2007	115	5	3
3	Yukichi Chuganji, Japan	23 Mar 1889	28 Sep 2003	114	6	5
4	Joan Riudavets, Spain	15 Dec 1889	5 Mar 2004	114	2	19
5	Fred H. Hale, USA	1 Dec 1890	19 Nov 2004	113	11	18
6	Johnson Parks, USA	15 Oct 1884	17 Jul 1998	113	9	2
7	John Ingram McMorran, USA	19 Jun 1889	24 Feb 2003	113	8	5
8	Tomoji Tanabe, Japan	18 Sep 1895	#	113	6	27
9	Frederick L. Frazier, USA	27 Jan 1880	14 Jun 1993	113	4	18
10	Walter Richardson, USA	7 Nov 1885	25 Dec 1998	113	1	18

* Includes only men whose birth and death dates are undisputed
# Alive as at 27 April 2009

Joan Riudavets
Europe's longest-lived man was a retired cobbler from Minorca, Spain.

Life & Death

TOP 10 COUNTRIES WITH THE HIGHEST LIFE EXPECTANCY

COUNTRY	MALE	LIFE EXPECTANCY AT BIRTH (2010) FEMALE	BOTH
(1) Andorra	80.30	84.55	82.36
(2) Japan	78.87	85.66	82.17
(3) = San Marino	78.63	81.75	82.06
= Singapore	79.45	84.87	82.06
(5) Australia	79.33	84.25	81.72
(6) Canada	78.72	84.00	81.29
(7) France	77.91	84.44	81.09
(8) = Sweden	78.69	83.40	80.97
= Switzerland	78.14	83.95	80.97
(10) Iceland	78.63	83.04	80.79
UK	*76.66*	*81.80*	*79.16*
World average	*64.80*	*69.20*	*66.90*

Source: US Census Bureau, International Data Base

TOP 10 COUNTRIES WITH THE MOST BIRTHS

COUNTRY	ESTIMATED BIRTHS (2010)
(1) India	25,221,127
(2) China	19,216,255
(3) Nigeria	5,490,479
(4) Pakistan	4,829,240
(5) Indonesia	4,482,766
(6) USA	4,290,520
(7) Ethiopia	3,814,505
(8) Bangladesh	3,761,967
(9) Brazil	3,641,981
(10) Dem. Rep. of Congo	2,996,929
UK	*653,909*
World	*135,994,165*

Source: US Census Bureau, International Data Base

TOP 10 COUNTRIES WITH THE MOST CREMATIONS

COUNTRY	% OF DEATHS	CREMATIONS*
1 China#	50.00	4,543,795
2 Japan	99.81	1,193,697
3 USA	34.89	842,467
4 UK	72.49	417,920
5 Germany	40.10	338,469
6 Thailand	80.00	318,750
7 South Korea	58.91	144,255
8 France	27.33	141,862
9 Canada	56.00	120,714
10 Russia	46.50	113,110

* Estimated in latest year for which data available
# Including Taiwan

Source: The Cremation Society of Great Britain

THE 10 COUNTRIES WITH THE MOST DEATHS

COUNTRY	ESTIMATED DEATHS (2010)
1 China	9,567,701
2 India	7,199,270
3 USA	2,599,751
4 Nigeria	2,482,665
5 Russia	2,235,819
6 Indonesia	1,518,552
7 Bangladesh	1,435,238
8 Pakistan	1,349,241
9 Brazil	1,277,006
10 Japan	1,246,488
UK	*612,848*
Top 10 total	*30,911,731*
World	*55,956,426*

Source: US Census Bureau, International Data Base

The Top 10 countries account for some 55 per cent of all deaths in the world.

TOP 10 **COUNTRIES WITH THE GREATEST POPULATION GROWTH**

COUNTRY	GROWTH RATE % (2010)
① Niger	3.66
② =Uganda	3.56
=United Arab Emirates	3.56
④ Kuwait	3.50
⑤ Yemen	3.44
⑥ Ethiopia	3.20
⑦ Dem. Rep. of Congo	3.17
⑧ Burkina Faso	3.10
⑨ =Oman	3.07
=São Tomé and Príncipe	3.07
UK	*0.28*
World average	*1.16*

Source: US Census Bureau, International Data Base

Baby boom
With a growth rate of three times the world average, the population of Niger doubled between 1989 and 2009.

THE 10 **MOST SUICIDAL COUNTRIES**

COUNTRY	SUICIDES PER 100,000 PER ANNUM*		
	MALE	FEMALE	TOTAL
1 Lithuania	68.1	12.9	38.6
2 Belarus	63.3	10.3	35.1
3 Russia	58.1	9.8	32.2
4 Slovenia	42.1	11.1	26.3
5 Hungary	42.3	11.2	26.0
6 Kazakhstan	45.0	8.1	25.9
7 Latvia	42.0	9.6	24.5
8 South Korea	29.6	14.1	21.9
9 Guyana	33.8	11.6	22.9
10 Ukraine	40.9	7.0	22.6
UK	*10.4*	*3.2*	*6.8*

* In those countries/latest year for which data available

Source: World Health Organization

THE 10 **COUNTRIES WITH THE HIGHEST INFANT MORTALITY**

COUNTRY	ESTIMATED DEATH RATE PER 1,000 LIVE BIRTHS (2010)
1 Angola	178.13
2 Sierra Leone	152.42
3 Afghanistan	149.28
4 Liberia	136.06
5 Niger	114.50
6 Somalia	107.42
7 Mozambique	103.82
8 Mali	100.30
9 Zambia	99.92
10 Guinea-Bissau	98.05
UK	*4.78*
World average	*39.70*

Source: US Census Bureau, International Data Base

For Better or For Worse

TOP 10 COUNTRIES OF RESIDENCE FOR COUPLES MARRYING AT GRETNA GREEN

	COUNTRY OF RESIDENCE	BRIDE	GROOM	TOTAL (2007)
1	England	2,483	2,493	4,976
2	Scotland	492	495	987
3	Wales	159	161	320
4	Northern Ireland	74	74	148
5	Ireland	57	59	116
6	Germany	20	17	37
7	Australia	15	13	28
8 =	Spain	12	11	23
=	USA	14	9	23
10	France	11	10	21

Source: General Register Office for Scotland

In 2007, 4,452 marriages were registered at Gretna (a fall on the record year of 2005 with 5,555), with these representing the principal countries of origin.

TOP 10 YEARS FOR MARRIAGES IN ENGLAND AND WALES

	YEAR	MARRIAGES
1	1940	470,549
2	1939	439,694
3	1972	426,241
4	1970	415,487
5	1968	407,822
6	1971	404,737
7	1947	401,210
8	1973	400,435
9	1945	397,626
10	1948	396,891

Source: National Statistics

The number of marriages in England and Wales fell in 2007 to 231,450, the lowest total since 1895 (228,204), and the lowest rate (21.6 per 1,000 men and 19.7 per 1,000 women) since records began in 1862. As the Top 10 indicates, there was a flurry of marriages at the outset and end of World War II, just as there had been at the end of World War I, with 369,411 marriages recorded in 1919.

TOP 10 COUNTRIES WITH THE MOST MARRIAGES

	COUNTRY	MARRIAGES PER ANNUM*
1	USA	2,160,000
2	Bangladesh	1,181,000
3	Russia	1,001,589
4	Vietnam	964,701
5	Japan	757,331
6	Brazil	710,120
7	Iran	650,960
8	Ethiopia	630,290
9	Mexico	570,060
10	Egypt	525,412
	UK	305,912

* In those countries/latest year for which data available

Source: United Nations

THE 10 **COUNTRIES WITH THE HIGHEST DIVORCE RATES**

	COUNTRY	DIVORCE RATE PER 1,000*
1	Russia	5.30
2	Aruba	5.27
3	USA	4.19
4	Ukraine	3.79
5	Belarus	3.77
6	Moldova	3.50
7	Cuba	3.16
8	Czech Republic	3.11
9 =	Lithuania	3.05
=	South Korea	3.05
	UK	*2.58*

* In those countries/latest year
for which data available

Source: United Nations

THE 10 **COUNTRIES WITH THE LOWEST MARRIAGE RATE**

	COUNTRY	MARRIAGES PER 1,000 PER ANNUM*
1	Colombia	1.7
2 =	Dominican Republic	2.8
=	St Lucia	2.8
=	Venezuela	2.8
5 =	Andorra	2.9
=	Peru	2.9
7	United Arab Emirates	3.1
8 =	Argentina	3.2
=	Slovenia	3.2
10	Panama	3.3

* In 2005 or latest year in those countries
for which data available

Source: United Nations

THE 10 **COUNTRIES WITH THE LOWEST DIVORCE RATES**

	COUNTRY	DIVORCE RATE PER 1,000*
1	Guatemala	0.12
2	Belize	0.17
3	Mongolia	0.28
4	Libya	0.32
5	Georgia	0.40
6	Chile	0.42
7	Saint Vincent and the Grenadines	0.43
8	Jamaica	0.44
9	Armenia	0.47
10	Turkey	0.49

* In those countries/latest year for which
data available

Source: United Nations

The countries that figure among those with the lowest rates represent a range of cultures and religions, which either condone or condemn divorce to varying extents, thus affecting its prevalence or otherwise. In some countries, legal and other obstacles make divorce difficult or costly, while in certain societies – such as Jamaica, where the marriage rate is also low – partners often separate without the formality of divorce.

Names of the Decades

TOP 10 FIRST NAMES IN ENGLAND AND WALES
1900s

BOYS		GIRLS
William	1	Mary
John	2	Florence
George	3	Doris
Thomas	4	Edith
Arthur	5	Dorothy
James	6	Annie
Charles	7	Margaret
Frederick	8	Alice
Albert	9	Elizabeth
Ernest	10	Elsie

TOP 10 FIRST NAMES IN ENGLAND AND WALES
1910s

BOYS		GIRLS
John	1	Mary
William	2	Margaret
George	3	Doris
Thomas	4	Dorothy
James	5	Kathleen
Arthur	6	Florence
Frederick	7	Elsie
Albert	8	Edith
Charles	9	Elizabeth
Robert	10	Winifred

TOP 10 FIRST NAMES IN ENGLAND AND WALES
1920s

BOYS		GIRLS
John	1	Margaret
William	2	Mary
George	3	Joan
James	4	Joyce
Thomas	5	Dorothy
Ronald	6	Kathleen
Kenneth	7	Doris
Robert	8	Irene
Arthur	9	Elizabeth
Frederick	10	Eileen

TOP 10 FIRST NAMES IN ENGLAND AND WALES
1930s

BOYS		GIRLS
John	1	Margaret
Peter	2	Jean
William	3	Mary
Brian	4	Joan
David	5	Patricia
James	6	Sheila
Michael	7	Barbara
Ronald	8	Doreen
Kenneth	9	June
George	10	Shirley

TOP 10 FIRST NAMES IN ENGLAND AND WALES
1940s

BOYS		GIRLS
John	1	Margaret
David	2	Patricia
Michael	3	Christine
Peter	4	Mary
Robert	5	Jean
Anthony	6	Ann
Brian	7	Susan
Alan	8	Janet
William	9	Maureen
James	10	Barbara

TOP 10 FIRST NAMES IN ENGLAND AND WALES
1950s

BOYS		GIRLS
David	1	Susan
John	2	Linda
Stephen	3	Christine
Michael	4	Margaret
Peter	5	Janet
Robert	6	Patricia
Paul	7	Carol
Alan	8	Elizabeth
Christopher	9	Mary
Richard	10	Anne

TOP 10 FIRST NAMES IN ENGLAND AND WALES
1960s

BOYS		GIRLS
David	1	Susan
Paul	2	Julie
Andrew	3	Karen
Mark	4	Jacqueline
John	5	Deborah
Michael	6	Tracey
Stephen	7	Jane
Ian	8	Helen
Robert	9	Diane
Richard	10	Sharon

TOP 10 FIRST NAMES IN ENGLAND AND WALES
1970s

BOYS		GIRLS
Paul	1	Sarah
Mark	2	Claire
David	3	Nicola
Andrew	4	Emma
Richard	5	Lisa
Christopher	6	Joanne
James	7	Michelle
Simon	8	Helen
Michael	9	Samantha
Matthew	10	Karen

TOP 10 FIRST NAMES IN ENGLAND AND WALES
1980s

BOYS		GIRLS
Christopher	1	Sarah
James	2	Laura
David	3	Gemma
Daniel	4	Emma
Michael	5	Rebecca
Matthew	6	Claire
Andrew	7	Victoria
Richard	8	Samantha
Paul	9	Rachel
Mark	10	Amy

Changing Fashions

These popular first names are those recorded in the midpoint in each decade. Where boys' names are concerned, tradition rules: three of the top names of the 1900s appear among those of the 2000s, whereas none of the girls' names do. Certain names are redolent of their era and have fallen out of favour: Ernest dropped out of the Top 100 in the 1940s and Albert in the 1970s, while Mary, long the most common girl's name, dropped out of the Top 100 in 1997. The stock of girls' names is larger and more susceptible to changes in fashion.

Source (all lists): Office for National Statistics

TOP 10 FIRST NAMES IN ENGLAND AND WALES
1990s

BOYS		GIRLS
Thomas	1	Rebecca
James	2	Lauren
Jack	3	Jessica
Daniel	4	Charlotte
Matthew	5	Hannah
Ryan	6	Sophie
Joshua	7	Amy
Luke	8	Emily
Samuel	9	Laura
Jordan	10	Emma

TOP 10 FIRST NAMES IN ENGLAND AND WALES
2000s

BOYS		GIRLS
Jack	1	Emily
Joshua	2	Ellie
Thomas	3	Jessica
James	4	Sophie
Daniel	5	Chloe
Samuel	6	Lucy
Oliver	7	Olivia
William	8	Charlotte
Benjamin	9	Katie
Joseph	10	Megan

Names Around the World

TOP 10 SURNAMES IN FRANCE

SURNAME / NO.		
1	Martin	235,846
2	Bernard	105,132
3	Dubois	95,998
4	Thomas	95,387
5	Robert	91,393
6	Richard	90,689
7	Petit	88,318
8	Durand	84,252
9	Leroy	78,868
10	Moreau	78,177

TOP 10 SURNAMES IN SPAIN

SURNAME / NO.		
1	García	813,257
2	Fernández	503,142
3	González	499,596
4	Rodríguez	482,448
5	López	467,681
6	Martínez	449,954
7	Sánchez	433,030
8	Pérez	421,997
9	Martín	278,261
10	Gómez	261,776

TOP 10 SURNAMES IN GERMANY

NAME / NO.		
1	Müller	78,107
2	Schmidt	56,730
3	Schneider	32,887
4	Fischer	28,776
5	Meyer	27,131
6	Weber	24,665
7 =	Schulz	22,199
=	Wagner	22,199
=	Becker	22,199
10	Hoffmann	21,377

TOP 10 SURNAMES IN ITALY

SURNAME	
1	Rossi
2	Russo
3	Ferrari
4	Esposito
5	Bianchi
6	Romano
7	Colombo
8	Ricci
9	Marino
10	Greco

TOP 10 SURNAMES IN DENMARK

SURNAME / NO.		
1	Jensen	288,050
2	Nielsen	283,928
3	Hansen	238,251
4	Pedersen	178,578
5	Andersen	168,761
6	Christensen	128,168
7	Larsen	125,438
8	Sørensen	119,929
9	Rasmussen	101,154
10	Jørgensen	95,244

Source: Statistics Denmark

TOP 10 SURNAMES IN POLAND

SURNAME / NO.		
1	Nowak	203,506
2	Kowalski	139,719
3	Wisniewski	109,855
4	Wójcik	99,509
5	Kowalczyk	97,796
6	Kaminski	94,499
7	Lewandowski	92,449
8	Zielinski	91,043
9	Szymanski	89,091
10	Wozniak	88,039

Source: Jaroslaw Maciej Zawadzki, *1000 Najpopularniejszych Nazwisk w Polsce* (2002)

TOP 10 **SURNAMES IN THE UK**

	SURNAME / NO.	
1	Smith	729,862
2	Jones	578,261
3	Taylor	458,268
4	Williams	411,385
5	Brown	380,443
6	Davies	316,982*
7	Evans	231,844
8	Wilson	227,652
9	Thomas	220,228
10	Roberts	219,694

* There are also 108,041 people bearing the surname Davis

TOP 10 **SURNAMES IN THE USA**

	SURNAME / NO.	
1	Smith	2,376,206
2	Johnson	1,857,160
3	Williams	1,534,042
4	Brown	1,380,145
5	Jones	1,362,755
6	Miller	1,127,803
7	Davis	1,072,335
8	Garcia	858,289
9	Rodriguez	804,240
10	Wilson	783,051

Source: US Census Bureau, Census 2000

TOP 10 **SURNAMES IN AUSTRALIA***

	SURNAME / NO.	
1	Smith	114,997
2	Jones	56,698
3	Williams	55,555
4	Brown	54,896
5	Wilson	46,961
6	Taylor	45,328
7	Johnson	33,435
8	White	31,099
9	Martin	31,058
10	Anderson	30,910

* Based on occurrences on Australian electoral rolls

TOP 10 **SURNAMES IN CHINA**

	SURNAME
1	Wáng
2	Li
3	Zhang
4	Liú
5	Chén
6	Yáng
7	Huáng
8	Zhào
9	Zhou
10	Wú

Source: Ministry of Public Security

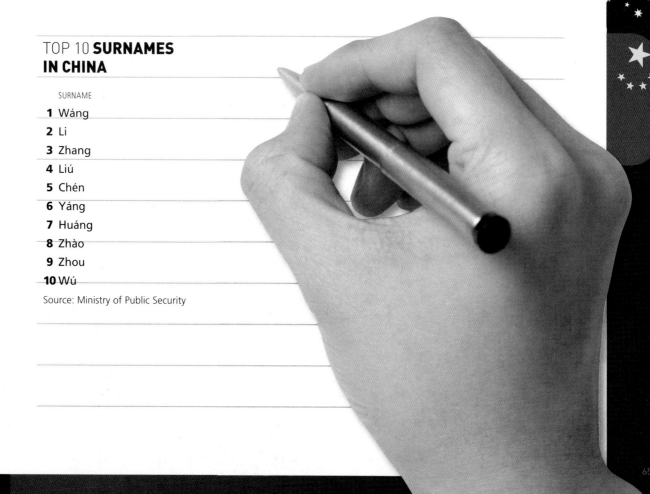

Royalty

TOP 10 **LONGEST-REIGNING QUEENS***

1 THRONE = 10 YEARS	MONARCH	COUNTRY	REIGN	AGE AT ACCESSION	REIGN		
					YRS	MTHS	DAYS
	1 Victoria	UK	20 Jun 1837–22 Jan 1901	18	63	7	2
	2 Wilhelmina	Netherlands	23 Nov 1890–4 Sep 1948	10	57	9	12
	3 Elizabeth II	UK	6 Feb 1952–#	25	57	1	25
	4 Salote Tupou III	Tonga	5 Apr 1918–16 Dec 1965	18	47	8	11
	5 Elizabeth I	England	17 Nov 1558–24 Mar 1603	25	44	4	7
	6 Maria Theresa	Hungary	20 Oct 1740–29 Nov 1780	23	40	1	9
	7 Maria I	Portugal	24 Feb 1777–20 Mar 1816	42	39	25	0
	8 Joanna I	Naples	20 Jan 1343–12 May 1382	16	39	3	22
	9 Isabella II	Spain	29 Sep 1833–30 Sep 1868†	2	35	0	1
	10 Catharine II	Russia	28 Jun 1762–17 Nov 1796	32	34	4	20

* Queens and empresses who ruled in their own right, not as consorts of kings or emperors, during past 1,000 years, excluding earlier rulers of dubious authenticity
\# Current; as at 31 March 2009 † Exiled; later abdicated

TOP 10 **LONGEST-REIGNING BRITISH MONARCHS**

MONARCH	REIGN	YRS	REIGN* MTHS	DAYS
1 Victoria	20 Jun 1837–22 Jan 1901	63	7	2
2 George III	25 Oct 1760–29 Jan 1820	59	3	4
3 Elizabeth II	6 Feb 1952–	57	1	25
4 Henry III	18 Oct 1216–16 Nov 1272	56	0	29
5 Edward III	25 Jan 1327–21 Jun 1377	50	4	27
6 Elizabeth I	17 Nov 1558–24 Mar 1603	44	4	7
7 Henry VI	31 Aug 1422–4 Mar 1461/ 31 Oct 1470–11 Apr 1471	38	11	15
8 Henry VIII	22 Apr 1509–28 Jan 1547	37	9	6
9 Charles II	30 Jan 1649–3 Sep 1651#/ 29 May 1660–6 Feb 1685	36	7	0
10 Henry I	2 Aug 1100–1 Dec 1135	35	3	29

* As at 31 March 2009
\# Reign in Scotland; discounting 1649–60 Interregnum

Young ruler
Crowned at the age of 28, King Jigme Khesar Namgyal Wangchuck of Bhutan became the world's youngest reigning monarch and head of state.

TOP 10 **LONGEST-REIGNING LIVING MONARCHS**

	MONARCH	COUNTRY*	ACCESSION	REIGN# YRS	MTHS	DAYS
1	Bhumibol Adulyadej	Thailand	9 Jun 1946	62	7	28
2	Elizabeth II	UK	6 Feb 1952	57	1	25
3	Malietoa Tanumafili II	Samoa	1 Jan 1962†	47	1	5
4	Haji Hassanal Bolkiah	Brunei	5 Oct 1967	41	4	1
5	Sayyid Qaboos ibn Said al-Said	Oman	23 Jul 1970	38	6	14
6	Margrethe II	Denmark	14 Jan 1972	37	0	23
7	Carl XVI Gustaf	Sweden	15 Sep 1973	35	4	22
8	Juan Carlos	Spain	22 Nov 1975	33	2	15
9	Beatrix	Netherlands	30 Apr 1980	28	9	7
10	Mswati	Swaziland	25 Mar 1986	22	8	12

* Sovereign states only
# As at 31 March 2009
† Sole ruler since 15 April 1963

THE 10 **LATEST MONARCHS TO ASCEND THE THRONE**

	MONARCH	COUNTRY*	ACCESSION
1	King Jigme Khesar Namgyal Wangchuck	Bhutan	15 Dec 2006
2	Sultan Mizan Zainal Abidin	Malaysia	13 Dec 2006
3	King George Tupou V	Tonga	11 Sep 2006
4	Emir Sabah Al-Ahmad Al-Jaber Al-Sabah	Kuwait	29 Jan 2006
5	Emir Mohammed bin Rashid Al Maktoum	Dubai	4 Jan 2006
6	King Abdullah	Saudi Arabia	1 Aug 2005
7	Prince Albert II	Monaco	6 Apr 2005
8	King Norodom Sihamoni	Cambodia	14 Oct 2004
9	Grand Duke Henri	Luxembourg	7 Oct 2000
10	Mohammed VI	Morocco	23 Jul 1999

* Sovereign states only

Malaysia has a unique system of 'revolving monarchy', which was established following Malaysia's independence from Britain in 1957. Each of the nine state sultans takes a five-year turn as king.

Politics

THE 10 YOUNGEST US PRESIDENTS

	PRESIDENT	TOOK OFFICE	AGE ON TAKING OFFICE		
			YRS	MTHS	DAYS
1	Theodore Roosevelt	14 Sep 1901	42	10	18
2	John F. Kennedy	20 Jan 1961	43	7	22
3	Bill Clinton	20 Jan 1993	46	5	1
4	Ulysses S. Grant	4 Mar 1869	46	10	5
5	Barack Obama	20 Jan 2009	47	5	16
6	Grover Cleveland	4 Mar 1893	47	11	14
7	Franklin Pierce	4 Mar 1804	48	3	9
8	James A. Garfield	4 Mar 1881	49	3	13
9	James K. Polk	4 Mar 1845	49	4	2
10	Millard Fillmore	10 Jul 1850	50	6	3

Roosevelt became president following the assassination of William McKinley, while Kennedy was the youngest to be elected. US presidents must be at least 35 years old.

TOP 10 LONGEST-SERVING BRITISH PRIME MINISTERS

PRIME MINISTER (LIFE DATES) / PERIOD(S) IN OFFICE	TOTAL DURATION		
	YRS	MTHS	DAYS
1 Sir Robert Walpole (1676–1745) 3 Apr 1721–8 Feb 1742	20	10	5
2 William Pitt the Younger (1759–1806) 19 Dec 1783–14 Mar 1801 10 May 1804–23 Jan 1806	18	11	8
3 Earl of Liverpool (1770–1828) 7 Jun 1812–17 Feb 1827	14	8	10
4 Marquess of Salisbury (1830–1903) 23 Jun 1885–28 Jan 1886 26 Jul 1886–11 Aug 1892 25 Jun 1895–11 Jul 1902	13	8	6
5 William Gladstone (1809–98) 4 Dec 1868–17 Feb 1874 23 Apr 1880–9 Jun 1885 1 Feb 1886–20 Jul 1886 15 Aug 1892–2 Mar 1894	12	4	3
6 Lord North (1732–79) 28 Jan 1770–20 Mar 1782	12	1	20
7 Margaret Thatcher (b. 1925) 4 May 1979–29 Nov 1990	11	6	25
8 Henry Pelham (1694–1754) 27 Aug 1743–6 Mar 1754	10	6	7
9 Tony Blair (b. 1953) 2 May 1997–27 Jun 2007	10	1	25
10 Viscount Palmerston (1784–1865) 6 Feb 1855–21 Feb 1858 12 Jun 1859–18 Oct 1865	9	4	24

President Obama
The average age of US presidents on taking office is 55 years 1 month – only four have been younger than Barack Obama.

TOP 10 **PARLIAMENTS WITH THE HIGHEST PERCENTAGE OF WOMEN MEMBERS** *

PARLIAMENT (LATEST ELECTION)	WOMEN MEMBERS	TOTAL MEMBERS	% WOMEN
1 Rwanda (2008)	45	80	56.3
2 Sweden (2006)	164	349	47.0
3 Cuba (2008)	265	614	43.2
4 Finland (2007)	83	200	41.5
5 Argentina (2007)	102	255	40.0
6 Netherlands (2003)	59	150	39.3
7 Denmark (2007)	68	179	38.0
8 Angola (2008)	82	220	37.3
9 Costa Rica (2006)	21	57	36.8
10 Spain (2008)	127	350	36.3
UK (2005)	*126*	*646*	*19.5*

* As at 28 February 2009

Source: Inter-Parliamentary Union

This list is based on the most recent general election results for 136 democratic countries, based on the lower chamber where the parliament or equivalent body comprises two chambers. A total of 102 countries have at least 10 per cent female members of parliament, 57 more than 20 per cent, 22 over 30 per cent and five over 40 per cent. Rwanda is the first – and to date only – country with more than 50 per cent female members. Nine countries have no women members.

Cuban parliament
Women won 43.2 per cent of the seats in the 2008 elections to Cuba's National Assembly.

THE 10 **FIRST COUNTRIES TO GIVE WOMEN THE VOTE**

	COUNTRY	YEAR
1	New Zealand	1893
2	Australia (South Australia 1894; Western Australia 1898; Australia united in 1901)	1902
3	Finland (then a Grand Duchy under the Russian Crown)	1906
4	Norway (restricted franchise; all women over 25 in 1913)	1907
5	Denmark and Iceland (a Danish dependency until 1918)	1915
6 =	Netherlands	1917
=	USSR	1917
8 =	Austria (granted; enacted 1919)	1918
=	Azerbaijan	1918
=	Canada	1918
=	Estonia	1918
=	Germany	1918
=	Great Britain and Ireland (Ireland part of the United Kingdom until 1921; women over 30 only, lowered to 21 in 1928)	1918
=	Latvia	1918
=	Poland	1918

Nobel Prizes

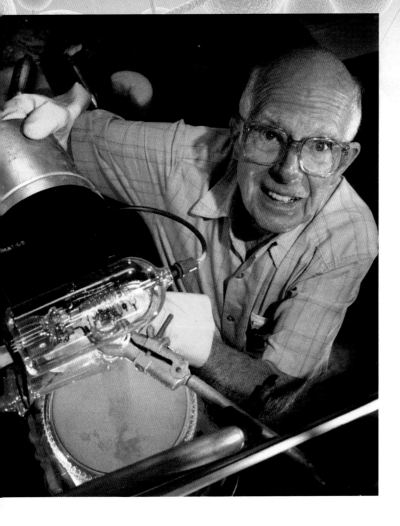

TOP 10 OLDEST NOBEL PRIZE WINNERS

WINNER / COUNTRY / AWARD	DATE OF BIRTH	AGE* YRS	MTHS	DAYS
1 Leonid Hurwicz (USA) Economics 2007	21 Aug 1917	90	3	28
2 Raymond Davis Jr (USA) Physics 2002	14 Oct 1914	88	1	26
3 Doris Lessing (UK) Literature 2007	22 Oct 1919	88	1	18
4 Yoichiro Nambu (Japan) Physics 2008	18 Jan 1921	87	10	22
5 Vitaly L. Ginzburg (Russia) Physics 2003	4 Oct 1916	87	2	6
6 Peyton Rous (USA) Medicine 1966	5 Oct 1879	87	2	5
7 Joseph Rotblat (UK) Peace 1995	4 Nov 1908	87	1	6
8 Karl von Frisch (Germany) Medicine 1973	20 Nov 1886	87	0	20
9 Ferdinand Buisson (France) Peace 1927	20 Dec 1841	85	11	20
10 John B. Fenn (USA) Chemistry 2002	15 Jun 1917	85	5	25

* At date of award ceremony – prizes are announced in October, but awarded annually on 10 December, Alfred Nobel's birthday

Senior scientist
American scientist Raymond Davis Jr (1914–2006), head of the Homestake Experiment that detected neutrinos in the Sun, became the oldest-ever winner of the Nobel Physics prize for his work.

THE 10 YOUNGEST NOBEL PRIZE WINNERS

WINNER / COUNTRY	DATE OF BIRTH	AWARD	AGE* YRS	MTHS	DAYS
1 William Lawrence Bragg (UK)	31 Mar 1890	Physics 1915	25	8	10
2 Werner Karl Heisenberg (Germany)	5 Dec 1901	Physics 1932	31	0	5
3 Tsung-Dao Lee (China)	24 Nov 1926	Physics 1957	31	0	16
4 Carl David Anderson (USA)	3 Sept 1905	Physics 1936	31	3	7
5 Paul Adrien Maurice Dirac (UK)	8 Aug 1902	Physics 1933	31	4	2
6 Frederick Grant Banting (Canada)	14 Nov 1891	Medicine 1923	32	0	26
7 Rudolf Ludwig Mössbauer (West Germany)	31 Jan 1929	Physics 1961	32	10	10
8 Mairead Corrigan (UK)	27 Jan 1944	Peace 1976	32	10	13
9 Joshua Lederberg (USA)	23 May 1925	Medicine 1958	33	6	17
10 Betty Williams (UK)	22 May 1943	Peace 1976	33	6	18

* At date of award ceremony

TOP 10 NOBEL PRIZE-WINNING COUNTRIES*

COUNTRY	NOBEL PRIZES	PRIZES PER MILLION
1 Switzerland	25	3.27
2 Iceland	1	3.13
3 Sweden	28	3.04
4 Denmark	13	2.37
5 Norway	11	2.30
6 Austria	19	2.28
7 UK	114	1.86
8 Ireland	8	1.81
9 Germany	101	1.23
10 Netherlands	18	1.09

* Ranked by prizes per million of population

THE 10 **FIRST WOMEN TO WIN A NOBEL PRIZE**

WINNER	COUNTRY	PRIZE	YEAR
1 Marie Curie* (1867–1934)	Poland	Physics	1903
2 Bertha von Suttner (1843–1914)	Austria	Peace	1905
3 Selma Lagerlöf (1858–1940)	Sweden	Literature	1909
4 Marie Curie (1867–1934)	Poland	Chemistry	1911
5 Grazia Deledda (1875–1936)	Italy	Literature	1926#
6 Sigrid Undset (1882–1949)	Norway	Literature	1928
7 Jane Addams† (1860–1935)	USA	Peace	1931
8 Irène Joliot-Curie§ (1897–1956)	France	Chemistry	1935
9 Pearl Buck (1892–1973)	USA	Literature	1938
10 Gabriela Mistral (1899–1957)	Chile	Literature	1945

* Shared half with husband Pierre Curie; other half to Henri Becquerel
\# Awarded 1927
† Shared with Nicholas Murray Butler
§ Shared with husband Frédéric Joliot-Curie

Medical pioneer
Institut Pasteur virologist Françoise Barré-Sinoussi received her 2008 Nobel Prize for Medicine for her discovery of HIV/AIDS.

THE 10 **LATEST WOMEN TO WIN A NOBEL PRIZE**

WINNER / COUNTRY	PRIZE	YEAR
1 Françoise Barré-Sinoussi (France, b. 1947) France	Medicine	2008
2 Doris Lessing (b. 1919) UK	Literature	2007
3 = Linda B. Buck (b. 1947) USA	Medicine	2004
= Elfriede Jelinek (b. 1946) Austria	Literature	2004
= Wangari Maathai (b. 1940) Kenya	Peace	2004
6 Shirin Ebadi (b. 1947) Iran	Peace	2003
7 Jody Williams (b. 1950) USA	Peace	1997
8 Wislawa Szymborska (b. 1923) Poland	Literature	1996
9 Christiane Nüsslein-Volhard (b. 1942) Germany	Medicine	1995
10 Toni Morrison (b. 1931) USA	Literature	1993

Women have won a total of 34 Nobel Prizes, 12 of them for Peace, 11 for Literature, seven for Physiology or Medicine, three for Chemistry and two for Physics.

World War I

TOP 10 **LARGEST ARMED FORCES OF WORLD WAR I**

	COUNTRY	MOBILIZED*
1	Russia	12,000,000
2	Germany	11,000,000
3	British Empire#	8,904,467
4	France	8,410,000
5	Austria-Hungary	7,800,000
6	Italy	5,615,000
7	USA	4,355,000
8	Turkey	2,850,000
9	Bulgaria	1,200,000
10	Japan	800,000

* Total at peak strength
# Including Australia, Canada, India, New Zealand, South Africa, etc.

Russia's armed forces were relatively small in relation to the country's population – some six per cent, compared with 17 per cent in Germany. Several other European nations had forces that were similarly substantial in relation to their populations: Serbia's army was equivalent to 14 per cent of its population. In total, more than 65,000,000 combatants were involved in fighting some of the costliest battles – in terms of numbers killed – that the world has ever known.

THE 10 **SMALLEST ARMED FORCES OF WORLD WAR I**

	COUNTRY	MOBILIZED*
1	Montenegro	50,000
2	Portugal	100,000
3	Greece	230,000
4	Belgium	267,000
5	Serbia	707,343
6	Romania	750,000
7	Japan	800,000
8	Bulgaria	1,200,000
9	Turkey	2,850,000
10	USA	4,355,000

* Total at peak strength

THE 10 **COUNTRIES SUFFERING THE GREATEST MILITARY LOSSES IN WORLD WAR I**

	COUNTRY	MOBILIZED*	WOUNDED	MISSING/POW	DEAD
1	Germany	11,000,000	4,216,058	1,152,800	1,773,700
2	Russia	12,000,000	4,950,000	2,500,000	1,700,000
3	France	8,410,000	4,266,000	537,000	1,375,800
4	Austria-Hungary	7,800,000	3,620,000	2,200,000	1,200,000
5	British Empire#	8,904,467	2,090,212	191,652	908,371
6	Italy	5,615,000	947,000	600,000	650,000
7	Romania	750,000	120,000	80,000	335,706
8	Turkey	2,850,000	400,000	250,000	325,000
9	USA	4,355,000	234,300	4,526	126,000
10	Bulgaria	1,200,000	152,390	27,029	87,500

1 cross = 10,000 dead

* Total at peak strength
# Including Australia, Canada, India, New Zealand, South Africa, etc.

THE 10 COUNTRIES WITH THE HIGHEST PROPORTIONS OF MILITARY VICTIMS IN WORLD WAR I*

	COUNTRY	WOUNDED (%)	MISSING/POW (%)	DEAD (%)
1	Romania	16.00	10.67	44.76
2	France	50.73	6.39	16.36
3	Germany	38.33	10.48	16.12
4	Austria-Hungary	46.41	28.21	15.38
5	Russia	41.25	20.83	14.17
6	Italy	16.87	10.69	11.58
7	Turkey	14.04	8.77	11.40
8	Great Britain	23.47	2.15	10.20
9	Bulgaria	12.70	2.25	7.29
10	Portugal	13.75	12.32	7.22

* As percentage of troops mobilized

Memorials to the Missing

In addition to the graves of known victims of World War I, Commonwealth War Graves Commission memorials alone record a total of 526,974 names of those who have no known graves: the Thiepval Memorial (Somme) lists 72,090 names, the Menin Gate, Ypres, 54,896 and Tyne Cot, near Passendale, 34,984.

Below: Line of fire
Of all the German troops mobilized, nearly 65 per cent were killed, wounded or captured in the course of World War I.

TOP 10 AIR ACES OF WORLD WAR I

	PILOT	NATIONALITY	KILLS CLAIMED*
1	Rittmeister Manfred Albrecht Freiherr von Richthofen#	German	80
2	Capitaine René Paul Fonck	French	75
3	Major William Avery Bishop	Canadian	72
4	Major Edward Corringham 'Mick' Mannock#	British	68
5 =	Major Raymond Collishaw	Canadian	62†
=	Oberleutnant Ernst Udet	German	62
7	Major James Thomas Byford McCudden#	British	57
8 =	Captain Anthony Wetherby Beauchamp-Proctor	South African	54
=	Captain Donald Roderick MacLaren	Canadian	54
=	Capitaine George Marie Ludovic Jules Guynemer#	French	54

* Approximate – some kills disputed
\# Killed in action
† Including two in Russian Civil War, 1919

The term 'ace' – a pilot who had brought down at least five enemy aircraft – first appeared in print in *The Times* of 14 September 1917.

Right: Red Baron
25-year-old air ace Manfred von Richthofen's reign of aerial terror ended when he was shot down on 21 April 1918.

World War II

THE 10 COUNTRIES SUFFERING THE GREATEST MILITARY LOSSES IN WORLD WAR II

COUNTRY	KILLED
1 USSR	13,600,000*
2 Germany	3,300,000
3 China	1,324,516
4 Japan	1,140,429
5 British Empire# (UK 264,000)	357,116
6 Romania	350,000
7 Poland	320,000
8 Yugoslavia	305,000
9 USA	292,131
10 Italy	279,800
Total	21,268,992

* Total, of which 7.8 million battlefield deaths
# Including Australia, Canada, India, New Zealand, etc.

The precise numbers of World War II military victims and civilian war deaths will never be known, these figures representing only authoritative estimates.

THE 10 SMALLEST ARMED FORCES OF WORLD WAR II

COUNTRY	PERSONNEL*
1 Costa Rica	400
2 Liberia	1,000
3 = El Salvador	3,000
= Honduras	3,000
= Nicaragua	3,000
6 Haiti	3,500
7 Dominican Republic	4,000
8 Guatemala	5,000
9 = Bolivia	8,000
= Paraguay	8,000
= Uruguay	8,000

* Total at peak strength

The smallest European force was that of Denmark, some 15,000, 13 of whom were killed during the one-day German invasion of 9 April 1940, when Denmark became the second country to be occupied.

THE 10 AREAS OF EUROPE MOST BOMBED BY ALLIED AIRCRAFT* IN WORLD WAR II

AREA / BOMBS DROPPED (TONS)

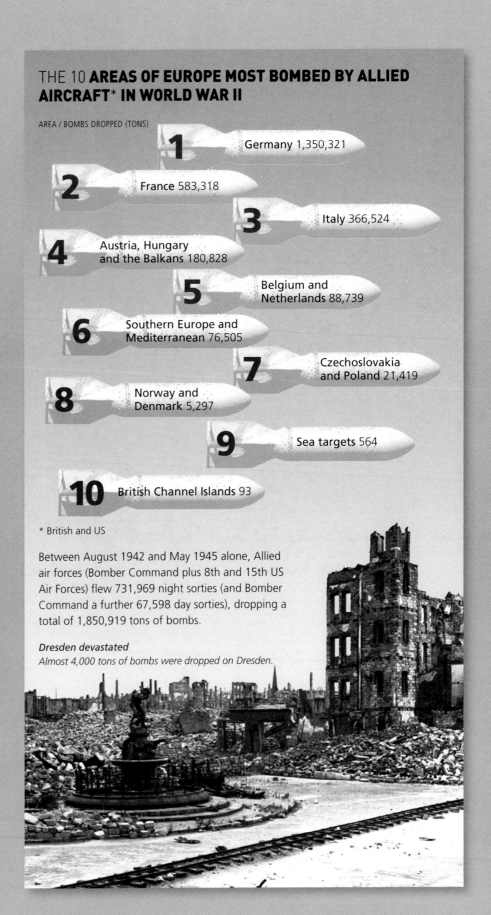

1 Germany 1,350,321

2 France 583,318

3 Italy 366,524

4 Austria, Hungary and the Balkans 180,828

5 Belgium and Netherlands 88,739

6 Southern Europe and Mediterranean 76,505

7 Czechoslovakia and Poland 21,419

8 Norway and Denmark 5,297

9 Sea targets 564

10 British Channel Islands 93

* British and US

Between August 1942 and May 1945 alone, Allied air forces (Bomber Command plus 8th and 15th US Air Forces) flew 731,969 night sorties (and Bomber Command a further 67,598 day sorties), dropping a total of 1,850,919 tons of bombs.

Dresden devastated
Almost 4,000 tons of bombs were dropped on Dresden.

THE 10 **SUBMARINE FLEETS WITH THE GREATEST LOSSES IN WORLD WAR II**

COUNTRY / SUBMARINES SUNK

- **10** Greece 4
- **9** Norway 5
- **8** Netherlands 10
- **7** France 23
- **1** Germany 787
- **2** Japan 130
- **6** USA 50
- **5** UK 77
- **3** USSR 103
- **4** Italy 85

U-boat loss
German submarine U-185 sank in the mid-Atlantic on 24 August 1943 after sustained attack by US aircraft.

THE 10 **COUNTRIES SUFFERING THE GREATEST AIRCRAFT LOSSES IN WORLD WAR II**

COUNTRY / AIRCRAFT LOST

- **10** New Zealand 684
- **9** France 2,100
- **8** Canada 2,389
- **1** Germany 116,584
- **2** USSR 106,652
- **3** USA 59,296
- **7** Italy 5,272
- **4** Japan 49,485
- **6** Australia 7,160
- **5** UK 33,090

While many reports are vague, very precise combat-loss figures exist for the Battle of Britain: during the period from 10 July to 31 October 1940, 1,065 RAF aircraft were destroyed, compared with 1,922 Luftwaffe fighters, bombers and other aircraft.

Modern Military

TOP 10 **LARGEST ARMED FORCES**

COUNTRY	ARMY	ESTIMATED ACTIVE FORCES NAVY	AIR	TOTAL
1 China	1,600,000	255,000	330,000	2,185,000
2 USA	632,245	339,453	340,530	1,539,587*
3 India	1,100,000	55,000	120,000	1,281,200#
4 North Korea	950,000	46,000	110,000	1,106,000
5 Russia	360,000	142,000	160,000	1,027,000†
6 South Korea	560,000	68,000	64,000	692,000
7 Pakistan	550,000	22,000	45,000	617,000
8 Iran	350,000	18,000	30,000	523,000§
9 Turkey	402,000	48,600	60,000	510,600
10 Egypt	340,000	18,500	30,000	468,500‡
UK	*95,780*	*30,880*	*33,620*	*160,280*

* Includes 186,661 Marine Corps and 40,698 Coast Guard
\# Includes 6,200 Coast Guard
† Includes 35,000 Airbone Army, 80,000 Strategic Deterrent Forces and 250,000 Command and Support
§ Includes 125,000 Islamic Revolutionary Guard Corps
‡ Includes 80,000 Air Defence Command

Source: The International Institute for Strategic Studies,
The Military Balance 2008

TOP 10 **MILITARY EXPENDITURE COUNTRIES**

COUNTY	% OF WORLD TOTAL	MILITARY SPENDING (US$MILLION)*
1 USA	48.51	713,100
2 France	4.19	61,571
3 UK	4.17	61,281
4 China	4.16	61,000
5 Russia	3.40	50,000
6 Japan	3.32	48,860
7 Germany	3.12	45,930
8 Italy	2.72	40,050
9 Saudi Arabia	2.11	31,050
10 Turkey	2.10	30,936
Top 10 total	*77.80*	*1,143,778*
World total	*100*	*1,470,000*

* 2009 or latest available year

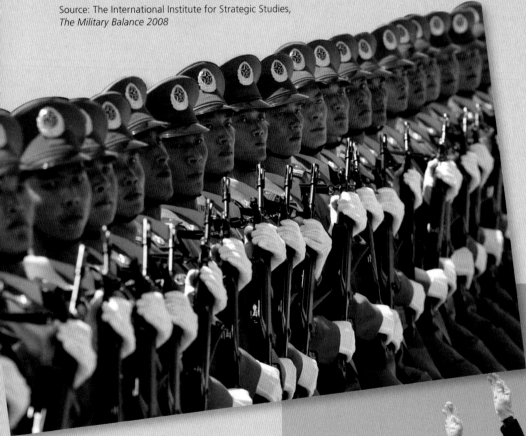

Show of arms
Recruits to the Jammu and Kashmir Light Infantry Regiment at a passing-out parade. The JKLIR, which celebrated its fiftieth anniversary in 2008, is a component of the million-plus Indian army.

Fighting force
The Chinese People's Liberation Army combines the country's serving land, sea and air personnel in a vast organization of over two million troops.

Chinese

TOP 10 RANKS OF THE ROYAL NAVY, ARMY AND ROYAL AIR FORCE

	ROYAL NAVY	ARMY	ROYAL AIR FORCE
1	Admiral	General	Air Chief Marshal
2	Vice-Admiral	Lieutenant-General	Air Marshal
3	Rear-Admiral	Major-General	Air Vice-Marshal
4	Commodore	Brigadier	Air Commodore
5	Captain	Colonel	Group Captain
6	Commander	Lieutenant-Colonel	Wing Commander
7	Lieutenant-Commander	Major	Squadron Leader
8	Lieutenant	Captain	Flight Lieutenant
9	Sub-Lieutenant	Lieutenant	Flying Officer
10	Acting Sub-Lieutenant	Second Lieutenant	Pilot Officer

In February 1996 the three most senior ranks in all three services – Admiral of the Fleet, Field Marshal and Marshal of the Royal Air Force – were abolished, in the cases of the first two ending a tradition that dates back several centuries. The names given to some ranks date back to medieval times – in the case of Admiral of the Fleet, for example, its earliest use in English has been dated to c. 1425, while Admiral was used even earlier to mean a prince or other military ruler in the service of a Sultan. The first recorded use of General was in 1576, and it appeared in Shakespeare's plays soon afterwards. The term Brigadier dates from 1678, and Field Marshal first appeared in print in 1736, when the Duke of Argyll and the Earl of Orkney were both appointed as Field Marshals of the British Army.

TOP 10 COUNTRIES WITH THE MOST BATTLE TANKS

	COUNTRY		TANKS
1	Russia		28,381
2	USA		7,821
3	China		7,580
4	Turkey		4,205
5	Syria		4,100
6	India		3,978
7	Ukraine		3,784
8	Egypt		3,680
9	Israel		3,650
10	North Korea		3,500
	UK		393

Fire power
The USA's main battle tank, the M1A1 Abrams. At an average cost of $3.325 million each, they represent a total cost of $26 billion.

Crime

THE 10 COUNTRIES WITH THE HIGHEST MURDER RATES

COUNTRY	MURDERS PER 100,000 POP.*
El Salvador	55.3
Honduras	49.9
Jamaica	49.0
Venezuela	48.0
Guatemala	45.2
South Africa	38.6
Colombia	37.0
Belize	30.8
Trinidad & Tobago	30.4
Brazil	25.7

* Recorded in 2006/2007

THE 10 AREAS OF ENGLAND AND WALES WITH THE HIGHEST CRIME RATES*

AREA*	CRIMES RECORDED (2007–08)
1 London (Met)	862,032
2 Greater Manchester	297,977
3 West Midlands	248,235
4 West Yorkshire	228,195
5 Thames Valley	196,008
6 Hampshire	164,940
7 South Yorkshire	145,769
8 Avon and Somerset	144,970
9 Kent	131,269
10 Merseyside	126,934
England & Wales total	*4,950,671*
Top 10 total	*2,546,329*

* England & Wales police areas

Source: Home Office, *Crime in England and Wales 2007/08*

THE 10 MOST COMMON CRIMES IN ENGLAND AND WALES

CRIME	NO. RECORDED (2007–08)
1 Theft and handling stolen goods (excl. car theft)	1,121,104
2 Criminal damage	1,036,246
3 Violence against the person	961,188
4 Car theft (incl. theft from vehicles)	656,549
5 Burglary (excl. domestic)	302,995
6 Domestic burglary	280,704
7 Drug offences	228,958
8 Fraud and forgery	155,358
9 Robbery	84,706
10 Sexual offences	53,540
Top 10 total	*4,881,348*
Total (including those not in Top 10)	*4,950,671*

Source: Home Office, *Crime in England and Wales 2007/08*

THE 10 MOST COMMON CRIMES IN ENGLAND AND WALES 100 YEARS AGO

OFFENCE	NO. REPORTED
1 Larcenies	68,483
2 Burglary and housebreaking	10,627
3 Frauds	4,345
4 Attempted suicide	2,443
5 Crimes of violence (other than murder)	1,828
6 Crimes against morals	1,643
7 Receiving	1,283
8 Forgery	383
9 Arson	296
10 Robbery and extortion	268

These are the annual averages of indictable crimes (calling for a trial before a jury) in England and Wales in 1903–07. Falling just below them are the almost defunct crime of 'coining' – the forgery of coins – (158 cases) and murder (132).

THE 10 MOST CORRUPT COUNTRIES

	COUNTRY	RATING
1	Somalia	1.0
2	= Iraq	1.3
	= Myanmar	1.3
4	Haiti	1.4
5	Afghanistan	1.5
6	= Chad	1.6
	= Guinea	1.6
	= Sudan	1.6
9	= Dem. Rep. of Congo	1.7
	= Equatorial Guinea	1.7

Source: Transparency International, *Corruption Perceptions Index 2008*

The Corruption Perceptions Index ranks countries by how likely they are to accept bribes, as perceived by the general public, business people and risk analysts. They are ranked on a scale of 0–10, the higher the score, the 'cleaner', or less corrupt, the country. A total of 180 countries were covered by the latest survey.

THE 10 LEAST CORRUPT COUNTRIES

	COUNTRY	RATING
1	= Denmark	9.3
	= New Zealand	9.3
	= Sweden	9.3
4	Singapore	9.2
5	= Finland	9.0
	= Switzerland	9.0
7	= Iceland	8.9
	= Netherlands	8.9
9	= Australia	8.7
	= Canada	8.7
	UK	*7.7*

Source: Transparency International, *Corruption Perceptions Index 2008*

Somali pirate
With little law and order, Somalia is considered the world's most corrupt country, with piracy an ongoing threat to international shipping.

Executions

THE 10 **LAST PEOPLE BURNED AT THE STAKE IN ENGLAND**

VICTIM / CIRCUMSTANCES	DATE

1 Christian (or Catherine) Murphy (or Bowman) — 18 Mar 1789
A female member of a gang of coiners, she was strangled and then burnt at Newgate, London.

2 Margaret Sullivan — 25 Jun 1788
Burned at Newgate for coining.

3 Phebe (or Phoebe) Harris — 21 Jun 1786
Burned at Newgate for coining.

4 Mary Bailey — 8 Mar 1784
Strangled and burnt at Winchester, Hampshire, along with John Quinn, for the murder of Cornelius Bailey. She was the last person to be burned at the stake for 'petty treason' (husband murder).

5 Rebecca Downing — 29 Jun 1782
A servant burned at Exeter, Devon, for murdering her mistress.

6 Isabella Condon — 27 Oct 1779
Burned at Tyburn for coining.

7 Ann Cruttenden — 8 Aug 1776
80-year-old Cruttenden was burned at the stake at Horsham, Sussex, for the murder of her husband.

8 Elizabeth Bordingham — 30 Mar 1776
Burned in York for murdering her husband.

9 Margaret Ryan — 18 Mar 1776
Burned at Maidstone, Kent, for husband murder.

10 Elizabeth Herring — 13 Sep 1773
Burned at Tyburn for husband murder.

Burning at the stake was the punishment reserved for women found guilty of treason, which included coining (forging coins), a crime for which men were customarily hanged, drawn and quartered, and 'petty treason', which included the murder of husbands and of masters and mistresses by servants. This punishment was abolished on 5 June 1790.

THE 10 **LAST PEOPLE EXECUTED AT THE TOWER OF LONDON**

VICTIM / CIRCUMSTANCES	DATE

1 Josef Jakobs — 15 Aug 1941
A German spy, parachuted into England posing as James Rymer, a British civilian, but was captured by the Home Guard. He was tried and shot at the Tower of London at 7.15 a.m. on 15 August 1941 – seated in a chair, as he had broken his ankle. He was the only World War II spy and the last person to be executed at the Tower of London.

2 Ludovico Hurwitz-y-Zender — 11 Apr 1916
A spy of Peruvian descent charged with sending information to Germany about British troop movements.

3 Albert Meyer — 2 Dec 1915
Meyer was a German spy who posed as a commercial traveller.

4 Irving Guy Ries — 27 Oct 1915
Like Meyer, Ries claimed to be a commercial traveller.

5 Georg Traugott Breeckow — 26 Oct 1915
Posing as an American, Reginald Rowland, with a forged passport, he was caught when he sent a parcel containing secret messages, but addressed in German style – with country and town name preceding that of the street.

6 Fernando Buschman — 19 Oct 1915
Posing as a Dutch violinist, Buschman spied while offering entertainment at Royal Navy bases.

7 Augusto Alfredo Roggen — 17 Sep 1915
A German who attempted to escape the death penalty by claiming to be Uruguayan, Roggen was found guilty of spying on tests of a new torpedo at Loch Lomond, sending information in invisible ink.

8 Ernst Waldemar Melin — 10 Sep 1915
A German spy, shot after a General Court Martial.

9 Haicke Petrus Marinus Janssen — 30 Jul 1915
Janssen was an accomplice of Roos, who used the same methods. They were tried together, with Janssen shot 10 minutes after Roos, at 6.10 a.m.

10 Wilhem Johannes Roos — 30 Jul 1915
A Dutchman who had posed as a cigar salesman, sending coded messages to a firm in Holland detailing ship movements in British ports, Roos was the third spy of World War I to be shot at the Tower of London.

German spy Carl Hans Lody was the first foreign spy and, since Simon Fraser, Lord Lovat in 1747, the first person to be executed at the Tower when he was shot on 6 November 1914, having been found guilty of relaying British naval secrets. He was followed on 23 June 1915 by Carl Fredrick Muller, a spy who had transmitted messages in cipher and invisible ink.

THE 10 **LAST PUBLIC HANGINGS IN THE UK**

VICTIM / CIRCUMSTANCES	DATE
1 Joseph Phillip Le Brun	11 Aug 1875

Found guilty of the murder of his sister Nancy Laurence, Le Brun was hanged in Jersey by British executioner William Marwood. Jersey was not yet covered by the law now in force in the rest of the UK.

2 Michael Barrett — 26 May 1868

Barrett, 27, was hanged at the Old Bailey, London, for the murder of Sarah Ann Hodgkinson, one of 12 victims of a Fenian (Irish nationalist) bombing in Clerkenwell, London. His was the last public hanging on the UK mainland.

3 Robert Smith — 12 May 1868

Nineteen-year-old Smith was hanged at Dumfries, Scotland, for the murder of nine-year-old Thomasina Scott. Smith's was the last public hanging in Scotland – although the crowd was held back from the scaffold.

4 Richard Bishop — 30 Apr 1868

Bishop, 21, was hanged in Maidstone, Kent, for the fatal stabbing of Alfred Cartwright.

5 Frederick Parker — 4 Apr 1868

Parker, a 21-year-old bricklayer, was executed in York for the murder of Daniel Driscoll near Selby, Yorkshire.

6 Timothy Faherty — 4 Apr 1868

Faherty was hanged at the New Bailey prison, Salford, Manchester, by hangman William Calcraft for the murder of Mary Hanmer.

7 Miles Weatherill — 4 Apr 1868

Weatherhill was executed at the New Bailey, Salford, immediately after Faherty for the murder of the Reverend Anthony Plow and his maid Jane Smith.

8 Frances Kidder — 2 Apr 1868

Twenty-five-year-old Kidder's hanging at Maidstone for the murder of her stepdaughter, 12-year-old Louisa Kidder-Staple, was the last public hanging of a woman in the UK.

9 William Worsley — 31 Mar 1868

Worsley was executed in Bedford for the murder of William Bradbury.

10 John Mapp — 22 Mar 1868

Mapp, aged 35, was hanged in Shrewsbury, Wiltshire, for the murder of nine-year-old Catherine Lewis.

Public hangings were a common sight in Britain's towns and cities until 29 May 1868, when the Capital Punishment (Amendment) Act was passed, after which all hangings took place behind prison walls. William Calcraft (1800–79), the official hangman in this transitional period, undertook the last public hangings on the British mainland and the first in private.

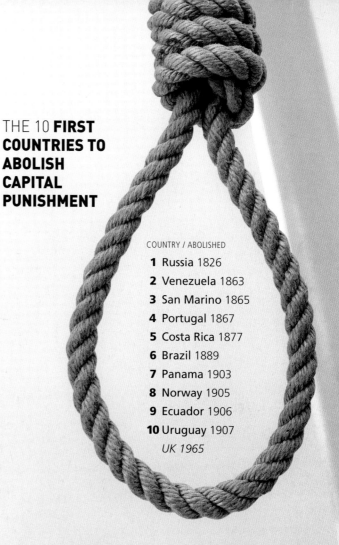

THE 10 **FIRST COUNTRIES TO ABOLISH CAPITAL PUNISHMENT**

COUNTRY / ABOLISHED	
1 Russia	1826
2 Venezuela	1863
3 San Marino	1865
4 Portugal	1867
5 Costa Rica	1877
6 Brazil	1889
7 Panama	1903
8 Norway	1905
9 Ecuador	1906
10 Uruguay	1907
UK	*1965*

THE 10 **LAST MEN HANGED IN THE UK**

	VICTIM	PRISON	DATE
1 =	Peter Anthony Allen	Liverpool	13 Aug 1964
=	John Robson Welby*	Manchester	13 Aug 1964
3 =	Russell Pascoe	Bristol	17 Dec 1963
=	Dennis John Whitty	Winchester	17 Dec 1963
5	Henry John Burnett	Aberdeen	15 Aug 1963
6	James Smith	Manchester	28 Nov 1962
7	Oswald Augustus Grey	Birmingham	20 Nov 1962
8	James Hanratty	Bedford	4 Apr 1962
9	Robert Andrew McGladdery	Belfast	20 Dec 1961
10	Hendryk Niemasz	Wandsworth	8 Sep 1961

* Or Walby, aka Gwynne Owen Evans

Capital punishment was abolished in the UK on 9 November 1965. Welby and Allen, the last two men to be hanged, were executed on the same day but at different prisons after being found guilty of stabbing John Alan West to death during a robbery. The last woman hanged in the UK was Ruth Ellis, executed on 13 July 1955 for shooting David Blakely.

World Religions

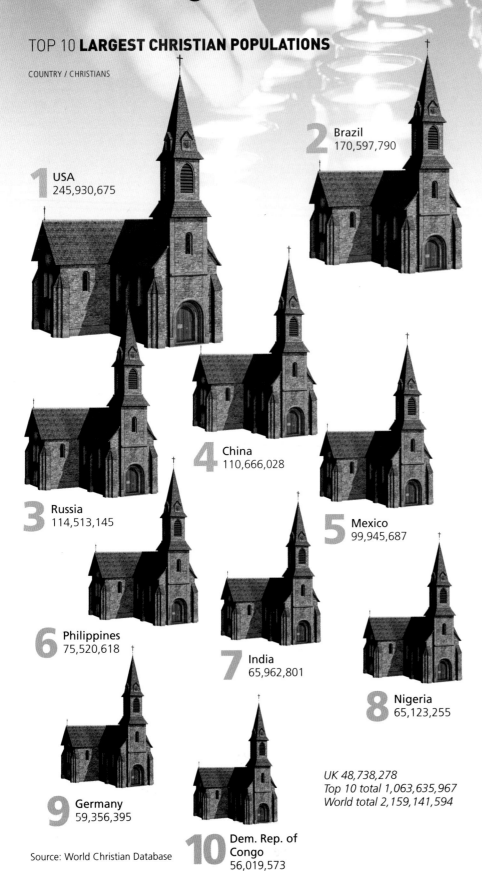

TOP 10 **LARGEST CHRISTIAN POPULATIONS**

COUNTRY / CHRISTIANS

1 USA
245,930,675

2 Brazil
170,597,790

3 Russia
114,513,145

4 China
110,666,028

5 Mexico
99,945,687

6 Philippines
75,520,618

7 India
65,962,801

8 Nigeria
65,123,255

9 Germany
59,356,395

10 Dem. Rep. of Congo
56,019,573

UK 48,738,278
Top 10 total 1,063,635,967
World total 2,159,141,594

Source: World Christian Database

TOP 10 **LARGEST JEWISH POPULATIONS**

	COUNTRY	JEWS
1	USA	5,760,530
2	Israel	4,843,655
3	France	609,905
4	Argentina	512,671
5	Canada	418,315
6	UK	282,306
7	Germany	224,963
8	Russia	187,916
9	Ukraine	182,425
10	Brazil	140,925
	Top 10 total	*13,163,611*
	World total	*14,692,748*

Source: World Christian Database

Although not an independent country, the West Bank and Gaza are together reckoned to have 444,707 Jewish inhabitants.

TOP 10 **LARGEST HINDU POPULATIONS**

	COUNTRY	HINDUS
1	India	817,112,705
2	Nepal	18,725,504
3	Bangladesh	14,751,609
4	Indonesia	7,217,099
5	Sri Lanka	2,515,776
6	Pakistan	2,053,374
7	Malaysia	1,607,947
8	USA	1,337,734
9	South Africa	1,141,006
10	Myanmar	818,250
	UK	*604,436*
	Top 10 total	*867,281,004*
	World total	*872,921,745*

Source: World Christian Database

Hindus constitute some 72.03 per cent of the population of India and 69.11 per cent of that of Nepal, but only 9.62 per cent of that of Bangladesh and as little as 3.19 per cent of Indonesia.

Buddhist shrine
A Buddhist monk at the feet of the giant Buddha of Wat Intharawihan, Thailand.

Left: Riding high
Followers celebrate the week-long Hola Mohalla festival in India, the foremost centre of Sikhism.

TOP 10 **LARGEST SIKH POPULATIONS**

COUNTRY	SIKHS
1 India	21,274,191
2 UK	384,906
3 Canada	330,773
4 USA	269,862
5 Thailand	51,032
6 Saudi Arabia	45,336
7 Malaysia	42,481
8 Pakistan	40,627
9 Australia	35,171
10 Kenya	32,566
Top 10 total	*22,506,945*
World total	*22,782,827*

Source: World Christian Database

TOP 10 **LARGEST MUSLIM POPULATIONS**

COUNTRY	MUSLIMS
1 India	155,115,142
2 Pakistan	151,806,340
3 Bangladesh	135,690,886
4 Indonesia	127,753,305
5 Turkey	71,054,050
6 Iran	68,243,783
7 Nigeria	62,408,926
8 Egypt	61,769,354
9 Algeria	32,198,881
10 Morocco	29,991,256
UK	*1,539,737*
Top 10 total	*896,031,923*
World total	*1,358,290,337*

Source: World Christian Database

TOP 10 **LARGEST BUDDHIST POPULATIONS**

COUNTRY	BUDDHISTS
1 China	116,774,700
2 Japan	71,795,145
3 Thailand	54,158,633
4 Vietnam	41,401,771
5 Myanmar	35,476,781
6 Sri Lanka	12,999,238
7 Cambodia	11,901,352
8 India	7,789,140
9 South Korea	7,233,870
10 Laos	3,001,939
UK	*191,724*
Top 10 total	*362,532,569*
World total	*378,724,109*

Source: World Christian Database

TOWN & COUNTRY

Country Facts

THE 10 **LARGEST COUNTRIES IN THE AMERICAS**

	COUNTRY	SQ KM	SQ MILES
			AREA
1	Canada	9,984,670	3,855,103
2	USA	9,629,091	3,717,813
3	Brazil	8,514,877	3,287,613
4	Argentina	2,780,400	1,073,519
5	Mexico	1,964,375	758,450
6	Peru	1,285,216	496,225
7	Colombia	1,138,914	439,737
8	Bolivia	1,098,581	424,165
9	Venezuela	912,050	352,145
10	Chile	756,102	291,933

Source: United Nations

Geographically, Greenland – with an area of 2,166,086 sq km (836,331 sq miles), which would place it fifth in this list – is considered part of the Americas, but being under Danish control, does not qualify as an independent country.

TOP 10 **LARGEST COUNTRIES IN EUROPE**

	COUNTRY	SQ KM	SQ MILES
			AREA
1	Russia*	3,960,000	1,528,965
2	Ukraine	603,500	233,013
3	France	551,500	212,935
4	Spain	505,992	195,365
5	Sweden	450,295	173,860
6	Germany	357,022	137,849
7	Finland	338,145	130,559
8	Norway	323,802	125,021
9	Poland	312,685	120,728
10	Italy	301,318	116,340

* In Europe; total area 17,098,242 sq km (6,601,669 sq miles)

Source: United Nations

The United Kingdom falls just outside the Top 10 at 242,900 sq km (93,784 sq miles), the 78th largest in the world.

THE 10 **MOST RECENT INDEPENDENT COUNTRIES**

	COUNTRY	INDEPENDENCE
1	Abkhazia	26 Aug 2008*
2	South Ossetia	8 Aug 2008*
3	Kosovo	17 Feb 2008*
4	= Serbia	3 Jun 2006
	= Montenegro	3 Jun 2006
6	East Timor	20 May 2002
7	Palau	1 Oct 1994
8	Eritrea	24 May 1993
9	= Czech Republic	1 Jan 1993
	= Slovakia	1 Jan 1993

* Not recognized internationally

New country
Although it awaits full international recognition, Kosovo became one of the world's newest countries when it declared independence in 2008.

TOP 10 **COUNTRIES WITH MOST NEIGHBOURS**

COUNTRY / NEIGHBOURS   NO. OF NEIGHBOURS

1 Russia
Abkhazia, Azerbaijan, Belarus, China, Estonia, Finland, Georgia, Kazakhstan, Latvia, Lithuania, Mongolia, North Korea, Norway, Poland, South Ossetia, Ukraine   16

2 China
Afghanistan, Bhutan, India, Kazakhstan, Kyrgyzstan, Laos, Mongolia, Myanmar, Nepal, North Korea, Pakistan, Russia, Tajikistan, Vietnam   14

3 = Brazil
Argentina, Bolivia, Colombia, Guyana, Paraguay, Peru, Suriname, Uruguay, Venezuela   9

= Dem Rep of Congo
Angola, Burundi, Central African Republic, Congo, Rwanda, Sudan, Tanzania, Uganda, Zambia   9

= Germany
Austria, Belgium, Czech Republic, Denmark, France, Luxembourg, Netherlands, Poland, Switzerland   9

= Sudan
Central African Republic, Chad, Dem. Rep. of Congo, Egypt, Eritrea, Ethiopia, Kenya, Libya, Uganda   9

7 = Austria
Czech Republic, Germany, Hungary, Italy, Liechtenstein, Slovakia, Slovenia, Switzerland   8

= France
Andorra, Belgium, Germany, Italy, Luxembourg, Monaco, Spain, Switzerland   8

= Serbia
Albania, Bosnia-Herzegovina, Bulgaria, Croatia, Hungary, Republic of Macedonia, Montenegro, Romania   8

= Tanzania
Burundi, Dem. Rep. of Congo, Kenya, Malawi, Mozambique, Rwanda, Uganda, Zambia   8

= Turkey
Armenia, Azerbaijan, Bulgaria, Georgia, Greece, Iran, Iraq, Syria   8

= Zambia
Angola, Botswana, Dem. Rep. of Congo, Malawi, Mozambique, Namibia, Tanzania, Zimbabwe   8

It should be noted that some countries have more than one discontinuous border with the same country, each of which has been counted only once. Borders with overseas territories are discounted – if included, France, with borders such as that with Brazil and French Guyana, could be considered as bordering a total of 11 countries. Countries connected only by bridges or tunnels (Bahrain/Saudi Arabia, Denmark/Sweden, Singapore/Malaysia and UK/France) are also excluded.

TOP 10 **LARGEST COUNTRIES**

COUNTRY / AREA SQ KM/SQ MILES / % OF WORLD TOTAL

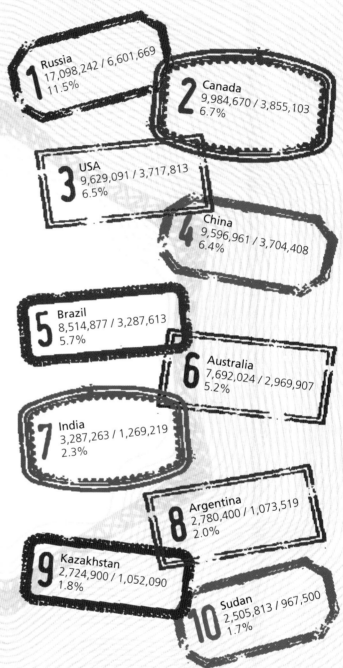

1 Russia 17,098,242 / 6,601,669 11.5%

2 Canada 9,984,670 / 3,855,103 6.7%

3 USA 9,629,091 / 3,717,813 6.5%

4 China 9,596,961 / 3,704,408 6.4%

5 Brazil 8,514,877 / 3,287,613 5.7%

6 Australia 7,692,024 / 2,969,907 5.2%

7 India 3,287,263 / 1,269,219 2.3%

8 Argentina 2,780,400 / 1,073,519 2.0%

9 Kazakhstan 2,724,900 / 1,052,090 1.8%

10 Sudan 2,505,813 / 967,500 1.7%

UK 242,900 / 93,784 0.16%
World 148,939,063 / 57,505,700 100.0%

Source: United Nations Statistics Division

This list is based on the total area of a country within its borders, including offshore islands, inland water such as lakes and rivers, and reservoirs. It may thus differ from versions of this list in which such features are excluded.

People Counting

Top town
London, the world's most populous city in 1910, was overtaken by New York a decade later.

Gene pool
Although one-fifth of the world's population lives in China, it is scheduled to be overtaken by India.

TOP 10 **MOST POPULATED COUNTRIES**

	COUNTRY	% OF WORLD TOTAL	POPULATION (2010 EST.)
1	China	19.62	1,347,563,498
2	India	17.24	1,184,090,490
3	USA	4.50	309,162,581
4	Indonesia	3.54	242,968,342
5	Brazil	2.93	201,103,330
6	Pakistan	2.62	179,659,223
7	Bangladesh	2.33	159,765,367
8	Nigeria	2.22	152,217,341
9	Russia	2.03	139,390,205
10	Japan	1.85	126,804,433
	UK	*0.89*	*61,284,806*
	Top 10 total	*58.87*	*4,042,724,810*
	World	*100.00*	*6,866,880,431*

Source: US Census Bureau, International Data Base

In 2009, the population of Nigeria overtook that of Russia, the only country in the Top 10 whose population is declining. Mexico, with a projected 2010 population of 112,468,855, is the only other country in the world with a population of more than 100 million.

TOP 10 **MOST POPULOUS CITIES IN THE WORLD, 1910**

	CITY	POPULATION
1	London, UK	6,580,616
2	Paris, France	2,763,393
3	Tokyo, Japan	2,186,079
4	Vienna, Austria	2,085,888
5	Berlin, Germany	2,040,148
6	St Petersburg, Russia	1,678,000
7	Peking, China	1,600,000
8	Moscow, Russia	1,359,254
9	Osaka, Japan	1,226,590
10	Buenos Aires, Argentina	1,189,252

World Population Milestones
The world's population 2,000 years ago is estimated to have been about 200 million. Having climbed to one billion by 1804, it took 123 years – until 1927 – for it to attain two billion. It hit three billion in 1960, four billion in 1974, five billion in 1987 and six billion in 1999. It is estimated that world population will increase to 6.9 billion in 2010, seven billion in 2012, eight billion in 2025 and nine billion in 2040.

TOP 10 **URBAN POPULATION COUNTRIES**

	COUNTRY	%	URBAN POPULATION TOTAL
1	China	45	594,794,000
2	India	28	327,316,000
3	USA	79	240,544,000
4	Brazil	83	162,452,000
5	Indonesia	48	115,510,000
6	Russia	73	103,526,000
7	Japan	79	100,516,000
8	Mexico	76	82,158,000
9	Nigeria	47	69,149,000
10	Germany	73	60,280,000
	UK	*80*	*49,033,000*

Source: Population Reference Bureau, *2008 World Population Data Sheet*

TOP 10 **COUNTRIES WITH THE BIGGEST POPULATION DECREASE**

COUNTRY / ESTIMATED POPULATION DECREASE 2008–50 (NO. / %)

1 Bulgaria	**2** Swaziland	**3** Guyana	**4** Georgia	**=** Ukraine	**6** Tonga	**7** Japan	**8** Moldova	**9** Russia	**10** Serbia
-2,648,000	-378,000	-226,000	-1,306,000	-12,805,000	-28,000	-32,568,000	-964,000	-31,775,000	-1,535,000
-35%	-33%	-29%	-28%	-28%	-27%	-25%	-23%	-22%	-21%

Source: Population Reference Bureau, *2008 World Population Data Sheet*

TOP 10 **COUNTRIES WITH THE BIGGEST POPULATION INCREASE**

COUNTRY / ESTIMATED POPULATION INCREASE 2008–50 (NO. / %)

1 Uganda	**2** Niger	**3** Burundi	**4** Liberia	**5** Guinea-Bissau	**6** Dem. Rep. of Congo	**7** Timor-Leste	**8** Mayotte	**9** Mali	**10** Somalia
76,855,000	38,432,000	19,459,000	8,518,000	3,578,000	122,796,000	1,935,000	325,000	21,515,000	14,859,000
263%	261%	220%	216%	205%	185%	179%	174%	169%	166%
									UK
									15,658,000
									26%

Source: Population Reference Bureau, *2008 World Population Data Sheet*

TOP 10 **MOST POPULOUS CITIES IN THE UK AT THE 1901 CENSUS**

CITY	POPULATION
1 London	4,536,063
2 Liverpool	684,947
3 Manchester	543,969
4 Birmingham	522,182
5 Leeds	428,953
6 Sheffield	380,717
7 Bristol	328,842
8 Bradford	279,809
9 West Ham	267,308
10 Kingston-upon-Hull	240,618

TOP 10 **MOST POPULOUS CITIES IN THE UK AT THE 2001 CENSUS**

CITY	POPULATION
1 London	7,172,091
2 Birmingham	970,892
3 Glasgow	629,501
4 Liverpool	469,017
5 Leeds	443,247
6 Sheffield	439,866
7 Edinburgh	430,082
8 Bristol	420,556
9 Manchester	394,269
10 Leicester	330,574

* Cities, excluding conurbation for all except London

Source: National Statistics

TOP 10 **MOST POPULATED ISLAND COUNTRIES**

	COUNTRY	POPULATION (2010 EST.)
1	Indonesia	242,968,342
2	Japan	126,804,433
3	Philippines	99,900,177
4	Malaysia	26,160,256
5	Sri Lanka	21,513,990
6	Madagascar	21,281,844
7	Cuba	11,477,459
8	Dominican Republic	9,794,487
9	Haiti	9,203,083
10	Papua New Guinea	6,182,390

Source: US Census Bureau, International Data Base

Place Names

TOP 10 **LONGEST PLACE NAMES***

NAME / LETTERS

1 Krung Thep Mahanakhon Amon Rattanakosin Mahinthara Ayuthaya Mahadilok Phop Noppharat Ratchathani Burirom Udomratchaniwet Mahasathan Amon Piman Awatan Sathit Sakkathattiya Witsanukam Prasit (168)

It means 'The city of angels, the great city, the eternal jewel city, the impregnable city of God Indra, the grand capital of the world endowed with nine precious gems, the happy city, abounding in an enormous Royal Palace that resembles the heavenly abode where reigns the reincarnated god, a city given by Indra and built by Vishnukarn'. When the poetic name of Bangkok, capital of Thailand, is used, it is usually abbreviated to 'Krung Thep' (city of angels).

2 Taumatawhakatangihangakoauauotamateaturipu kakapikimaungahoronukupokaiwhenuakitanatahu (85)

This is the longer version (the other has a mere 83 letters) of the Maori name of a hill in New Zealand. It translates as 'The place where Tamatea, the man with the big knees, who slid, climbed and swallowed mountains, known as land-eater, played on the flute to his loved one'.

3 Gorsafawddachaidraigddanheddogleddollôn penrhynareurdraethceredigion (67)

A name contrived by the Fairbourne Steam Railway, Gwynedd, North Wales, for publicity purposes and in order to outdo its rival, No. 4. It means 'The Mawddach station and its dragon teeth at the Northern Penrhyn Road on the golden beach of Cardigan Bay'.

4 Llanfairpwllgwyngyllgogerychwyrndrobwllllanty siliogogogoch (58)

This is the place in Gwynedd famed for the length of its railway tickets. Its name means 'St Mary's Church in the hollow of the white hazel near to the rapid whirlpool of the church of St Tysilo near the Red Cave'. It appears to have been a hoax perpetrated in the 1860s by an unnamed tailor.

5 El Pueblo de Nuestra Señora la Reina de los Ángeles de la Porciúncula (57)

The site of a Franciscan mission and the full Spanish name of Los Angeles; it means 'The town of Our Lady the Queen of the Angels of the Little Portion'. Nowadays it is customarily known by its initial letters, 'LA', making it also one of the shortest-named cities in the world.

6 Chargoggagoggmanchaugagoggchaubunag ungamaug (43)

America's longest placename, a lake near Webster, Massachusetts, is claimed to mean 'You fish on your side, I'll fish on mine, and no one fishes in the middle'. It is, however, a hoax name devised in about 1921 by local journalist Larry Daly.

7 = Lower North Branch Little Southwest Miramichi = Villa Real de la Santa Fé de San Francisco de Asis (40)

Canada's longest placename – a short river in New Brunswick. The full Spanish name of Santa Fe, New Mexico, translates as, 'Royal city of the holy faith of St Francis of Assisi'.

9 Te Whakatakanga-o-te-ngarehu-o-te-ahi-a-Tamatea (38)

The hyphenated or single-word Maori name of Hammer Springs, New Zealand. Like the second name in this list, it refers to a legend of Tamatea, explaining how the springs were warmed by 'the falling of the cinders of the fire of Tamatea'.

10 Meallan Liath Coire Mhic Dhubhghaill (32)

The longest multiple name in Scotland, a place near Aultanrynie, Highland, alternatively spelled Meallan Liath Coire Mhic Dhughaill (30 letters).

* Including single-word, hyphenated and multiple names

Above: Brasília
The National Congress, Brasília: the purpose-built city replaced Rio de Janeiro as Brazil's capital in 1960.

Above right: South American giant
At the Rio carnival, Brazil celebrates with a float depicting Simón Bolivar, the founder of its neighbour Bolivia.

TOP 10 **LARGEST COUNTRIES WHOSE NAMES ARE INCLUDED IN THOSE OF THE CAPITAL CITY**

	CAPITAL	COUNTRY	POPULATION
1	Brasília	Brazil	188,001,000
2	Mexico City	Mexico	106,682,500
3	Algiers	Algeria	33,858,000
4	Guatemala City	Guatemala	13,354,000
5	Tunis	Tunisia	10,327,000
6	Santo Domingo	Dominican Republic	9,760,000
7	Singapore	Singapore	4,839,400
8	Panama City	Panama	3,343,000
9	Kuwait	Kuwait	2,851,000
10	Bissau	Guinea Bissau	1,695,000

These are the only 10 countries in the world with populations of more than one million where the country names are identical to or are incorporated in those of its capital cities. In some instances the city took its name from the country, while in others it was the other way round. Among smaller countries exhibiting this phenomenon are Djibouti (Djibouti), Luxembourg (Luxembourg), São Tomé (São Tomé and Príncipe), Andorra la Vella (Andorra), Monaco (Monaco), San Marino (San Marino) and Vatican City (Vatican City).

TOP 10 **LARGEST COUNTRIES NAMED AFTER REAL PEOPLE**

		AREA	
	COUNTRY / NAMED AFTER	SQ KM	SQ MILES
1	United States of America Amerigo Vespucci (Italy; 1451–1512)	9,166,601	3,539,245
2	Saudi Arabia Abdul Aziz ibn-Saud (Nejd;1882–1953)	2,149,690	830,000
3	Bolivia Simón Bolivar (Venezuela;1783–1830)	1,084,389	418,685
4	Colombia Christopher Columbus (Italy; 1451–1506)	1,038,699	401,044
5	Philippines Philip II (Spain; 1527–98)	298,171	115,124
6	Swaziland Mswati II (Swaziland; c. 1820–68)	17,364	6,704
7	Falkland Islands Lucius Cary, 2nd Viscount Falkland (Britain; c. 1610–43)	12,173	4,700
8	Mauritius Maurice of Nassau (Orange; 1567–1625)	2,040	787
9	Kiribati Thomas Gilbert (British; fl. 1780s)	726	280
10	Northern Mariana Maria Theresa (Austria; 1717–80)	477	184

Many countries were named after mythical characters, or saints of dubious historical authenticity – often because they were discovered on the saint's day – but these are all named after real people. The origin of the name 'America' is uncertain, some authorities citing a Richard Amerike (c. 1445–1503) as its true source.

Capital Cities

TOP 10 **LARGEST CAPITAL CITIES**

CITY / COUNTRY	ESTIMATED POPULATION (2009)
1 Tokyo Japan	33,800,000
2 Seoul, South Korea	23,900,000
3 Mexico City, Mexico	22,900,000
4 Delhi*, India	21,500,000
5 Manila, Philippines	19,200,000
6 Cairo, Egypt	14,800,000
7 Jakarta, Indonesia	15,100,000
8 Buenos Aires, Argentina	13,800,000
9 Moscow, Russia	13,500,000
10 Beijing, China	13,200,000

* Capital New Delhi

Source: Th. Brinkhoff: *The Principal Agglomerations of the World*, www.citypopulation.de

TOP 10 **LARGEST NON-CAPITAL CITIES**

CITY / COUNTRY	CAPITAL	POPULATION (2009)
1 Mumbai, India	Delhi	22,300,000
2 New York, USA	Washington DC	21,900,000
3 São Paulo, Brazil	Brasília	21,000,000
4 Los Angeles, USA	Washington DC	18,000,000
5 Shanghai, China	Beijing	17,900,000
6 Osaka, Japan	Tokyo	16,700,000
7 Kolkata*, India	Delhi	16,000,000
8 Karachi*, Pakistan	Islamabad	15,700,000
9 Guangzhou, China	Beijing	15,300,000
10 Rio de Janeiro*, Brazil	Brasília	12,500,000

* Former capital

Source: Th. Brinkhoff: *The Principal Agglomerations of the World*, www.citypopulation.de

Northern Lights
Reykjavik, Iceland – the most northerly capital city – is situated 7,134 km (4,432 miles) from the North Pole.

TOP 10 **MOST NORTHERLY CAPITAL CITIES**

	CAPITAL	COUNTRY	LATITUDE
1	Reykjavik	Iceland	64° 08′ N
2	Helsinki	Finland	60° 12′ N
3	Olso	Norway	59° 56′ N
4	Tallin	Estonia	59° 26′ N
5	Stockholm	Sweden	59° 21′ N
6	Riga	Latvia	56° 58′ N
7	Moscow	Russia	55° 45′ N
8	Copenhagen	Denmark	55° 43′ N
9	Vilnius	Lithuania	54° 41′ N
10	Dublin	Ireland	53° 21′ N

At 55° 57′ N, Scotland's capital Edinburgh is more northerly than half of the cities in the Top 10, while London is not far below, at 51° 30′ N.

TOP 10 **CAPITAL CITIES CLOSEST TO THE EQUATOR**

	CAPITAL	COUNTRY	LATITUDE
1	Quito	Ecuador	0° 15′ S
2	Kampala	Uganda	0° 19′ N
3	São Tomé	São Tomé and Príncipe	0° 20′ N
4	Libreville	Gabon	0° 23′ N
5	=Nairobi	Kenya	1° 17′ S
	=Singapore City	Singapore	1° 17′ N
7	Kigali	Rwanda	1° 57′ S
8	Mogadishu	Somalia	2° 04′ N
9	Kuala Lumpur	Malaysia	3° 08′ N
10	Bujumbura	Burundi	3° 23′ S

TOP 10 **MOST SOUTHERLY CAPITAL CITIES**

	CAPITAL	COUNTRY	LATITUDE
1	Wellington	New Zealand	41° 17′ S
2	Canberra	Australia	35° 17′ S
3	Montevideo	Uruguay	34° 53′ S
4	Buenos Aires	Argentina	34° 40′ S
5	Santiago	Chile	33° 27′ S
6	Maseru	Lesotho	29° 18′ S
7	Mbabane	Swaziland	26° 19′ S
8	Asuncíon	Paraguay	25° 16′ S
9	Maputo	Mozambique	25° 58′ S
10	Pretoria	South Africa	25° 44′ S

Although the Falkland Islands is a self-governing British Overseas Territory, rather than a country, its capital Stanley lies at 51° 41′ – making it as far south as London is to the north (51° 30′).

Tallest by Decade

100 years ago
The world's highest building in 1909 was the Metropolitan Life Tower, New York. Since then it has been overtaken as the heights of the tallest skyscrapers have almost quadrupled, with construction of record-breaking buildings increasingly shifting to Asia.

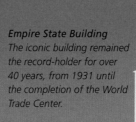

Chrysler Building
The Chrysler Building briefly held the title of world's tallest, from 28 May 1930 to 1 May 1931.

Empire State Building
The iconic building remained the record-holder for over 40 years, from 1931 until the completion of the World Trade Center.

TOP 10 **TALLEST HABITABLE BUILDINGS IN** 1930

BUILDING / LOCATION	YEAR COMPLETED	STOREYS	HEIGHT M	HEIGHT FT
1 Chrysler Building, New York, USA	1930	77	282	925
spire			*319*	*1,046*
2 40 Wall Street (Trump Building, formerly Bank of Manhattan Trust), New York, USA	1930	71	264	866
spire			*283*	*927*
3 Woolworth Building, New York, USA	1913	57	241	792
4 Terminal Tower, Cleveland, USA	1930	52	216	708
spire			*235*	*771*
5 Metropolitan Life Tower, New York, USA	1909	50	213	700
6 Lincoln Building, New York	1930	53	205	673
7 Chanin Building, New York, USA	1929	56	198	649
spire			*207*	*680*
8 Mercantile Building (10 East 40th Street), New York, USA	1929	48	193	632
9 New York Life Building, New York, USA	1928	33	187	615
spire			*203*	*665*
10 Singer Building*, New York, USA	1908	47	187	612

* Demolished 1968

TOP 10 **TALLEST HABITABLE BUILDINGS IN** 1960

BUILDING / LOCATION	YEAR COMPLETED	STOREYS	HEIGHT M	HEIGHT FT
1 Empire State Building, New York, USA	1931	102	381	1,250
spire			*449*	*1,472*
2 Chrysler Building, New York, USA	1929	77	282	925
spire			*319*	*1,046*
3 40 Wall Street, New York, USA	1929	71	264	866
spire			*283*	*927*
4 GE Building (formerly RCA Building), New York, USA	1933	70	259	850
5 American International Building, New York, USA	1932	67	252	826
spire			*290*	*952*
6 1 Chase Manhattan Plaza, New York, USA	1960	60	248	813
7 Woolworth Building, New York, USA	1913	57	241	792
8 MV Lomonosov State University, Moscow, Russia	1953	39	239	784
9 Palace of Culture and Science, Warsaw, Poland	1955	42	231	758
10 City Bank-Farmers Trust Company Building (20 Exchange Place), New York, USA	1931	57	226	741
spire			*228*	*748*

Sears Tower
Chicago's Sears Tower took the world's tallest crown in 1974 and remains America's highest habitable building.

Burj Dubai
Topped off in 2009, the Burj Dubai ('Dubai Tower') has broken every height record, even overtaking the tallest mast.

TOP 10 **TALLEST HABITABLE BUILDINGS IN** 1990

	BUILDING / LOCATION	YEAR COMPLETED	STOREYS	HEIGHT M	HEIGHT FT
1	Sears Tower, Chicago, USA	1974	108	442	1,450
	spire			527	1,730
2	1 World Trade Center*, New York, USA	1972	110	417	1,368
	spire			526	1,727
3	2 World Trade Center*, New York, USA	1973	110	415	1,363
4	Empire State Building, New York, USA	1931	102	381	1,250
	spire			449	1,472
5	Aon Center (formerly Amoco Building), Chicago, USA	1973	83	346	1,136
6	John Hancock Center, Chicago, USA	1968	100	344	1,127
	spire			427	1,500
7	Library Tower, Los Angeles, USA	1990	73	310	1,018
8	JPMorgan Chase Tower (formerly Texas Commerce Tower), Houston, USA	1982	75	305	1,002
9	Bank of China Tower, Hong Kong	1989	70	305	1,001
	spires			367	1,205
10	First Canadian Place, Toronto, Canada	1975	72	298	978
	spire			355	1,165

* Destroyed by 9/11 terrorist attacks

TOP 10 **TALLEST HABITABLE BUILDINGS IN** 2010

	BUILDING / LOCATION	YEAR COMPLETED	STOREYS	HEIGHT M	HEIGHT FT
1	Burj Dubai, Dubai, UAE	2009	162	818	2,684
2	Taipei 101, Taipei, China	2004	101	448	1,470
	spire			509	1,671
3	Shanghai World Financial Center, Shanghai, China	2008	101	492	1,614
4	International Commerce Centre, Hong Kong, China	2010*	118	484	1,588
5	Abraj Al Bait Towers, Mecca, Saudi Arabia	2010*	76	460	1,509
	spire			595	1,952
6	Petronas Towers, Kuala Lumpur, Malaysia	1998	88	452	1,483
7	Sears Tower, Chicago, USA	1974	108	442	1,450
	spire			527	1,730
8	West Tower, Guangzhou, China	2009	110	432	1,417#
9	Jin Mao Building, Shanghai, China	1998	88	383	1,255
	spire			421	1,380
10	2 International Finance Centre, Hong Kong, China	2003	90	415	1,362

* Under construction – scheduled completion
\# Helipad takes height to 437.5 m (1,435 ft)

Tallest by Type

TOP 10 **TALLEST BUILDINGS WITH NARROW BASES**

	BUILDING / LOCATION	YEAR COMPLETED	STOREYS	HEIGHT M	HEIGHT FT
1	The Center, Hong Kong, China	1998	73	292	958
	spire			*346*	*1,135*
2	Citigroup Center, New York, USA	1977	59	279	915
3	Alberta Plaza, Calgary, Canada	1984	75	277	909
4	Tower 42, London, UK	1980	47	183	600
5	First National Bank, Boston, Massachussets, USA	1971	37	180	591
6	Dalian Hope Mansion, Dalian, China	1999	38	171	561
7	MCI Plaza, Denver, Colorado, USA	1981	42	159	522
8	Rainier Tower, Seattle, Washington, USA	1977	31	156	512
9	Tour du Midi, Brussels, Belgium	1967	38	150	492
10	Kwa Dukuza Egoli Hotel Tower 1, Johannesburg, South Africa	1985	40	140	459

TOP 10 **TALLEST REINFORCED CONCRETE BUILDINGS**

	BUILDING / LOCATION	YEAR COMPLETED	STOREYS	HEIGHT M	HEIGHT FT
1	Mekkah Royal Hotel Tower, Mekkah, Saudi Arabia	2010*	76	485	1,591
2	Dubai Towers, Doha, Qatar	2010*	84	437	1,434
3	Trump International Hotel & Tower, Chicago, USA	2009*	96	415	1,362
4	Princess Tower, Dubai, United Arab Emirates	2009*	101	414	1,358
5 =	Al Hamra Tower, Kuwait City, Kuwait	2009*	77	412	1,352
=	Marina 101, Dubai, United Arab Emirates	2010*	101	412	1,352
7	Emirates Park Towers Hotel & Spa 1, Dubai, United Arab Emirates	2010*	77	395	1,296
8	Emirates Park Towers Hotel & Spa 2, Dubai, United Arab Emirates	2010*	77	395	1,296
9	CITIC Plaza, Guangzhou, China	1996	80	391	1,283
10	23 Marina, Dubai, United Arab Emirates	2009*	90	389	1,276

* Under construction – scheduled completion

Left: Skyscraper on stilts
New York's Citigroup Center has a distinctive stilt-like narrow base.

Right: Trumping its rivals
The Trump International Hotel and Tower, Chicago, is the USA's second tallest building.

TOP 10 **TALLEST CYLINDRICAL BUILDINGS**

	BUILDING / LOCATION	YEAR COMPLETED	STOREYS	HEIGHT M	HEIGHT FT
1	8 Shenton Way (formerly Treasury Building), Singapore	1986	52	235	770
2	Tun Abdul Razak Building, Penang, Malaysia	1985	61	232	760
3	Westin Peachtree Plaza, Atlanta, USA	1973	71	220	721
4	Renaissance Centre, Detroit, USA	1977	73	219	718
5	Hopewell Centre Hong Kong, China	1980	64	215	705
6	Marina City Apartments (twin towers), Chicago, USA	1969	61	179	588
7	Australia Square Tower, Sydney, Australia	1968	46	170	560
8	Amartapura Condominium 1, Tangerang, Indonesia	1996	54	163	535
9	Shenzen City Plaza, Shenzen, China	1996	37	150	490
10	Amartapura Condominium 2, Tangerang, Indonesia	1997	36	136	445

TOP 10 **TALLEST BUILDINGS WITH HOLES**

	BUILDING / LOCATION	YEAR COMPLETED	STOREYS	HEIGHT M	HEIGHT FT
1	Shanghai World Financial Center, Shanghai, China	2008	101	492	1,614
2	Tuntex 85 Sky Tower, Kaohsiung, China *spire*	1997	85	348 / *378*	1,142 / *1,240*
3	Gate of the Orient, Suzhou, China	2009*	66	301	
4	Kingdom Centre, Riyadh, Saudi Arabia	2002	41	300	984
5	The HarbourSide, Hong Kong, China	2003	74	255	837
6	Repsol Tower, Madrid, Spain	2008	45	250	823
7	Chelsea Tower, Dubai, United Arab Emirates *spire*	2005	49	230 / *251*	755 / *823*
8	CCTV Headquarters, Beijing, China	2008	51	234	768
9	The Arch, Hong Kong, China	2005	65	231	758
10	Centerpoint Energy Plaza, Houston, Texas, USA	1974	53	226	741

* Under construction – scheduled completion

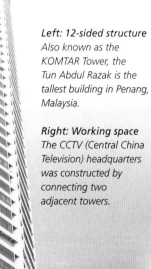

Left: 12-sided structure
Also known as the KOMTAR Tower, the Tun Abdul Razak is the tallest building in Penang, Malaysia.

Right: Working space
The CCTV (Central China Television) headquarters was constructed by connecting two adjacent towers.

Megastructures

TOP 10 **TALLEST TELECOMMUNICATIONS TOWERS**

TOWER / LOCATION	YEAR COMPLETED	HEIGHT* M	FT
1 **Tokyo Sky Tree**, Tokyo, Japan	2011#	610.58	2,001
2 **Guangzhou TV & Sightseeing Tower**, Guangzhou, China	2009#	610.0	2,001
3 **Jakarta TV Tower**, Jakarta, Indonesia	2010#	558.0	1,831
4 **CN Tower**, Toronto, Canada	1975	555.0	1,821
5 **Ostankino Tower**†, Moscow, Russia	1967	537.0	1,762
6 **Broadcasting, Telephone and TV-tower**, Xian, China	2008	470	1,542
7 **Oriental Pearl Broadcasting Tower**, Shanghai, China	1995	467.9	1,535
8 **Borj-e Milad Telecommunications Tower**, Tehran, Iran	2007	435.0	1,427
9 **Menara Telecom Tower**, Kuala Lumpur, Malaysia	1996	421.0	1,381
10 **Tianjin Radio and Television Tower**, Tianjin, China	1991	415.2	1,362

* To tip of antenna
\# Under construction – scheduled completion
† Severely damaged by fire 27 August 2000, restored and reopened 2004

All the towers listed are self-supporting, rather than masts braced with guy wires, and all have observation facilities. A flurry of tower construction in recent years has evicted the Eiffel Tower (1889, 324.0 m/10.063 ft) – which long headed the list – from the Top 10.

Ancient and modern
Symbolizing an early Chinese poem that refers to pearls, the Oriental Pearl Tower, Shanghai, China, a high-tech structure with a revolving restaurant, was once China's tallest structure.

Mighty Mosques
The world's tallest religious building is the Hassan II Mosque, Casablanca, Morocco. Completed in 1993, its minaret stands 210 m (689 ft) high. The world's largest mosque is the Masjid al-Haram ('Sacred Mosque'), Mecca, which covers 356,800 sq m (3,840,570 sq ft).

Gateway to the West
The Gateway Arch, St Louis, USA, is a monument commemorating the nation's westward expansion.

TOP 10 **TALLEST MONUMENTS**

MONUMENT	LOCATION	YEAR	HEIGHT M	HEIGHT FT
1 Gateway Arch	St Louis, Missouri, USA	1965	192	630
2 San Jacinto Monument	La Porte, Texas, USA	1939	174	570
3 Crazy Horse Memorial	Thunderhead Mountain, South Dakota, USA	u/c*	172	563
4 Juche Tower	Pyongyang, North, Korea	1982	170	558
5 Washington Monument	Washington, DC, USA	1884	169	555
6 Cruz de los Caidos	San Lorenzo de El Escorial, Spain	1956	150	492
7 Victory Monument	Moscow, Russia	1995	142	465
8 Pyramid of Khufu	Giza Egypt	2560 BC	139	455
9 National Monument	Jakarta, Indonesia	1975	137	449
10 Pyramid of Khafre	Giza, Egypt	2532 BC	136	448

* Under construction

TOP 10 **HIGHEST DAMS**

DAM / RIVER / LOCATION	YEAR COMPLETED	HEIGHT M	HEIGHT FT
1 **Rogun**, Vakhsh, Tajikistan	1985	335	1,099
2 **Nurek**, Vakhsh, Tajikistan	1980	300	984
3 **Xiaowan**, Lancangjiang, China	2012*	292	958
4 **Grande Dixence**, Dixence, Switzerland	1962	285	935
5 **Xiluodu**, China	2015*	273	896
6 **Inguri**, Inguri, Georgia	1984	272	892
7 **Vaiont**, Vaiont, Italy	1961	262	860
8 = **Manuel Moreno Torres**, Chicoasén, Grijalva, Mexico	1981	261	856
= **Tehri**, Bhagirathi, India	2006	261	856
10 **Álvaro Obregón**, Mextiquic, Mexico	1946	260	853

* Under construction – scheduled completion

Source: International Commission on Large Dams (ICOLD), *World Register of Dams*

TOP 10 **TALLEST CHIMNEYS**

CHIMNEY / LOCATION	YEAR	HEIGHT M	HEIGHT FT
1 **GRES-2 power station**, Ekibastuz, Kazakhstan	1987	420	1,378
2 **Inco Superstack**, International Nickel Company, Copper, Hill Sudbury, Ontario, Canada	1971	381	1,250
3 **Homer City Generating Station Unit 3**, Minersville, Pennsylvania, USA	1977	371	1,217
4 = **Kennecott Copper Corporation**, Magna, Utah, USA	1974	370	1,214
= **Beryozovskaya GRES**, Shaypovo, Russia	1985	370	1,214
6 **Mitchell Power Plant**, Moundsville, West Virginia, USA	1971	368	1,207
7 **Zasavje power station**, Trbovlje, Slovenia	1976	360	1,181
8 **Endesa Termic**, La Coruña, Spain	1974	356	1,168
9 **Phoenix Copper Smelter**, Baia Mare, Romania	n/a	352	1,155
10 **Syrdarya Power Plant Units 5–10**, Syrdarya, Uzbekistan	1975	350	1,148

Bridges & Tunnels

TOP 10 **LONGEST ARCH BRIDGES**

	BRIDGE / LOCATION	YEAR COMPLETED	LENGTH OF MAIN SPAN	
			M	FT
1	Chaotianmen, Chongqing, China	2008	552	1,811
2	Lupu, Shanghai, China	2003	550	1,804
3	New River Gorge, Fayetteville, West Virginia, USA	1977	518	1,699
4	Bayonne, Kill Van Kull, New Jersey/New York, USA	1931	504	1,654
5	Sydney Harbour, Sydney, Australia	1932	503	1,650
6	Chenab, Bakkal, India	2009	480	1,575
7	Wushan, Chongqing, China	2005	460	1,509
8	Xinguang, Guangzhou, China	2008	428	1,405
9	= Wanxian, Wanxian, China	1997	420	1,378
	= Caiyuanba, Chongqing, China	2007	420	1,378

Over-arching
Connecting Luwan and Pudong – hence its name – the Lupu Bridge, Shanghai, China, took the record as the world's longest arch bridge.

Sky high
While the giant pylons of the Millau Viaduct, France, are taller, the Royal Gorge Bridge, Colorado, USA, has the highest road deck.

TOP 10 **LONGEST RAIL TUNNELS**

	TUNNEL / LOCATION	YEAR COMPLETED	LENGTH	
			KM	MILES
1	AlpTransit Gotthard, Switzerland	2018*	57.1	35.6
2	Seikan, Japan	1988	53.9	33.6
3	Channel Tunnel, France/England	1994	50.5	31.5
4	Moscow Metro (Serpukhovsko-Timiryazevskaya line), Russia	2002	41.5	25.9
5	Moscow Metro (Kaluzhsko-Rizhskaya line), Russia	1990	37.6	23.4
6	Lötschberg Base, Switzerland	2007	34.6	21.6
7	Berlin U-Bahn (U7 line)	1984	31.8	19.8
8	Guadarrama, Spain	2007	28.4	17.7
9	Taihang, China	2008	27.9	17.4
10	London Underground (East Finchley/Morden, Northern Line), UK	1939	27.8	17.3

* Under construction – scheduled completion

The world's longest rail tunnel, the AlpTransit Gotthard, Switzerland, was proposed as early as 1947 and given the go-ahead in 1998 after a referendum of the Swiss electorate. When completed, trains will travel through it at 250 km/h (155 mph).

TOP 10 **LONGEST TUNNELS IN THE UK***

	TUNNEL / LOCATION	TYPE	YEAR COMPLETED	LENGTH	
				M	FT
1	Stratford West (Channel Tunnel rail link)	Rail	2007	10,105	33,152
2	Stratford East (Channel Tunnel rail link)	Rail	2007	7,555	24,786
3	Severn, Avon/Gwent	Rail	1886	7,008	22,992
4	Totley, South Yorkshire	Rail	1893	5,596	18,359
5	Standedge, Manchester/West Yorkshire	Canal	1811	5,210	17,093
6	Woodhead New#, South Yorkshire	Rail	1953	4,888	16,036
7	Standedge, Manchester/West Yorkshire	Rail	1949	4,886	16,030
8	Woodhead Old I#, South Yorkshire	Rail	1845	4,848	15,905
9	Woodhead Old II#, South Yorkshire	Rail	1852	4,840	15,879
10	Chipping Sodbury, Avon	Rail	1902	4,063	13,330

* Excluding underground railways
# Disused

TOP 10 **TALLEST BRIDGES**

	BRIDGE	LOCATION	YEAR	HEIGHT* M	FT
1	Royal Gorge	Colorado, USA	1929	321	1,053
2	Millau Viaduct	Millau, France	2004	270	886
3	New River Gorge	West Virginia, USA	1977	267	876
4	Foresthill	California, USA	1973	223	732
5	Mala Rijeka viaduct#	Montenegro	1973	200	656
6	Europabrücke	Patsch, Austria	1963	190	623
7	Kocher Valley	Geislingen am Kocher, Germany	1979	185	607
8	Đurđevića Tara	Montenegro	1940	172	564
9	Verrazano Narrows	New York City, USA	1964	69	226
10	Golden Gate	San Francisco, USA	1937	67	220

* Clearance above water
\# Rail; all others road

TOP 10 **LONGEST SUSPENSION BRIDGES**

	BRIDGE / LOCATION	YEAR COMPLETED	LENGTH OF MAIN SPAN M	FT
1	Akashi-Kaikyō, Kobe-Naruto, Japan	1998	1,991	6,532
2	Xihoumen, China	2007	1,650	5,413
3	Great Belt, Denmark	1997	1,624	5,328
4	Ryungyang, China	2005	1,490	4,888
5	Humber Estuary, UK	1980	1,410	4,625
6	Jiangyin, China	1998	1,385	4,543
7	Tsing Ma, Hong Kong, China	1997	1,377	4,518
8	Verrazano-Narrows, New York, USA	1964	1,298	4,260
9	= Golden Gate, San Francisco, USA	1937	1,280	4,200
	= Yangluo, Wuhan, China	2007	1,280	4,200

TOP 10 **LONGEST ROAD TUNNELS**

	TUNNEL / LOCATION	YEAR COMPLETED	LENGTH M	FT
1	Lærdal, Norway	2000	24,510	80,413
2	Zhongnanshan, China	2007	18,040	59,186
3	St Gotthard, Switzerland	1980	16,918	55,505
4	Arlberg, Austria	1978	13,972	45,850
5	Hsuehshan, Taiwan	2006	12,900	42,323
6	Fréjus, France/Italy	1980	12,895	42,306
7	Mont-Blanc, France/Italy	1965	11,611	38,094
8	Gudvangen, Norway	1991	11,428	37,493
9	Folgefonn, Norway	2001	11,100	36,417
10	Kan-Etsu II (southbound), Japan	1991	11,010	36,122

* Under construction – scheduled completion

Nos. 1, 3, 4 and 7 have all held the record as 'world's longest road tunnel'. Previous record-holders include the 5,854-m (19,206-ft) Grand San Bernardo (Italy-Switzerland; 1964); the 5,133-m (16,841-ft) Alfonos XIII or Viella (Spain; 1948); the 3,237-m (10,620-ft) Queensway (Mersey) Tunnel (connecting Liverpool and Birkenhead, UK; 1934); and the 3,186-m (10,453-ft) Col de Tende (France-Italy; 1882).

Going underground
Engineering advances have enabled the construction of increasingly long subterranean and underwater tunnels.

CULTURE & LEARNING

Words & Language

TOP 10 **LANGUAGES INTO WHICH MOST BOOKS ARE TRANSLATED**

LANGUAGE / TRANSLATIONS 1979–2008

1 German 270,484

2 Spanish 206,779

3 French 203,559

4 Japanese 117,769

5 English 115,710

6 Dutch 101,763

7 Portuguese 71,291

8 Polish 64,119

9 Russian 62,983

10 Danish 59,014

Source: UNESCO,
Index Translationum
(1979–2008)

TOP 10 **LANGUAGES FROM WHICH MOST BOOKS ARE TRANSLATED**

LANGUAGE / TRANSLATIONS 1979–2008

1 English 1,000,758

2 French 186,036   **3** German 169,387   **4** Russian 93,779

| **5** Italian 55,397 | **6** Spanish 43,365 | **7** Swedish 30,738 | **8** Latin 16,602 | **9** Danish 16,222 | **10** Czech 16,050 |

Source: UNESCO,
Index Translationum (1979–2008)

TOP 10 **LANGUAGES MOST SPOKEN IN THE UK**

LANGUAGE / APPROX. NO. OF SPEAKERS*

1 English 58,190,000

2 Welsh 582,000

3 Eastern Panjabi 471,000

4 = Bengali 400,000

= Urdu 400,000

6 = Chinese (Cantonese) 300,000

= Sylheti# 300,000

8 = Greek 200,000

= Italian 200,000

10 Caribbean Creole 170,000

* As primary language
# Spoken in Bangladesh

TOP 10 **MOST COMMON WORDS IN ENGLISH**

WRITTEN		SPOKEN
the	**1**	be
of	**2**	the
and	**3**	I
a	**4**	you
in	**5**	and
to	**6**	it
is	**7**	have
was	**8**	a
it	**9**	not
for	**10**	do

Source: British National Corpus

A survey of a wide range of texts containing a total of almost 90 million words indicated that, in written English, one word in every 16 is 'the'.

TOP 10 **LANGUAGES OFFICIALLY SPOKEN IN THE MOST COUNTRIES**

LANGUAGE / COUNTRIES

English 55

French 29

Arabic 24

Spanish 20

Portuguese 10

German 7

= Albanian 4
= Italian 4
= Russian 4
= Serbian 4

World English
English has become the lingua franca *in countries that have a multiplicity of local languages.*

TOP 10 **MOST-SPOKEN LANGUAGES***

LANGUAGE	SPEAKERS
1 Chinese (Mandarin)	873,014,298
2 Spanish	322,299,171
3 English	309,352,280
4 Hindi	180,764,791
5 Portuguese	177,457,180
6 Bengali	171,070,202
7 Russian	145,031,551
8 Japanese	122,433,899
9 German	95,392,978
10 Chinese (Wu)	77,175,000

* Primary speakers only

Source: Gordon, Raymond G., Jr. (ed.), *Ethnologue: Languages of the World*, Fifteenth edition. Dallas, Tex.: SIL International, 2005. Online version: www.ethnologue.com

Schools

TOP 10 COUNTRIES WITH MOST PRIMARY SCHOOL PUPILS

	COUNTRY	PRIMARY SCHOOL PUPILS (2006)
1	India	139,170,000
2	China	108,925,000
3	Indonesia	28,983,000
4	USA	24,319,000
5	Nigeria	22,115,000
6	Brazil	18,661,000
7	Pakistan	17,979,000
8	Bangladesh	17,953,000
9	Mexico	14,595,000
10	Philippines	13,007,000
	UK	*4,518,000*
	Top 10 total	*405,707,000*
	World total	*688,608,000*

Source: UNESCO, *Global Education Digest 2008*

TOP 10 COUNTRIES WITH MOST PRIMARY SCHOOL TEACHERS

	COUNTRY	AVERAGE CLASS SIZE	PRIMARY SCHOOL TEACHERS (2006)
1	China	18	5,968,000
2	India	64	2,189,000
3	USA	14	1,761,000
4	Indonesia	20	1,428,000
5	Brazil	21	887,000
6	Nigeria	37	599,000
7	Mexico	28	521,000
8	Pakistan	40	450,000
9	Japan	19	386,000
10	Philippines	35	376,000
	UK	*18*	*250,000*
	World	*25*	*27,216,000*

Source: UNESCO, *Global Education Digest 2008*

A class of their own
Almost 140 million children
attend primary school in India,
one in eight of its population.

TOP 10 **OLDEST SCHOOLS IN THE WORLD**

	SCHOOL	FOUNDED
1	Shishi Middle School, Chengdu, China	143–141 BC
2	The King's School, Canterbury, UK	597
3	The King's School, Rochester, UK	604
4	St Peter's School, York, UK	627
5	Beverley Grammar School, UK	700
6	Gymnasium Paulinum, Münster, Germany	797
7	Gymnasium Carolinum in Osnabrück, Germany	804
8	Warwick School, UK	914
9	St Alban's School, UK	948
10	The King's School, Ely, UK	970

TOP 10 **COUNTRIES WITH THE MOST SECONDARY SCHOOL PUPILS**

	COUNTRY	SECONDARY SCHOOL PUPILS (2006)
1	China	101,195,000
2	India	91,529,000
3	Brazil	24,863,000
4	USA	24,552,000
5	Indonesia	16,798,000
6	Russia	11,548,000
7	Mexico	10,883,000
8	Bangladesh	10,355,000
9	Vietnam	9,975,000
10	Egypt	8,330,000
	UK	5,358,000
	Top 10 total	310,028,000
	World total	513,766,000

High school
Although close behind
Brazil in numbers of
pupils in secondary
school, the population
of the USA is more than
one-third higher.

Further Education

Allama Iqbal Open University,
Islamabad, Pakistan
1,850,643

**Indira Gandhi National
Open University,**
New Delhi, India
1,800,000

Islamic Azad University,
Tehran, Iran
1,300,000

Anadolu University,
Eskisehir, Turkey
884,081

**Bangladesh
Open University,**
Eskisehir, Turkey
884,081

**University System
of Ohio,**
Ohio, USA
800,000

**Dr Babasaheb
Ambedkar Open
University,**
Andhra Pradesh, India
450,000

**State University
of New York,**
New York, USA
418,000

**California State
University,**
California, USA
417,000

University of Delhi,
India
400,000

TOP 10 **COUNTRIES WITH THE MOST UNIVERSITY STUDENTS**

COUNTRY / % FEMALE /
STUDENTS IN TERTIARY
EDUCATION (2006)

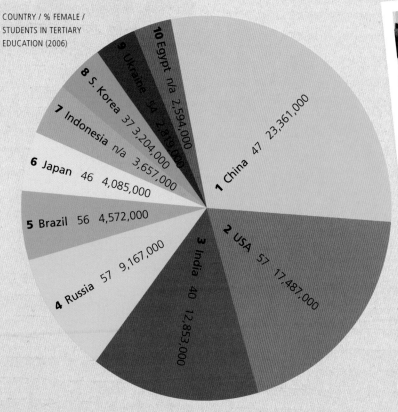

- **9** Ukraine 54 2,819,000
- **10** Egypt n/a 2,594,000
- **8** S. Korea 37 3,204,000
- **7** Indonesia n/a 3,657,000
- **6** Japan 46 4,085,000
- **5** Brazil 56 4,572,000
- **4** Russia 57 9,167,000
- **3** India 40 12,853,000
- **2** USA 57 17,487,000
- **1** China 47 23,361,000

High flyers
*A graduation ceremony in China, now at the
forefront of higher education.*

TOP 10 OLDEST UNIVERSITIES*

	UNIVERSITY	COUNTRY	FOUNDED
1	Parma	Italy	1064
2	Bologna	Italy	1088
3	Oxford	England	1117
4	Paris	France	1150
5	Modena	Italy	1175
6	Cambridge	England	1209
7	Salamanca	Spain	1218
8	Padua	Italy	1222
9	Naples	Italy	1224
10	Toulouse	France	1229

* Only those in continuous operation since founding

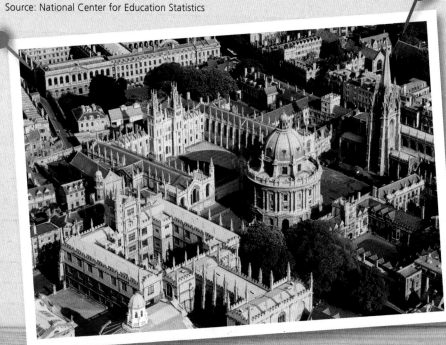

Alma mater
One of the world's oldest universities, Bologna's former students include Renaissance astronomer Nicolaus Copernicus.

TOP 10 OLDEST UNIVERSITIES IN THE UK

	UNIVERSITY	FOUNDED
1	Oxford	1117
2	Cambridge	1209
3	St Andrews	1411
4	Glasgow	1451
5	Aberdeen	1495
6	Edinburgh	1583
7	Dublin*	1592
8	Durham#	1832
9	London†	1836
10	Manchester	1851

* Ireland then part of England
# A short-lived Cromwellian establishment was set up in 1657
† Constituent colleges founded earlier: University College 1826, King's College 1828

Although its constituent colleges were founded earlier – Lampeter 1822, Aberystwyth 1872, Cardiff 1883, Bangor 1884 – the University of Wales dates from 1893.

Dreaming spires
Oxford was Britain's first university and is the oldest outside Italy.

TOP 10 OLDEST UNIVERSITIES AND COLLEGES IN THE USA

	UNIVERSITY / LOCATION	YEAR CHARTERED
1	Harvard University, Massachusetts	1636
2	College of William and Mary, Virginia	1692
3	Yale University, Connecticut	1701
4	University of Pennsylvania, Pennsylvania	1740
5	Moravian College, Pennsylvania	1742
6	Princeton University, New Jersey	1746
7	Washington and Lee University, Virginia	1749
8	Columbia University, New York	1754
9	Brown University, Rhode Island	1764
10	Rutgers, the State University of New Jersey	1766

Source: National Center for Education Statistics

Books & Libraries

TOP 10 MOST DOWNLOADED ENGLISH-LANGUAGE AUTHORS

	AUTHOR	DOWNLOADS*
1	Charles Dickens	37,541
2	Mark Twain	32,273
3	Jane Austen	27,979
4	William Shakespeare	27,678
5	Sir Arthur Conan Doyle	26,007
6	J. Arthur Thomson	23,069
7	Oscar Wilde	14,551
8	Lewis Carroll	13,790
9	Edgar Allan Poe	13,563
10	L. Frank Baum	13,355

* Based on 30-day sample on Project Gutenberg

THE 10 FIRST PUBLIC LIBRARIES IN THE UK

	LIBRARY	FOUNDED
1	Canterbury	1847
2	Warrington	1848
3	Salford	1849
4	Winchester	1851
5	= Manchester Free	1852
	= Liverpool	1852
7	= Bolton	1853
	= Ipswich	1853
9	Oxford	1854
10	= Cambridge	1855
	= Kidderminster	1855

TOP 10 BESTSELLING ENGLISH-LANGUAGE AUTHORS

	AUTHOR / COUNTRY / DATES	MAX. ESTIMATED SALES
1	= Agatha Christie (UK, 1890–1976)	4,000,000,000
	= William Shakespeare (England, 1664–1616)	4,000,000,000
3	Barbara Cartland (UK, 1901–2000)	1,000,000,000
4	Harold Robbins (USA, 1916–97)	750,000,000
5	Enid Blyton (UK, 1897–1968)	600,000,000
6	Danielle Steel (USA, b. 1947)	570,000,000
7	Dr Seuss (Theodor Seuss Geisel; USA, 1904–91)	500,000,000
8	= Horatio Alger Jr (USA, 1832–99)	400,000,000
	= Jackie Collins (UK, b. 1937)	400,000,000
	= J. K. Rowling (UK, b. 1965)	400,000,000
	= R. L. Stine (USA, b. 1943)	400,000,000

Estimates of book sales are fraught with difficulty: records have often been lost, publishers may either withhold information or exaggerate for publicity purposes, while taking account of all editions, including hardbacks, paperbacks and translations, compounds the problem. This list should therefore be regarded as a tentative attempt to indicate the total sales of the oeuvre of some of the bestselling writers of all time in the English language, according to authorities on the respective writers and their work. The omission, through lack of sales evidence, of such writers as Charles Dickens suggests that it should not be taken as definitive.

TOP 10 **LARGEST LIBRARIES**

* Founded as part of the British Museum, 1753; became an independent body in 1973
# Formed in 1990 through the unification of the Deutsche Bibliothek, Frankfurt (founded 1947) and the Deutsche Bucherei, Leipzig
† Founded 1862 as Rumyantsev Library, formerly State V. I. Lenin Library

	LIBRARY	LOCATION	FOUNDED	BOOKS
1	Library of Congress	Washington DC, USA	1800	32,124,001
2	British Library*	London, UK	1753	29,000,000
3	Library of the Russian Academy of Sciences	St Petersburg, Russia	1714	20,500,000
4	National Library of Canada	Ottawa, Canada	1953	19,500,000
5	Deutsche Bibliothek#	Frankfurt, Germany	1990	22,200,000
6	Russian State Library†	Moscow, Russia	1862	17,000,000
7	Harvard University Library	Cambridge, Massachusetts, USA	1638	15,826,570
8	Boston Public Library	Boston, Massachusetts, USA	1895	15,686,902
9	Vernadsky National Scientific Library of Ukraine	Kiev, Ukraine	1919	15,000,000
10	National Library of Russia	St Petersburg	1795	14,799,267

Library of Congress
The vast range of the collections of the Library of Congress is exemplified by the figures that surmount the eight columns in its reading room, which represent Religion, Commerce, History, Art, Philosophy, Poetry, Law and Science.

TOP 10 **BOOKS FOUND IN MOST LIBRARIES**

BOOK / TOTAL LIBRARY HOLDINGS*

* Based on WorldCat listings of all editions of books held in 53,000 libraries in 96 countries

Source: OCLC (Online Computer Library Center)

1 Bible 796,882
2 US Census 460,628
3 Mother Goose 67,663
4 Dante Alighieri, Divine Comedy 62,414
5 Homer, The Odyssey 45,551
6 Homer, The Iliad 44,093
7 Mark Twain, Huckleberry Finn 42,724
8 J. R. R. Tolkien, Lord of the Rings (trilogy) 40,907
9 William Shakespeare, Hamlet 39,521
10 Lewis Carroll, Alice's Adventures in Wonderland 39,277

Literary Prizes

THE 10 **LATEST KATE GREENAWAY MEDAL WINNERS**

YEAR   ILLUSTRATOR / TITLE

2008 Emily Gravett, Little Mouse's Big Book of Fears
2007 Mini Grey, The Adventures of the Dish and the Spoon
2005 Emily Gravett, Wolves
2004 Chris Riddell, Jonathan Swift's Gulliver
2003 Shirley Hughes, Ella's Big Chance
2002 Bob Graham, Jethro Byrde, Fairy Child
2001 Chris Riddell (text by Richard Platt), Pirate Diary
2000 Lauren Child, I Will Not Ever Never Eat a Tomato
1999 Helen Oxenbury, Alice's Adventures in Wonderland
1998 Helen Cooper, Pumpkin Soup

The Kate Greenaway Medal, named after the English illustrator (1846–1901), has been awarded annually since 1956 for the most distinguished work in the illustration of children's books published in the UK.

THE 10 **LATEST CARNEGIE MEDAL WINNERS**

YEAR   AUTHOR / TITLE

2008 Philip Reeve, Here Lies Arthur
2007 Meg Rosoff, Just in Case
2005 Mal Peet, Tamar
2004 Frank Cottrell Boyce, Millions
2003 Jennifer Donnelly, A Gathering Light
2002 Sharon Creech, Ruby Holler
2001 Terry Pratchett, Amazing Maurice and his Educated Rodents
2000 Beverley Naidoo, The Other Side of Truth
1999 Aidan Chambers, Postcards from No Man's Land
1998 David Almond, Skellig

Established in 1937, the Carnegie Medal is awarded annually by the Library Association for an outstanding English language children's book published during the previous year. It is named in honour of Scots-born millionaire Andrew Carnegie, who was a notable library benefactor. In its early years, winners included such distinguished authors as Arthur Ransome, Noel Streatfeild, Walter de la Mare and C. S. Lewis, while among notable post-war winners are books such as *Watership Down* by Richard Adams.

THE 10 **LATEST WINNERS OF HUGO AWARDS FOR BEST SCIENCE FICTION NOVEL**

YEAR   AUTHOR / TITLE

2008 Michael Chabon, The Yiddish Policeman's Union
2007 Vernor Vinge, Rainbows End
2006 Robert Charles Wilson, Spin
2005 Susanna Clarke, Jonathan Strange & Mr Norrell
2004 Lois McMaster Bujold, Paladin of Souls
2003 Robert J. Sawyer, Hominids
2002 Neil Gaiman, American Gods
2001 J.K. Rowling, Harry Potter and the Goblet of Fire
2000 Vernor Vinge, A Deepness in the Sky
1999 Connie Willis, To Say Nothing of the Dog

Hugo Awards for science-fiction novels, short stories and other fiction and non-fiction works are presented by the World Science Fiction Society. Named in honour of Hugo Gernsback, the 'father of magazine science fiction', they were established in 1953 as 'Science Fiction Achievement Awards for the best science fiction writing'. The prize in the Awards' inaugural year was presented to Alfred Bester for *The Demolished Man*.

Michael Chabon
Having received the Pulitzer Prize for Fiction in 2001, US author Michael Chabon won the 2008 Hugo Award.

THE 10 **LATEST WINNERS OF THE NOBEL PRIZE IN LITERATURE**

YEAR	WINNER / COUNTRY
2008	J. M. G. Le Clézio, France
2007	Doris Lessing, UK
2006	Orhan Pamuk, Turkey
2005	Harold Pinter, UK
2004	Elfriede Jelinek, Austria
2003	J. M. Coetzee, South Africa
2002	Imre Kertész, Hungary
2001	Sir V. S. Naipaul, UK
2000	Gao Xingjian, China
1999	Günter Grass, Germany

Le Clezio
Jean-Marie Gustave Le Clézio (left) receives his Nobel Prize from King Carl XVI Gustaf of Sweden.

THE 10 **LATEST WINNERS OF THE COSTA*** **'BOOK OF THE YEAR' AWARD**

YEAR	AUTHOR / TITLE
2008	Sebastian Barry, The Secret Scripture
2007	A. L. Kennedy, Day
2006	William Boyd, Restless: A Novel
2005	Hilary Spurling, Matisse The Master
2004	Andrea Levy, Small Island
2003	Mark Haddon, The Curious Incident of the Dog in the Night-Time
2002	Claire Tomalin, Samuel Pepys: The Unequalled Self
2001	Philip Pullman, The Amber Spyglass
2000	Matthew Kneale, English Passengers
1999	Seamus Heaney, Beowulf

* Whitbread until 2006

Nobel Prize Winners

Since it was first awarded in 1901, there have been 105 recipients of the Nobel Prize in Literature. As it is in effect a lifetime achievement award, it is not presented to young writers – Rudyard Kipling (UK, 1907 winner) was the youngest at 42. The first woman to receive the Prize was Selma Lagerlöf (Sweden, 1909), since when another 10 women have won. Twelve born or naturalized British and the same number of American writers have won it.

THE 10 **LATEST MAN BOOKER PRIZE WINNERS**

YEAR	AUTHOR / TITLE
2008	Aravind Adiga, White Tiger
2007	Anne Enright, The Gathering
2006	Kiran Desai, The Inheritance of Loss
2005	John Banville, The Sea
2003	Alan Hollinghurst, The Line of Beauty
2002	D.B.C. Pierre, Vernon God Little
2001	Yann Martel, Life of Pi
2000	Peter Carey, True History of the Kelly Gang
1999	Margaret Atwood, The Blind Assassin
1998	J. M. Coetzee, Disgrace

The Press

TOP 10 **DAILY NEWSPAPERS**

	NEWSPAPER	COUNTRY	AVERAGE DAILY CIRCULATION (2008)*
1	Yomiuri Shimbun	Japan	10,021,000
2	Asahi Shimbun	Japan	8,054,000
3	Mainichi Shimbun	Japan	3,945,646
4	Bild	Germany	3,548,000
5	Canako Xiaoxi (Beijing)	China	3,183,000
6	The Times of India	India	3,146,000
7	The Sun	UK	3,121,000
8	Nihon Keizai Shimbun	Japan	3,034,481
9	People's Daily	China	2,808,000
10	Chunichi Shimbun	Japan	2,763,602

* Morning edition if published twice daily

Source: World Association of Newspapers 2008 or latest Audit Bureau of Circulations figure

Yomiuri Shimbun was founded in Japan 1874. It became the country's and the world's bestselling daily newspaper when, in 1998, it achieved a record average sale of 14,532,694 copies a day, including its morning and evening editions.

The Times of India *The world's most-read English-language newspaper.*

TOP 10 **ENGLISH-LANGUAGE DAILY NEWSPAPERS**

	NEWSPAPER	COUNTRY	AVERAGE DAILY CIRCULATION (2008)
1	The Times of India	India	3,146,000
2	The Sun	UK	3,121,000
3	USA Today	USA	2,284,219
4	Daily Mail	UK	2,241,788
5	The Wall Street Journal	USA	2,069,463
6	Daily Mirror	UK	1,494,000
7	Hindustan Times	India	1,143,000
8	The Hindu	India	1,102,783
9	Deccan Chronicle	India	1,003,171
10	The New York Times	USA	1,000,665

Source: World Association of Newspapers 2008 or latest Audit Bureau of Circulations figure

The world's bestselling English-language dailies represent both long-established publications and relative newcomers: the *Daily Herald*, the first paper to ever sell two million copies, was launched in 1911, became *The Sun* in 1964 and was re-launched as a tabloid in 1969. The *Daily Mail* started in 1896, absorbing the *News Chronicle* in 1960 and *Daily Sketch* in 1971. *USA Today*, launched in 1982, was one of the first newspapers to use computers and to transmit editions for simultaneous publication around the world. *The Times of India* began in 1838 as *The Bombay Times* and *Journal of Commerce*, changing to its present name in 1861.

TOP 10 **DAILY NEWSPAPERS IN THE UK**

NEWSPAPER	AVERAGE NET CIRCULATION*
1 The Sun	3,146,006
2 The Daily Mail	2,228,897
3 The Mirror	1,366,891
4 The Daily Telegraph	842,912
5 Daily Star	768,534
6 Daily Express	736,340
7 The Times	617,483
8 Financial Times	432,944
9 The Guardian	358,844
10 Daily Record (Scotland)	354,302

* As at 25 January 2009

Source: Audit Bureau of Circulations Ltd

TOP 10 **CHILDREN'S AND TEEN MAGAZINES IN THE UK**

MAGAZINE	AVERAGE CIRCULATION PER ISSUE*
1 Sky Kids	762,254
2 Sugar	153,721
3 Disney High School Musical	148,514
4 Top of the Pops	125,558
5 The Simpsons Comics	112,393
6 Bliss	90,767
7 Doctor Who Adventures Magazine	82,205
8 Shout	81,904
9 Fun to Learn	79,400
10 Mizz	58,302

* In six-month period to 31 December 2008

Source: Audit Bureau of Circulation

Applied Science

Founded by artist-inventor Rufus Porter, *Scientific American* was first published on 28 August 1845 and is America's longest continuously published magazine. It originally included features on non-scientific topics, but its change of focus led to its becoming the world's most popular scientific journal.

Press censorship The military junta in Myanmar (Burma) severely restricts country's press.

THE 10 **COUNTRIES WITH THE LEAST PRESS FREEDOM**

COUNTRY	RATING
1 North Korea	98
2 Myanmar	97
3 Turkmenistan	96
4 = Cuba	94
= Eritrea	94
= Libya	94
7 Uzbekistan	92
8 Belarus	91
9 = Equatorial Guinea	89
= Zimbabwe	89

Source: Freedom House

This list is based on the Freedom House 2008 survey, which takes account of laws, political pressure, economic influence on and repressive actions against broadcast and print journalists; the higher the number, the worse the press freedom. The survey concludes that of a total of 195 countries, 72 have free press, 59 are partly free and 64 not free. The 'not free' category represents a population of 2,766,500,000, or 42 per cent of the world, and 'free' 1,177,090,000, or 18 per cent.

Reading frenzy
India's huge and literate population is served by a vast number of newspapers and magazines catering for its multiplicity of languages.

Art on Show

TOP 10 BEST-ATTENDED EXHIBITIONS AT THE NATIONAL GALLERY, LONDON*

EXHIBITION / YEAR	TOTAL ATTENDANCE
1 Manet to Picasso 2006–07	1,110,044
2 Seeing Salvation: The Image of Christ, 2000	355,175
3 Velázquez, 2006–07	302,520
4 Vermeer and the Delft School, 2001	276,164
5 Titian, 2003	267,939
6 Raphael: From Urbino to Rome, 2004–05	230,649
7 El Greco, 2004	219,000
8 Ron Mueck, 2003	193,320
9 Art in the Making: Degas 2004–05	186,181
10 Painted Illusions: Cornelius Gijsbrecht, 2000	173,272

* Twentieth century

TOP 10 MOST-VISITED GALLERIES AND MUSEUMS, 2008

GALLERY	TOTAL ATTENDANCE
1 Louvre Museum, Paris, France	8,500,000
2 British Museum, London, UK	5,930,000
3 National Gallery of Art, Washington, DC, USA	4,964,061
4 Tate Modern, London, UK	4,950,003
5 Metropolitan Museum of Art, New York, USA	4,821,079
6 Vatican Museums, Vatican City	4,441,734
7 National Gallery, London, UK	4,382,614
8 Musée d'Orsay, Paris, France	3,025,141
9 Musée d'Art Moderne Prado, Paris, France	2,981,000
10 Museum of Modern Art, New York, USA	2,900,157

Source: *Art Newspaper*

TOP 10 BEST-ATTENDED EXHIBITIONS AT THE ROYAL ACADEMY OF ARTS, LONDON

EXHIBITION / YEAR	TOTAL ATTENDANCE
1 The Genius of China 1974	771,466
2 Monet in the 20th Century 1999	739,324
3 Monet: The Series Paintings 1990	658,289
4 Pompeii AD79 1977	633,347
5 Post-Impressionism 1980	558,573
6 The Great Japan Exhibition 1982	523,005
7 The Genius of Venice 1983	452,885
8 Aztecs 2002–03	436,276
9 J. M. W. Turner 1975	424,629
10 From Russia 2008	388,628

TOP 10 BEST-ATTENDED EXHIBITIONS AT THE TATE MODERN, LONDON

EXHIBITION / YEAR	TOTAL ATTENDANCE
1 Matisse/Picasso 2002	467,166
2 Edward Hopper 2004–05	429,909
3 Frida Kahlo 2005	369,249
4 Rothko 2008–09	327,244
5 Kandinsky: The Path to Abstraction 2006	282,439
6 Andy Warhol 2002	218,801
7 Between Cinema and a Hard Place 2000	200,937
8 Henri Rousseau: Jungles in Paris 2005–06	190,795
9 Surrealism: Desire Unbound 2001–02	168,825
10 Dali and Film 2007	167,689

Ancient and Modern

Although controversial when it was built in 1989, the steel and glass Louvre pyramid, the design of Chinese-born architect I. M. Pei, has attracted increasing numbers of visitors to the museum. Once a royal palace, the Louvre was opened to the public in 1793, after the French Revolution. It is famous as the home of Leonardo da Vinci's *Mona Lisa*, which has been in France since 1516, when it was acquired by King Francis I.

Saleroom Record-breakers

TOP 10 **MOST EXPENSIVE PAINTINGS BY BRITISH ARTISTS**

PAINTING / ARTIST	SALE	PRICE (US$)
1 Triptych, Francis Bacon (1909–92)*	Sotheby's New York, 14 May 2008	86,281,000
2 Study from Innocent X, Francis Bacon	Sotheby's New York, 15 May 2007	52,680,000
3 Triptych, Francis Bacon	Christie's London, 6 Feb 2008	51,893,682 (£26,340,500)
4 Study for Bullfight No. 1, Francis Bacon	Sotheby's New York, 14 Nov 2007	45,961,000
5 Self-portrait, Francis Bacon	Sotheby's London, 21 Jun 2007	42,957,364 (£21,580,000)
6 Nude with Figure in a Mirror, Francis Bacon	Sotheby's London, 27 Feb 2008	39,320,704 (£19,956,000)
7 Giudecca, La Donna della Salute and San Giorgio, J. M. W. Turner (1775–1851)	Christies New York, 6 Apr 2006	35,856,000
8 Self-portrait, Francis Bacon	Christie's London, 30 Jun 2008	34,499,315 (£17,289,250)
9 Benefits Supervisor Sleeping, Lucian Freud (b. 1922)	Christie's New York, 13 May 2008	33,641,000
10 Self-portrait, Francis Bacon	Sotheby's New York, 14 Nov 2007	33,081,000

* Born Ireland, then part of UK

TOP 10 **MOST EXPENSIVE WORKS OF ART BY LIVING ARTISTS**

PAINTING / ARTIST	SALE	PRICE (US$)
1 Benefits Supervisor Sleeping, Lucian Freud (British; b. 1922)	Christie's New York, 13 May 2008	33,641,000
2 Balloon Flower – Magenta, Jeff Koons (American; b. 1955)	Christie's London, 30 Jun 2008	25,796,067 (£12,921,250)
3 Hanging Heart – Magenta/Gold, Jeff Koons	Sotheby's New York, 14 Nov 2006	23,561,000
4 Naked Portrait with Reflection, Lucian Freud	Christie's London, 30 Jun 2008	23,560,091 (£11,801,250)
5 IB and Her Husband, Lucian Freud	Christie's New York, 16 May 2007	19,361,000
6 Lullaby Spring, Damien Hirst (British; b. 1965)	Sotheby's London, 21 Jun 2007	19,075,098 (£9,652,000)
7 The Golden Calf, Damien Hirst	Sotheby's London, 15 Sep 2008	19,003,030 (£10,345,250)
8 The Kingdom, Damien Hirst	Sotheby's London, 15 Sep 2008	17,562,913 (£9,561,250)
9 Figure 4, Jasper Johns (American; b. 1930),	Christie's New York, 16 May 2007	17,400,000
10 False Start, Jasper Johns	Sotheby's New York, 10 Nov 1988	17,050,000

PRIVATE SALE RECORD-BREAKERS

The precise details of private (as contrasted with public auction) sales of works of art range from those that are totally secret to others where the vendor or purchaser deliberately publishes – and perhaps exaggerates – them in order to derive maximum publicity. In 2006, three paintings that were sold privately were claimed to have been the most expensive of all time: music mogul David Geffen sold Jackson Pollock's action painting *No. 5, 1948* for $140 million and Willem De Kooning's *Woman III* for $137.5 million, while Maria Altmann sold Gustav Klimt's *Portrait of Adele Bloch-Bauer I* to cosmetics magnate Ronald Lauder for $135 million. In the same year Pablo Picasso's *Le rêve* hit the headlines when its owner, Las Vegas casino owner Steve Wynn, agreed to sell it in a private transaction for $139 million. The sale was abandoned when Wynn accidentally damaged it by poking his elbow through the canvas. Picasso's *Garçon à la pipe* is the only other painting ever sold either privately or at auction for more than $100 million.

Monet market
Monet's waterlily painting was sold in 2008 for a record $80 million.

TOP 10 **MOST EXPENSIVE PAINTINGS EVER SOLD AT AUCTION**

PAINTING / ARTIST	SALE	PRICE (US$)
1 Garçon à la pipe, Pablo Picasso (Spanish; 1881–1973)	Sotheby's New York, 5 May 2004	104,168,000
2 Dora Maar au chat, Pablo Picasso	Sotheby's New York, 3 May 2006	95,216,000
3 Portrait of Adele Bloch-Bauer II, Gustav Klimt (Austrian; 1862–1918)	Christie's New York, 8 Nov 2006	87,936,000
4 Triptych, Francis Bacon (Irish; 1909–92)	Sotheby's New York, 14 May 2008	86,281,000
5 Portrait du Dr Gachet, Vincent van Gogh (Dutch; 1853–90)	Christie's New York, 15 May 1990	82,500,000
6 Le Bassin aux Nymphéas, Claude Monet (French; 1840–1926)	Christie's London, 24 Jun 2008	80,379,591 (£40,921,250)
7 Bal au Moulin de la Galette, Montmartre Pierre-Auguste Renoir (French; 1841–1919)	Sotheby's New York, 17 May 1990	78,100,000
8 The Massacre of the Innocents, Sir Peter Paul Rubens (Flemish; 1577–1640)	Sotheby's London, 10 Jul 2002	75,930,440 (£49,506,648)
9 White Center (Yellow, pink and lavender on rose), Mark Rothko (American; 1903–70)	Sotheby's New York, 15 May 2007	72,840,000
10 Green Car Crash – Green Burning Car I, Andy Warhol (American; 1928–87)	Christie's New York, 16 May 2007	71,720,000

TOP 10 **MOST EXPENSIVE PAINTINGS BY WOMEN ARTISTS**

PAINTING / ARTIST	SALE	SALE PRICE (US$)
1 Les Fleurs, Natalia Goncharova (Russian;1881–1962)	Christie's London, 24 Jun 2008	10,860,832 (£5,529,250)
2 Picking Apples, Natalia Goncharova	Christie's London, 18 Jun 2007	9,778,656 (£4,948,000)
3 The Visitor, Marlene Dumas (South African; b. 1953)	Sotheby's London, 1 Jul 2008	6,343,082 (£3,177,250)
4 Bluebells, Natalia Goncharova	Sotheby's London, 26 Nov 2007	6,229,793 (£3,044,500)
5 Children Playing with a Dog, Mary Cassatt (American; 1844–1926)	Christie's New York, 24 May 2007	6,200,000
6 Calla Lilies with Red Anemone, Georgia O'Keeffe (American; 1887–1986)	Christie's New York, 23 May 2001	6,166,000
7 Roots, Frida Kahlo (Mexican; 1907–54)	Sotheby's New York, 24 May 2006	5,616,000
8 Danseuses Espagnoles, Natalia Goncharova	Christie's London, 18 Jun 2007	5,573,122 (£2,820,000)
9 Cache-cache, Berthe Morisot (French; 1841–95)	Sotheby's New York, 2 Nov 2005	5,168,000
10 Chant 2, Bridget Riley (British; b. 1931)	Sotheby's London, 1 Jul 2008	5,113,296 (£2,561,250)

MUSIC

Singles

TOP 10 SINGLES OF ALL TIME

	TITLE / ARTIST	YEAR OF ENTRY	SALES EXCEED
1	'Candle in the Wind (1997)'/'Something About the Way You Look Tonight', Elton John	1997	37,000,000
2	'White Christmas', Bing Crosby	1942	30,000,000
3	'Rock Around the Clock', Bill Haley and His Comets	1954	17,000,000
4	'I Want to Hold Your Hand', The Beatles	1963	12,000,000
5 =	'It's Now or Never', Elvis Presley	1960	10,000,000
=	'Hey Jude', The Beatles	1968	10,000,000
=	'I Will Always Love You', Whitney Houston	1992	10,000,000
8 =	'Diana', Paul Anka	1957	9,000,000
=	'Hound Dog'/'Don't Be Cruel', Elvis Presley	1956	9,000,000
10 =	'(Everything I Do) I Do It For You', Bryan Adams	1991	8,000,000
=	'I'm a Believer', The Monkees	1966	8,000,000

Source: Music Information Database

In many countries, statistics on record sales were unavailable until recent times. Global sales are therefore notoriously difficult to calculate, with 'worldwide' customarily taken to mean minimum 'western world' sales. It took 55 years for a record to overtake Bing Crosby's 1942 'White Christmas', although including cover versions and sheet-music sales would place the song first in any list of bestsellers.

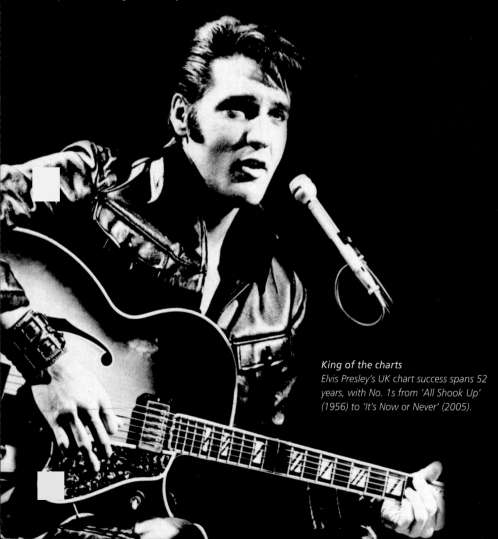

King of the charts
Elvis Presley's UK chart success spans 52 years, with No. 1s from 'All Shook Up' (1956) to 'It's Now or Never' (2005).

TOP 10 SINGLES IN THE UK 50 YEARS AGO

	TITLE	ARTIST
1	'It's Now or Never'	Elvis Presley
2	'Cathy's Clown'	Everly Brothers
3	'Apache'	Shadows
4	'Please Don't Tease'	Cliff Richard
5	'My Old Man's a Dustman'	Lonnie Donegan
6	'Handy Man'	Jimmy Jones
7	'Why'	Anthony Newley
8	'Poor Me'	Adam Faith
9	'A Mess of Blues'/ 'Girl of My Best Friend'	Elvis Presley
10	'I Love You'	Cliff Richard

Source: Music Information Database

In 1960, 'It's Now or Never' – initially prevented from release in the UK because of its apparent copyright infringement of 'O Sole Mio' – became the country's fastest-selling single, topping 1,000,000 in the UK within six weeks. The Everly Brothers' 'Cathy's Clown' was to be their all-time UK bestseller, as was the Shadows' 'Apache', their first success independent of Cliff Richard. (Apache, ironically dethroned Cliff's 'Please Don't Tease' from No. 1).

TOP 10 ARTISTS WITH THE MOST NO. 1 SINGLES IN THE UK

	ARTIST*	NO. 1 SINGLES
1	Elvis Presley (174)	21
2	The Beatles (54)	17
3 =	Cliff Richard (136)	14
=	Westlife (24)	14
5	Madonna (66)	13
6	Take That (21)	11
7 =	Abba (28)	9
=	Spice Girls (11)	9
9 =	Rolling Stones (55)	8
=	Oasis (25)	8

* Figures in brackets denote total chart hits

Source: Music Information Database

TOP 10 SINGLES IN THE UK IN 2008

	TITLE	ARTIST
1	'Hallelujah'	Alexandra Burke
2	'Hero'	X Factor Finalists
3	'Mercy'	Duffy
4	'I Kissed a Girl'	Katy Perry
5	'Rockstar'	Nickelback
6	'American Boy'	Estelle feat. Kanye West
7	'Sex on Fire'	Kings of Leon
8	'Now You're Gone'	Basshunter feat. DJ Mental Theo
9	'4 Minutes'	Madonna feat. Justin Timberlake
10	'Black and Gold'	Sam Sparro

Source: Official Charts Company

Sweet success
Madonna achieved her 13th UK No. 1 in 2008 on the eve of her 50th birthday and the launch of her Sticky & Sweet tour.

TOP 10 SINGLES IN THE UK IN THE PAST 10 YEARS

YEAR	TITLE	ARTIST
2008	'Hallelujah'	Alexandra Burke
2007	'Bleeding Love'	Leona Lewis
2006	'Crazy'	Gnarls Barkley
2005	'(Is This the Way to) Amarillo'	Tony Christie feat. Peter Kay
2004	'Do They Know It's Christmas'	Band Aid 20
2003	'Where Is the Love'	Black Eyed Peas
2002	'Anything is Possible'/'Evergreen'	Will Young
2001	'It Wasn't Me'	Shaggy feat. Rikrok
2000	'Can We Fix It'	Bob the Builder
1999	'Baby One More Time'	Britney Spears

Source: Official Charts Company

Of these bestselling artists, only four have had No. 1 hits since: Will Young (three), Britney Spears (two) and Elton John and Shaggy (once each). 'Where Is the Love' was Black Eyed Peas sole chart-topper.

TOP 10 SINGLES THAT STAYED LONGEST IN THE UK CHARTS

	TITLE / ARTIST*	FIRST CHART ENTRY	WEEKS IN CHART
1	'My Way', Frank Sinatra (42)	1969	124
2	'Chasing Cars', Snow Patrol (48)	2006	108
3	'Amazing Grace', Judy Collins (32)	1970	66
4	'Rule the World', Take That (30)	2007	63
5	'Relax', Frankie Goes to Hollywood (48)	1983	59
6	'Rehab', Amy Winehouse (34)	2006	58
7 =	'Rock Around the Clock', Bill Haley & His Comets (17)	1955	57
=	'Release Me', Engelbert Humperdinck (56)	1967	57
9	'Stranger on the Shore', Mr Acker Bilk (55)	1961	55
10	'Blue Monday', New Order (17)	1983	54

* Including reissues and remixes; numbers in brackets denote longest consecutive run on the charts

Source: Music Information Database

Albums

Golden age
Sales of Michael Jackson's Thriller *album were eclipsed in the UK, but it remains the world's bestselling.*

TOP 10 ALBUMS OF ALL TIME IN THE UK

TITLE / ARTIST / YEAR / SALES

1 Greatest Hits
Queen (1981)
5,407,587

2 Sgt. Pepper's Lonely Hearts Club Band
The Beatles (1967)
4,803,292

3 (What's the Story) Morning Glory
Oasis (1995)
4,303,504

4 Brothers in Arms
Dire Straits (1985)
3,946,931

5 Abba Gold
Abba (1992)
3,932,316

6 The Dark Side of the Moon
Pink Floyd (1973)
3,759,958

7 Greatest Hits II
Queen (1991)
3,631,321

8 Thriller
Michael Jackson (1982)
3,570,250

9 Bad
Michael Jackson (1987)
3,549,950

10 The Immaculate Collection
Madonna (1990)
3,364,785

Source: Official Charts Company

TOP 10 ALBUMS IN THE UK IN 2008

	TITLE	ARTIST
1	Rockferry	Duffy
2	The Circus	Take That
3	Only by the Night	Kings of Leon
4	Spirit	Leona Lewis
5	Viva La Vida	Coldplay
6	Good Girl Gone Bad	Rihanna
7	Day and Age	Killers
8	Out of Control	Girls Aloud
9	Funhouse	Pink
10	Scouting for Girls	Scouting for Girls

Source: Official Charts Company

TOP 10 ALBUMS IN THE UK IN THE PAST 10 YEARS

YEAR	TITLE	ARTIST
2008	Rockferry	Duffy
2007	Back to Black	Amy Winehouse
2006	Eyes Open	Snow Patrol
2005	Back to Bedlam	James Blunt
2004	Scissor Sisters	Scissor Sisters
2003	Life for Rent	Dido
2002	Escapology	Robbie Williams
2001	No Angel	Dido
2000	1	The Beatles
1999	Come on Over	Shania Twain

Source: Official Charts Company

Strong Rumours
Stevie Nicks and Lindsey Buckingham of Fleetwood Mac, whose
Rumours *entered the UK charts on 26 February 1977, last appearing*
on 24 September 2005.

THE 10 **SLOWEST UK ALBUM CHART RISES TO NO. 1**

TITLE / ARTIST	WEEKS TO REACH NO. 1
1 My People Were Fair and Had Sky in Their Hair, But Now They're Content to Wear Stars on Their Brows, Tyrannosaurus Rex	199
2 Abba Gold, Abba	117
3 40 Greatest Hits, Elvis Presley	114
4 Fame (Original Soundtrack), Various Artists	98
5 Come on Over, Shania Twain	88
6 Everybody Else is Doing It, So Why Can't We?, Cranberries	67
7 White Ladder, David Gray	66
8 Tubular Bells, Mike Oldfield	65
9 Happy Nation, Ace of Base	54
10 In Between Dreams, Jack Johnson	52

Source: Music Information Database

With the added distinction of having the longest title of any UK No. 1, the Tyrannosaurus Rex album originally charted in July 1968, but took until May 1972 to re-chart as half of a repackage with *Prophets, Seers and Sages, The Angels of the Ages,* when it hit UK No. 1.

TOP 10 **ALBUMS THAT STAYED LONGEST AT NO. 1 IN THE UK**

TITLE / ARTIST	WEEKS AT NO. 1
1 South Pacific, Soundtrack	115
2 The Sound of Music, Soundtrack	70
3 Bridge Over Troubled Water, Simon & Garfunkel	41
4 Please Please Me, The Beatles	30*
5 Sgt. Pepper's Lonely Hearts Club Band, The Beatles	27
6 G.I. Blues, Elvis Presley/Soundtrack	22
7 =With The Beatles, The Beatles	21*
=A Hard Day's Night, The Beatles/Soundtrack	21*
9 =Blue Hawaii, Elvis Presley/Soundtrack	18
=Saturday Night Fever, Soundtrack	18*

* Continuous run

Source: Music Information Database

Stayin' alive
Although it was released in 1977, no subsequent album has stayed
longer at UK No. 1 than the 18 consecutive weeks of the Saturday
Night Fever *soundtrack.*

TOP 10 **ALBUMS THAT STAYED LONGEST IN THE UK CHARTS**

TITLE / ARTIST*	FIRST CHART ENTRY	WEEKS IN CHART
1 Rumours, Fleetwood Mac (120)	1977	478
2 Bat Out of Hell, Meat Loaf (329)	1978	473
3 Greatest Hits, Queen (222)	1981	452
4 The Sound of Music, Soundtrack (318)	1965	382
5 The Dark Side of the Moon, Pink Floyd (135)	1973	366
6 Abba Gold, Abba (101)	1992	357
7 South Pacific, Soundtrack (153)	1960	319
8 Bridge Over Troubled Water, Simon & Garfunkel (244)	1970	307
9 Greatest Hits, Simon & Garfunkel (195)	1972	283
10 Tubular Bells, Mike Oldfield (128)	1973	276

* Numbers in brackets denote the longest consecutive run on the charts

Source: Music Information Database

Record Firsts

TOP 10 SINGLES IN THE FIRST UK TOP 10

TITLE / ARTIST

1 'Here in My Heart'
Al Martino

2 'You Belong to Me'
Jo Stafford

3 'Somewhere Along the Way'
Nat 'King' Cole

4 'Isle of Innisfree'
Bing Crosby

5 'Feet Up'
Guy Mitchell

6 'Half as Much'
Rosemary Clooney

7 = 'Forget Me Not'
Vera Lynn

= 'High Noon'
Frankie Laine

= 'Sugarbush'
Doris Day and Frankie Laine

= 'Blue Tango'
Ray Martin

8 'Homing Waltz'
Vera Lynn

9 'Auf Wiedersehen (Sweetheart)'
Vera Lynn

Source: New Musical Express

The first UK singles chart was published in the *New Musical Express* for the week ending 15 November 1952. Curiously, the Top 10 contained 12 entries because those of equal rank shared the same placing.

THE 10 FIRST SIMULTANEOUS US/UK CHART TOPPERS

	TITLE	ARTIST	DATE
1	'Oh Mein Papa'	Eddie Calvert	9 Jan 1954
2	'Cherry Pink and Apple Blossom White'	Perez Prado	7 May 1955
3	'Memories are Made of This'	Dean Martin	18 Feb 1956
4	'Singing the Blues'	Guy Mitchell	5 Jan 1957
5	'It's All in the Game'	Tommy Edwards	8 Nov 1958
6	'Cathy's Clown'	Everly Brothers	28 May 1960
7	'Can't Buy Me Love'	The Beatles	4 Apr 1964
8	'A Hard Day's Night'	The Beatles	1 Aug 1964
9	'Oh, Pretty Woman'	Roy Orbison	10 Oct 1964
10	'Baby Love'	The Supremes	21 Nov 1964

Source: Music Information Database

THE 10 **FIRST UK MALE ARTISTS TO TOP THE US SINGLES CHART**

TITLE / ARTIST	DATE AT NO. 1
1 'He's Got the Whole World (In His Hands)', Laurie London	19 Apr 1958
2 'Stranger on the Shore', Mr Acker Bilk	26 May 1962
3 'The Stripper', David Rose	7 Jul 1962
4 'Sunshine Superman', Donovan	3 Sep 1966
5 'My Sweet Lord'/'Isn't it a Pity', George Harrison	26 Dec 1970
6 'Maggie May'/'Reason to Believe', Rod Stewart	2 Oct 1971
7 'Crocodile Rock', Elton John	3 Feb 1973
8 'Photograph', Ringo Starr	26 Jan 1974
9 'I Shot the Sheriff', Eric Clapton	14 Sep 1974
10 'Whatever Gets You Thru the Night', John Lennon	16 Nov 1974

Source: Music Information Database

Transatlantic triumph
The Everly Brothers (above) and Guy Mitchell (below) were two of only 10 artists in a span of more than 12 years to achieve simultaneous US and UK chart-toppers.

THE 10 **FIRST FEMALE SINGERS TO HAVE A NO. 1 HIT IN THE UK**

ARTIST	TITLE	DATE AT NO. 1
1 Jo Stafford	'You Belong to Me'	17 Jan 1953
2 Kay Starr	'Comes A-Long A-Love'	24 Jan 1953
3 Lita Roza	'(How Much is That) Doggie in the Window?'	18 Apr 1953
4 Doris Day	'Secret Love'	17 Apr 1954
5 Kitty Kallen	'Little Things Mean a Lot'	11 Sep 1954
6 Vera Lynn	'My Son, My Son'	6 Nov 1954
7 Rosemary Clooney	'This Ole House'	27 Nov 1954
8 Ruby Murray	'Softly Softly'	19 Feb 1955
9 Alma Cogan	'Dreamboat'	16 Jul 1955
10 Anne Shelton	'Lay Down Your Arms'	22 Sep 1956

Source: Music Information Database

THE 10 **FIRST RECORDS TO ENTER THE UK CHART AT NO. 1**

ARTIST	TITLE	DATE AT NO. 1
1 Elvis Presley	'Jailhouse Rock'	25 Jan 1958
2 Elvis Presley	'It's Now or Never'	5 Nov 1960
3 Cliff Richard & the Shadows	'The Young Ones'	13 Jan 1962
4 Elvis Presley	'Can't Help Falling in Love/ Rock-A-Hula-Baby'	3 Mar 1962
5 The Beatles	'Get Back'	26 Apr 1969
6 Slade	'Cum On Feel the Noize'	3 Mar 1973
7 Slade	'Skweeze Me, Pleeze Me'	30 Jun 1973
8 Gary Glitter	'I Love You Love Me Love'	17 Nov 1973
9 Slade	'Merry Xmas Everybody'	15 Dec 1973
10 Jam	'Going Underground/ The Dreams of Children'	22 Mar 1980

Source: Music Information Database

In a changing of the times, more than 86 per cent of the chart-toppers in the twenty-first century have entered at No. 1. Al Martino's 'Here in My Heart' topped the first UK chart, and therefore has been excluded.

Record Lasts

THE 10 LAST NATIONALITIES TO TOP THE UK SINGLES CHART*

	NATIONALITY / ARTIST	TITLE	DATE AT NO. 1
1	Barbadian Rihanna	'Take a Bow'	1 Jun 2008
2	Swedish Basshunter	'Now You're Gone'	10 Feb 2008
3	Colombian Shakira (with Beyonce)	'Beautiful Liar'	6 May 2007
4	Lebanese Mika	'Grace Kelly'	18 Feb 2007
5	Dutch Fedde le Grand	'Put Your Hands Up for Detroit'	5 Nov 2006
6	Canadian Nelly Furtado	'Maneater'	25 Jun 2006
7	Irish U2	'Vertigo'	14 Nov 2004
8	Australian Kylie Minogue	'Slow'	9 Nov 2003
9	New Zealander Daniel Bedingfield	'Never Gonna Leave Your Side'	27 Jul 2003
10	German Tomcraft	'Loneliness'	4 May 2003

* Excluding US artists, as at 25 March 2009

Source: Music Information Database

Only three nationalities (Canadian, Irish and Australian) appear on both the first and last lists.

Rihanna
Barbadian singer Rihanna's 'Take a Bow' reached UK and US No. 1 in 2008, the year in which she also won her first Grammy Award.

THE 10 LAST SINGLES TO ENTER THE UK CHART AT NO. 1*

	TITLE / ARTIST	DATE AT NO. 1
1	'The Fear', Lily Allen	7 Feb 2009
2	'Hallelujah', Alexandra Burke	27 Dec 2008
3	'Run', Leona Lewis	13 Dec 2008
4	'Greatest Day', Take That	6 Dec 2008
5	'Hero', X Factor Finalists	8 Nov 2008
6	'The Promise', Girls Aloud	1 Nov 2008
7	'Sex on Fire', Kings of Leon	4 Oct 2008
8	'Dance Wiv Me', Dizzee Rascal feat. Calvin Harris & Chrome	12 Jul 2008
9	'Viva La Vida', Coldplay	28 Jun 2008
10	'That's Not My Name', Ting Tings	24 May 2008

* As at 25 March 2009

Source: Music Information Database

THE 10 LAST SINGLES BY FEMALE SINGERS AT NO. 1 IN THE UK*

	TITLE / ARTIST	DATE AT NO. 1
1	'Poker Face', Lady GaGa	13 Apr 2008
2	'The Fear', Lily Allen	7 Feb 2009
3	'Just Dance', Lady GaGa#	17 Jan 2009
4	'Hallelujah', Alexandra Burke	27 Dec 2008
5	'Run', Leona Lewis	13 Dec 2008
6	'If I Were a Boy', Beyonce	29 Nov 2008
7	'So What', Pink	19 Oct 2008
8	'I Kissed a Girl', Katy Perry	7 Sep 2008
9	'Take a Bow', Rihanna	1 Jun 2008
10	'4 Minutes', Madonna†	11 May 2008

* As at 27 April 2009
# Featuring Colby O'Donis
† With Justin Timberlake & Timbaland

Source: Music Information Database

Katy Perry
'I Kissed a Girl' was one of only two records to achieve simultaneous UK and US No. 1 positions in 2008.

Right: Coldplay
Coldplay's 'Viva la Vida' was the first US No. 1 single by a British group since the Spice Girls over 11 years earlier.

THE 10 **LAST UK ARTISTS TO TOP THE US SINGLES CHART***

	ARTIST	TITLE	DATE AT NO. 1
1	Coldplay	'Viva la Vida'	28 Jun 2008
2	Leona Lewis	'Bleeding Love'	5 Apr 2008
3	James Blunt	'You're Beautiful'	11 Mar 2006
4	Elton John	'Something About the Way You Look Tonight'/'Candle in The Wind 1997'	10 Jan 1998
5	The Spice Girls	'Wannabe'	15 Mar 1997
6	Seal	'Kiss from a Rose'	26 Aug 1995
7	Rod Stewart/Sting#	'All for Love'	5 Feb 1994
8	UB40	'Can't Help Falling in Love'	4 Sep 1993
9	Right Said Fred	'I'm Too Sexy'	22 Feb 1992
10	George Michael†	'Don't Let the Sun Go Down On Me'	1 Feb 1992

* As at 25 March 2009
\# With Bryan Adams
† With Elton John

Source: Music Information Database

THE 10 **LAST SIMULTANEOUS UK/US CHART TOPPERS***

	TITLE / ARTIST	DATE AT NO. 1
1	'Just Dance', Lady GaGa feat. Colby O'Donis	31 Jan 2009
2	'I Kissed a Girl', Katy Perry	16 Aug 2008
3	'Viva la Vida', Coldplay	28 Jun 2008
4	'Umbrella', Rihanna feat. Jay-Z	26 May 2007
5	'Give It to Me', Timbaland featuring Nelly Furtado	21 Apr 2007
6	'Sexyback', Justin Timberlake	9 Sep 2006
7	'Burn', Usher	17 Jul 2004
8	'Yeah', Usher feat. Ludacris & Lil Jon	27 Mar 2004
9	'Crazy in Love', Beyonce feat. Jay-Z	12 Jul 2003
10	'Lose Yourself', Eminem	14 Dec 2002

* As at 25 March 2009

Source: Music Information Database

Male Singers

Platinum for Diamond
Home Before Dark *went platinum in 2008.*

TOP 10 MALE ARTISTS WITH THE MOST PLATINUM ALBUMS IN THE UK

	ARTIST / GOLD TOTALS	PLATINUM ALBUMS
1	Robbie Williams (9)	56
2	Michael Jackson (14)	43
3	Phil Collins (13)	34
4	Elton John (24)	29
5	George Michael (8)	27
6	Rod Stewart (30)	20
7	Meat Loaf (10)	18
8	Eminem (7)	17
9	= Chris Rea (10)	15
	= Cliff Richard (25)	15

Source: Music Information Database

Platinum albums in the UK are those that have achieved sales of 300,000, roughly one for every 203 inhabitants, compared with the US ratio of 1:306.

TOP 10 BESTSELLING ALBUMS BY A MALE ARTIST IN THE UK

	TITLE / ARTIST	YEAR
1	Thriller, Michael Jackson	1982
2	Bad, Michael Jackson	1987
3	Back to Bedlam, James Blunt	2006
4	White Ladder, David Gray	2000
5	Bat Out of Hell, Meat Loaf	1978
6	But Seriously..., Phil Collins	1989
7	Tubular Bells, Mike Oldfield	1973
8	I've Been Expecting You, Robbie Williams	1998
9	Ladies & Gentlemen – The Best of, George Michael	1998
10	Sing When You're Winning, Robbie Williams	2000

Source: Official Charts Company

Michael Jackson's *Thriller* and *Bad* have both sold in excess of 3.5 million copies, meaning that approximately one in every six British households, or one in every 15 inhabitants, owns a copy of one or both of these mega-sellers. James Blunt's debut album is a long way behind, with sales of 2.8 million. Robbie Williams' nine albums have sold a combined 16 million-plus copies.

TOP 10 BESTSELLING ALBUMS BY MALE SOLO ARTISTS IN THE UK IN THE PAST 10 YEARS

YEAR / TITLE / ARTIST

2008 Home Before Dark, Neil Diamond

2007 Life in Cartoon Motion, Mika

2006 Undiscovered, James Morrison

2005 Back to Bedlam, James Blunt

2004 Greatest Hits, Robbie Williams

2003 Justified, Justin Timberlake

2002 Escapology, Robbie Williams

2001 Swing When You're Winning, Robbie Williams

2000 Sing When You're Winning, Robbie Williams

1999 I've Been Expecting You, Robbie Williams

Source: Music Information Database

Yellow Brick Road
Elton John has sustained a long run of hits, with UK chart albums spanning 1970 to 2007, including nine-times multi-platinum The Very Best of Elton John.

THE 10 LATEST NO. 1 SINGLES BY A FOREIGN MALE ARTIST IN THE UK*

TITLE / ARTIST / NATIONALITY	DATE
1 'Now You're Gone', Basshunter (Swedish)	13 Jan 2008
2 'Grace Kelly', Mika (Lebanese)	27 Jan 2007
3 'Put Your Hands up for Detroit', Fedde le Grande (Dutch)	11 Nov 2006
4 'Call on Me', Eric Prydz (Swedish)	25 Sep 2004
5 'Never Gonna Leave Your Side', Daniel Bedingfield (New Zealander)	2 Aug 2003
6 'Loneliness', Tomcraft (German)	10 May 2003
7 'If Tomorrow Never Comes', Ronan Keating (Irish)	18 May 2002
8 'Hero', Enrique Iglesias (Spanish)	2 Feb 2002
9 'Hey Baby', DJ Otzi (Austrian)	22 Sep 2001
10 'Angel', Shaggy (Jamaican)	9 Jun 2001

* Excluding US acts

Source: Music Information Database

TOP 10 SINGLES BY MALE SOLO SINGERS IN THE UK

TITLE / ARTIST	YEAR
1 'Candle in the Wind (1997)'/'Something About the Way You Look Tonight', Elton John	1997
2 'Anything Is Possible'/'Evergreen', Will Young	2002
3 'I Just Called to Say I Love You', Stevie Wonder	1984
4 '(Everything I Do) I Do It for You', Bryan Adams	1991
5 'Tears', Ken Dodd	1965
6 'Imagine', John Lennon	1975
7 'Careless Whisper', George Michael	1984
8 'Release Me', Engelbert Humperdinck	1967
9 'Unchained Melody', Gareth Gates	2002
10 'Diana', Paul Anka	1957

Source: Official Charts Company

This list represents a timeshaft through the history of British popular music, with singles from each decade reflecting the sometimes unpredictable taste of the British public.

Shaggy
Anglo-American artists so dominate the UK charts that No. 1s by singers of other nationalities are a relatively rare phenomenon.

Female Singers

Man eater
As well as her solo 2006 UK No. 1,
Nelly Furtado featured on Timbaland's
'Give It to Me' in 2007.

THE 10 LAST NO. 1 SINGLES BY A FOREIGN FEMALE ARTIST* IN THE UK

	TITLE / ARTIST / NATIONALITY	DATE
1	'Take a Bow', Rihanna (Barbadian)	31 May 2008
2	'Umbrella', Rihanna	26 May 2007
3	'Hips Don't Lie', Shakira (Colombian)	8 Jul 2006
4	'Man Eater', Nelly Furtado (Canadian)	17 Jun 2006
5	'Slow', Kylie Minogue (Australian)	15 Nov 2003
6	'Kiss Kiss', Holly Valance (Australian)	11 May 2002
7	'Can't Get You Out of My Head', Kylie Minogue	29 Sep 2001
8	'Spinning Around', Kylie Minogue	1 Jul 2000
9	'My Heart Will Go On', Celine Dion (Canadian)	21 Feb 1998
10	'Ooh Aah ... Just a Little Bit', Gina G (Australian)	25 May 1996

* Excluding US acts

Source: Music Information Database

TOP 10 FEMALE SOLO SINGERS IN THE UK

	SINGER	TOTAL CHART HITS
1	Madonna	65
2	Diana Ross	58
3	= Kylie Minogue	40
	= Donna Summer	40
5	= Janet Jackson	32
	= Tina Turner	32
7	Mariah Carey	31
8	= Shirley Bassey	29
	= Cher	29
10	Gloria Estefan	26

Source: Music Information Database

TOP 10 FEMALE ARTISTS WITH THE MOST PLATINUM ALBUMS IN THE UK

	ARTIST / GOLD TOTALS	PLATINUM ALBUMS
1	Madonna (21)	50
2	= Celine Dion (11)	22
	= Tina Turner (9)	22
4	Kylie Minogue (8)	21
5	Whitney Houston (5)	19
6	Dido (2)	16
7	Shania Twain (3)	15
8	= Mariah Carey (12)	13
	= Enya (6)	13
10	= Gloria Estefan (4)	12
	= Katie Melua (4)	12

Source: BPI

TOP 10 **SINGLES BY FEMALE SOLO SINGERS IN THE UK**

	TITLE / ARTIST	YEAR
1	'Believe', Cher	1998
2	'...Baby One More Time', Britney Spears	1999
3	'I Will Always Love You', Whitney Houston	1992
4	'The Power of Love', Jennifer Rush	1985
5	'My Heart Will Go On', Celine Dion	1998
6	'Think Twice', Celine Dion	1994
7	'Saturday Night', Whigfield	1994
8	'Can't Get You Out of My Head', Kylie Minogue	2001
9	'Don't Cry for Me Argentina', Julie Covington	1976
10	'Torn', Natalie Imbruglia	1997

Source: Official Charts Company

TOP 10 **BESTSELLING ALBUMS BY A FEMALE ARTIST IN THE UK**

	TITLE / ARTIST	YEAR
1	The Immaculate Collection, Madonna	1990
2	Come on Over, Shania Twain	1998
3	No Angel, Dido	2000
4	Life for Rent, Dido	2003
5	Jagged Little Pill, Alanis Morissette	1995
6	Come Away with Me, Norah Jones	2002
7	Tracy Chapman, Tracy Chapman	1998
8	Whitney, Whitney Houston	1987
9	Simply the Best, Tina Turner	1991
10	Spirit, Leona Lewis	2008

Source: Official Charts Company

Ross's record
Diana Ross's record span between UK No. 1s extends from 'I'm Still Waiting' (1971) to 'Chain Reaction' (1986).

Mariah Carey
Mariah Carey has had a UK chart hit almost every year since 1990.

TOP 10 **LONGEST GAPS BETWEEN UK NO. 1 HIT SINGLES BY FEMALE SOLO SINGERS**

	ARTIST	PERIOD	YRS	GAP MTHS	DAYS
1	Diana Ross	18 Sep 1971–1 Mar 1986	14	5	11
2	Kylie Minogue	3 Feb 1990–24 June 2000	10	5	21
3	Madonna	12 May 1990–28 Feb 1998	7	9	16
4	Pink	28 Sep 2002–11 Oct 2008	6	0	11
5	Petula Clark	4 Mar 1961–11 Feb 1967	5	11	7
6	Madonna	2 Sep 2000–19 Nov 2005	5	2	18
7	Jennifer Lopez	20 Jan 2001–26 Feb 2005	4	1	7
8	Whitney Houston	29 Oct 1988–28 Nov 1992	4	0	30
9	Britney Spears	20 May 2000–13 Mar 2004	3	9	22
10	Cher	8 Jun 1991–18 Mar 1995	3	9	10

Source: Music Information Database

Groups & Duos

TOP 10 SINGLES BY GROUPS AND DUOS IN THE UK

TITLE / GROUP	YEAR
1 'Bohemian Rhapsody', Queen	1975
2 'Mull of Kintyre'/'Girls' School', Wings	1977
3 'Rivers of Babylon'/'Brown Girl in the Ring', Boney M	1978
4 'You're the One That I Want', John Travolta & Olivia Newton-John	1978
5 'Relax', Frankie Goes To Hollywood	1984
6 'She Loves You', The Beatles	1963
7 'Unchained Melody'/'(There'll Be Bluebirds over the) White Cliffs of Dover', Robson Green & Jerome Flynn	1995
8 'Mary's Boy Child'/'Oh My Lord', Boney M	1978
9 'Love Is All Around', Wet Wet Wet	1994
10 'I Want to Hold Your Hand', The Beatles	1963

Source: Official Charts Company

Not only was Queen's 'Bohemian Rhapsody' the biggest-selling single by a group in the UK, but more than one poll has ranked it at the top of a list of '100 Greatest Singles' of all time. Its total sales in the UK alone are over 2.13 million.

TOP 10 ALBUMS BY GROUPS AND DUOS IN THE UK, 2008

TITLE	GROUP
1 The Circus	Take That
2 Only by the Night	Kings of Leon
3 Viva La Vida (Or Death and All His Friends)	Coldplay
4 Day and Age	Killers
5 Out of Control	Girls Aloud
6 Scouting for Girls	Scouting for Girls
7 All the Right Reasons	Nickelback
8 The Script	The Script
9 Best of – Decade in the Sun	Stereophonics
10 Dig Out Your Soul	Oasis

Source: Official Charts Company

TOP 10 SINGLES BY GROUPS AND DUOS IN THE UK, 2008

TITLE	GROUP
1 'Rockstar'	Nickelback
2 'Sex On Fire'	Kings of Leon
3 'The Promise'	Girls Aloud
4 'That's Not My Name'	Ting Tings
5 'Viva La Vida'	Coldplay
6 'The Man Who Can't Be Moved'	The Script
7 'Human'	Killers
8 'Stop and Stare'	OneRepublic
9 'Fascination'	Alphabeat
10 'Rule the World'	Take That

Source: Official Charts Company

Rockstar
Nickelback's 'Rockstar' took up residence in the UK charts for 50 weeks up to October 2008.

TOP 10 GROUPS AND DUOS WITH THE LONGEST SINGLES CHART CAREERS IN THE UK

	GROUP/DUO	CHART SPAN	YRS	MTHS	DAYS
1	Spencer Davis Group	7 Nov 1964–12 Apr 2008	43	5	6
2	The Rolling Stones	27 Jul 1963–2 Sep 2006	43	1	6
3	Status Quo	24 Aug 1968–27 Dec 2008	40	4	3
4	The Kinks	15 Aug 1964–25 Sep 2004	40	1	10
5	Slade	19 Jun 1971–3 Jan 2009	38	6	15
6	Wizzard	8 Dec 1973–3 Jan 2009	36	0	24
7	Bee Gees	29 Apr 1967–5 May 2001	35	0	6
8	Queen	9 Mar 1974–20 Sep 2008	34	6	11
9	Abba	20 Apr 1974–23 Aug 2008	34	4	4
10	The Beatles	13 Oct 1962–27 Apr 1996	33	6	14

Source: Music Information Database

TOP 10 ALBUMS BY GROUPS AND DUOS IN THE UK

	TITLE / GROUP	YEAR
1	Greatest Hits (Volume One), Queen	1981
2	Sgt. Pepper's Lonely Hearts Club Band, The Beatles	1967
3	(What's The Story) Morning Glory, Oasis	1995
4	Brothers in Arms, Dire Straits	1985
5	Gold - Greatest Hits, Abba	1992
6	The Dark Side Of The Moon, Pink Floyd	1973
7	Greatest Hits Volume II, Queen	1991
8	Stars, Simply Red	1991
9	Rumours, Fleetwood Mac	1977
10	Hopes And Fears, Keane	2004

Source: Official Charts Company

Rolling on
In addition to their sustained chart success, the Rolling Stones have been performing for over 47 years.

Music Greats

All-Time Greats

In issues published between 2003 and 2008, *Rolling Stone* magazine listed artists, songs, albums and performances in a variety of categories, ranked according to votes cast by their peers – fellow musicians, critics and prominent music-industry figures. The listings are dominantly Anglo-American: of the '500 Greatest Songs', 357 are by US singers and 117 by British artists.

TOP 10 **GREATEST SINGERS OF ALL TIME**

SINGER / COUNTRY / DATES

1 Aretha Franklin (USA; b. 1942)
2 Ray Charles (USA; 1930–2004)
3 Elvis Presley (USA; 1935–77)
4 Sam Cooke (USA; 1931–64)
5 John Lennon (UK; 1940–80)
6 Marvin Gaye (USA; 1939–84)
7 Bob Dylan (USA; b. 1941)
8 Otis Redding (USA; 1941–67)
9 Stevie Wonder (USA; b. 1950)
10 James Brown (USA; 1933–2006)

Source: *Rolling Stone*

Vocal perfection
Aretha Franklin topped the list of 'Greatest Singers' nominated by a panel of almost 200 experts.

TOP 10 **GREATEST ALBUMS OF ALL TIME**

ALBUM / ARTIST(S) / YEAR

1 Sgt. Pepper's Lonely Hearts Club Band, The Beatles (1967)
2 Pet Sounds, The Beach Boys (1966)
3 Revolver, The Beatles (1966)
4 Highway 61 Revisited, Bob Dylan (1965)
5 Rubber Soul, The Beatles (1965)
6 What's Going On, Marvin Gaye (1971)
7 Exile on Main Street, The Rolling Stones (1972)
8 London Calling, The Clash (1979)
9 Blonde on Blonde, Bob Dylan (1966)
10 The Beatles ('The White Album'), The Beatles (1968)

Source: *Rolling Stone*

TOP 10 **GREATEST MUSIC DVDS OF ALL TIME**

DVD / PRINCIPAL ARTIST / YEAR*

1 The Last Waltz, Bob Dylan (1976)
2 Monterey Pop, Various artists (1967)
3 A Hard Day's Night, The Beatles (1964)
4 Woodstock: Three Days of Peace and Music, Various artists (1969)
5 Metallica: Some Kind of Monster, Metallica (2004)
6 Gimme Shelter, Rolling Stones (1970)
7 Wild Style, Grandmaster Flash, *et al* (1983)
8 Stop Making Sense, Talking Heads (1983)
9 Purple Rain, Prince (1984)
10 No Direction Home, Bob Dylan (1966)

* Of original event or film; DVD release later

Source: *Rolling Stone*

Slow hand
Eric Clapton is the highest-ranked British guitarist on the Rolling Stone *list.*

TOP 10 GREATEST GUITARISTS OF ALL TIME

GUITARIST / COUNTRY / DATES

1 Jimi Hendrix (USA; 1942–70)
2 Duane Allman (USA; 1946–71)
3 B.B. King (USA; b. 1925)
4 Eric Clapton (UK; b. 1945)
5 Robert Johnson (USA; 1911–38)
6 Chuck Berry (USA; b. 1926)
7 Stevie Ray Vaughan (USA; 1954–90)
8 Ry Cooder (USA; b. 1947)
9 Jimmy Page (UK; b. 1944)
10 Keith Richards (UK; b. 1943)

Source: *Rolling Stone*

TOP 10 GREATEST SONGS OF ALL TIME

SONG / SINGER / FIRST RECORDING

1 'Like a Rolling Stone', Bob Dylan (1965)
2 'Satisfaction', The Rolling Stones (1965)
3 'Imagine', John Lennon (1971)
4 'What's Going On', Marvin Gaye (1970)
5 'Respect', Aretha Franklin (1967)
6 'Good Vibrations', The Beach Boys (1966)
7 'Johnny B. Goode', Chuck Berry (1958)
8 'Hey Jude', The Beatles (1968)
9 'Smells Like Teen Spirit', Nirvana (1991)
10 'What'd I Say', Ray Charles (1959)

Source: *Rolling Stone*

TOP 10 IMMORTALS

ARTIST / COUNTRY / DATES

1 The Beatles (UK; 1960–70)
2 Bob Dylan (USA; b. 1941)
3 Elvis Presley (USA; 1935–77)
4 The Rolling Stones (UK; 1962–)
5 Chuck Berry (USA; b. 1926)
6 Jimi Hendrix (USA; 1942–70)
7 James Brown (USA; 1933–2006)
8 Little Richard (USA; b. 1932)
9 Aretha Franklin (USA; b. 1942)
10 Ray Charles (USA; 1930–2004)

Source: *Rolling Stone*

Immortal Hendrix
Jimi Hendrix features both as the 'Greatest Guitarist' and among rock 'n' roll's 'Immortals'.

Music Awards

THE 10 **FIRST ARTISTS TO RECEIVE GRAMMY LIFETIME ACHIEVEMENT AWARDS**

	ARTIST	YEAR
1	Bing Crosby	1962
2	Frank Sinatra	1965
3	Duke Ellington	1966
4	Ella Fitzgerald	1967
5	Irving Berlin	1968
6	Elvis Presley	1971
7	= Louis Armstrong	1972
	= Mahalia Jackson	1972
9	= Chuck Berry	1984
	= Charlie Parker	1984

Source: NARAS

Grammy veterans
Bing Crosby (below), winner of the first Grammy Lifetime Achievement Award, and Quincy Jones (below right), who has been nominated for a record 79 Grammys with 27 wins.

THE 10 **LATEST WINNERS OF THE Q INSPIRATION AWARD**

YEAR	ACT
2008	Cocteau Twins
2007	Damon Albarn
2006	a-ha
2005	Björk
2004	The Pet Shop Boys
2003	The Cure
2002	Echo & the Bunnymen
2001	John Lydon
2000	Joe Strummer
1999	New Order

The Q Awards were launched by *Q* magazine in 1990. Awards are presented in conventional categories such as 'Best Album' and 'Lifetime Achievement', but also 'Legend', 'Idol' and 'Inspiration'.

THE 10 **ARTISTS WITH MOST GRAMMY AWARDS**

	ARTIST	AWARDS
1	Sir Georg Solti	31
2	Quincy Jones	27
3	= Pierre Boulez	26
	= Alison Krauss	26
5	= Vladimir Horowitz	25
	= Stevie Wonder	25
7	U2	22
8	John Williams	21
9	Henry Mancini	20
10	Bruce Springsteen	19

Source: NARAS

The Grammy Awards ceremony has been held annually in the USA since its inauguration on 4 May 1959, and are considered the most prestigious in the music industry. The presence of classical artists in this Top 10 (not least, conductor Sir George Solti) is largely attributable to the large number of classical award categories. Grammy winners are selected annually by the 7,000-member Recording Academy of NARAS (the National Academy of Recording Arts & Sciences).

THE 10 **LATEST GRAMMY RECORDS OF THE YEAR**

YEAR / RECORD / ARTIST(S)

2009
'Please Read the Letter'
Robert Plant and Alison Krauss

2008
'Rehab'
Amy Winehouse

2007
'Not Ready to Make Nice'
Dixie Chicks

2006
'Boulevard of Broken Dreams'
Green Day

2005
'Here We Go Again'
Ray Charles and Norah Jones

2004
'Clocks'
Coldplay

2003
'Don't Know Why'
Norah Jones

2002
'Walk On'
U2

2001
'Beautiful Day'
U2

2000
'Smooth'
Santana feat. Rob Thomas

The Grammys are awarded retrospectively. Thus the 51st awards presented in 2009 were in recognition of musical accomplishment during 2008.

THE 10 **LATEST WINNERS OF THE BRIT AWARD FOR BEST BRITISH BREAKTHROUGH ACT***

YEAR   ACT
2009 Duffy
2008 Mika
2007 The Fratellis
2006 Arctic Monkeys
2005 Keane
2004 Busted
2003 Will Young
2002 Blue
2001 A1
2000 S Club 7

* Formerly Best British Newcomer

Amy's Grammys
In 2008, Amy Winehouse was nominated for Grammy Awards in six categories, winning in five, including Record of the Year for 'Rehab'.

THE 10 **LATEST WINNERS OF THE BRIT AWARD FOR BEST INTERNATIONAL GROUP**

YEAR   GROUP
2009 Kings of Leon
2008 Foo Fighters
2007 The Killers
2006 Green Day
2005 Scissor Sisters
2004 The White Stripes
2003 Red Hot Chili Peppers
2002 Destiny's Child
2001 U2
2000 TLC

Movie Music

Dancing on ice
Recorded by Cab Calloway in 1930, Happy Feet was aptly used as the title of the animated film featuring tap-dancing penguins.

TOP 10 FILMS WITH TITLES DERIVED FROM SONG TITLES

	FILM	SONG*	FILM
1	Mamma Mia!	1975	2008
2	Happy Feet	1930	2006
3	American Pie	1972	1999
4	Walk the Line	1956	2005
5	Sweet Home Alabama	1976	2002
6	Bad Boys	1983	1995
7	Forever Young	1970	1992
8	Sea of Love	1959	1989
9	One Fine Day	1963	1996
10	My Girl	1965	1991

* Release of first hit version

Films with titles derived from those of songs date back to 'How Would You Like to Be the Ice Man?', a popular song before being appropriated for a film released on 21 April 1899. 'White Christmas', one of the most successful songs of all time, appeared in the film *Holiday Inn* (1942) before becoming the title of the 1954 film. Films with titles that are coincidentally the same as film titles, or not identical to those of the songs that inspired them, have been disregarded.

TOP 10 BEST SONG OSCAR-WINNING SINGLES IN THE UK

SONG TITLE / ARTIST / FILM (IF DIFFERENT)	YEAR
1 'I Just Called to Say I Love You', Stevie Wonder, *The Woman in Red*	1984
2 'Fame', Irene Cara	1980
3 'Take My Breath Away', Berlin, *Top Gun*	1986
4 'My Heart Will Go On', Celine Dion, *Titanic*	1997
5 'Flashdance...What a Feeling', Irene Cara, *Flashdance*	1983
6 'Evergreen', Barbra Streisand, *A Star is Born*	1976
7 'Streets of Philadelphia', Bruce Springsteen, *Philadelphia*	1994
8 'Moon River', Danny Williams, *Breakfast at Tiffany's*	1961
9 'Whatever Will Be, Will Be', Doris Day, *The Man Who Knew Too Much*	1956
10 'Raindrops Keep Fallin' on My Head', Sacha Distel, *Butch Cassidy and the Sundance Kid*	1969

Source: Music Information Database

TOP 10 JAMES BOND FILM THEMES IN THE UK

TITLE / FILM (IF DIFFERENT) / ARTIST	YEAR
1 'A View to a Kill', Duran Duran	1985
2 'We Have All the Time in the World' (from *On Her Majesty's Secret Service*), Louis Armstrong	1994
3 'The Living Daylights', a-ha	1987
4 'Licence to Kill', Gladys Knight	1989
5 'Nobody Does It Better' (from *The Spy Who Loved Me*), Carly Simon	1977
6 'For Your Eyes Only', Sheena Easton	1981
7 'Live and Let Die', Paul McCartney and Wings	1973
8 'GoldenEye', Tina Turner	1995
9 'You Only Live Twice', Nancy Sinatra	1967
10 'Die Another Day', Madonna	2002

Source: Music Information Database

Not all the James Bond themes have been major hits. Although all 10 in this list reached the Top 20, there has never been a Bond-associated UK No. 1. Themes from two films, *The Man with the Golden Gun* and *Moonraker*, failed to chart at all, even though major British artists (Lulu and Shirley Bassey) were involved. 'We Have All the Time in the World' also failed initially, taking 25 years (after a revival in a Guinness TV commercial) to gain Top 3 success.

TOP 10 MUSICAL FILMS

FILM	YEAR
1 Mamma Mia!	2008
2 Grease	1978
3 Chicago	2002
4 Saturday Night Fever	1977
5 High School Musical 3: Senior Year	2008
6 Hairspray	2007
7 Moulin Rouge!	2001
8 The Sound of Music	1965
9 The Phantom of the Opera	2004
10 Sweeney Todd: The Demon Barber of Fleet Street	2007

In recent years, animated films with an important musical content appear to have taken over from traditional musicals (films in which the cast actually sing), with *Beauty and the Beast, Aladdin, The Lion King, Pocahontas, The Prince of Egypt, Tarzan* and *Monsters, Inc.* all winning Best Original Song Oscars. However, the success of *Chicago* and *Mamma Mia!* suggests that the age of the blockbuster musical film is not yet over.

Money, money, money
With global box office income of almost $600 million, Mamma Mia! *is the highest-earning musical of all time.*

TOP 10 MUSICAL FILMS OF THE 1960S

FILM	YEAR
1 The Sound of Music	1965
2 Mary Poppins	1964
3 My Fair Lady	1964
4 Funny Girl	1968
5 Let's Make Love	1960
6 West Side Story	1961
7 Oliver!	1968
8 Thoroughly Modern Millie	1967
9 Hello Dolly!	1969
10 Paint Your Wagon	1969

TOP 10 ORIGINAL SOUNDTRACK ALBUMS IN THE UK

TITLE	YEAR OF RELEASE
1 The Sound of Music	1965
2 Dirty Dancing	1998
3 Grease	1978
4 Saturday Night Fever	1977
5 The Bodyguard	1992
6 South Pacific	1958
7 Titanic	1997
8 Bridget Jones's Diary	2001
9 Trainspotting	1996
10 The Commitments	1991

Source: Music Information Database

Classical Music & Opera

TOP 10 **CLASSICAL ALBUMS IN THE UK**

	TITLE	PERFORMER / ORCHESTRA	YEAR
1	The Three Tenors In Concert	José Carreras, Placido Domingo, Luciano Pavarotti	1990
2	The Essential Pavarotti	Luciano Pavarotti	1990
3	Vivaldi: The Four Seasons	Nigel Kennedy/English Chamber Orchestra	1989
4	The Three Tenors – In Concert 1994	José Carreras, Placido Domingo, Luciano Pavarotti, Zubin Mehta	1994
5	The Voice	Russell Watson	2000
6	Voice of an Angel	Charlotte Church	1998
7	Pure	Hayley Westenra	2003
8	Encore	Russell Watson	2002
9	The Essential Pavarotti, 2	Luciano Pavarotti	1991
10	The Pavarotti Collection	Luciano Pavarotti	1986

Source: Music Information Database

Sales of classical music boomed to unprecedented heights at the end of the 1980s and in the early 1990s, the rider to this being the records by tenors José Carreras, Placido Domingo and Luciano Pavarotti (particularly the latter, who even had a Top 3 single with *Nessun Dorma*), and young-gun violinist Nigel Kennedy, that soared way ahead of the field as a whole.

TOP 10 **MOST PROLIFIC CLASSICAL COMPOSERS**

	COMPOSER / NATIONALITY / DATES	HOURS OF MUSIC
1	Joseph Haydn (Austrian; 1732–1809)	340
2	George Friedrich Handel (German-English; 1685–1759)	303
3	Wolfgang Amadeus Mozart (Austrian; 1756–91)	202
4	Johann Sebastian Bach (German; 1685–1750)	175
5	Franz Schubert (German; 1797–1828)	134
6	Ludwig van Beethoven (German; 1770–1827)	120
7	Henry Purcell (English; 1659–95)	116
8	Giuseppe Verdi (Italian; 1813–1901)	87
9	Anton Dvorák (Czech; 1841–1904)	79
10 =	Franz Liszt (Hungarian; 1811–86)	76
=	Pyotr Ilyich Tchaikovsky (Russian; 1840–93)	76

This list is based on a survey conducted by *Classical Music* magazine, which ranked classical composers by the total number of hours of music each composed. If the length of the composer's working life is brought into the calculation, Schubert wins: his 134 hours were composed in a career of 18 years, giving an average of 7 hours 27 minutes per annum.

Most Prolific?

Georg Philipp Telemann (German; 1681–1767) has a claim as the most prolific composer of all time, with up to 3,000 works including more than 100 concertos and 50 operas, but since he lost count himself, only a proportion have survived and many misattributions have been discovered, his place in the world ranking must remain open to debate.

TOP 10 **COMPOSERS**

COMPOSER / WORKS*

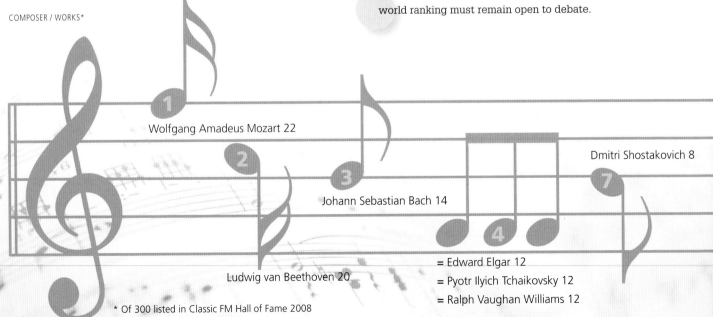

Wolfgang Amadeus Mozart 22

Dmitri Shostakovich 8

Johann Sebastian Bach 14

Ludwig van Beethoven 20

= Edward Elgar 12
= Pyotr Ilyich Tchaikovsky 12
= Ralph Vaughan Williams 12

* Of 300 listed in Classic FM Hall of Fame 2008

TOP 10 **OPERAS***

COMPOSER / OPERA

1 Piesco Mascagni,
Cavalleria Rusticana

2 Georges Bizet,
The Pearl Fishers

3 Wolfgang Amadeus Mozart,
The The Marriage of Figaro

4 Wolfgang Amadeus Mozart,
The Magic Flute

5 Giuseppe Verdi, Nabucco

6 Giacomo Puccini,
La Bohème

7 Giacomo Puccini,
Madama Butterfly

8 Léo Delibes,
Lakmé

9 Jules Massenet, Thaïs

10 Richard Wagner,
Tannhäuser

* Based on Classic FM Hall of Fame 2008

Mozart's magic

Mozart's first opera, Apollo et Hyacinthus, *had its debut in 1767, when he was just 11 years old. He died, aged 35, two months after the first performance of his last,* The Magic Flute, *since ranked as one his most-performed and most popular works.*

= Franz Schubert 6
= John Williams 6

= George Friedrich Handel 7
= Sergei Rachmaninov 7

THE 10 **LAST MOZART OPERAS**

	OPERA*	FIRST VENUE	PERFORMANCE
1	The Magic Flute (Die Zauberflöte)	Theater auf der Wieden, Vienna	30 Sep 1791
2	La Clemenza di Tito	Estates Theatre, Prague	6 Sep 1791
3	Così fan Tutte	Burgtheater, Vienna	26 Jan 1790
4	Don Giovanni	Estates Theatre, Prague	29 Oct 1787
5	The Marriage of Figaro	Burgtheater, Vienna	1 May 1786
6	The Impresario	Orangerie, Schönbrunn	7 Feb 1786
7	Die Entführung aus dem Serail	Burgtheater, Vienna	16 Jul 1782
8	Idomeneo	Court Theatre, Munich	29 Jan 1781
9	Die Gärtnerin aus Liebe	Komödienstadl, Augsburg	1 May 1780
10	Il re pastore	Archbishop's Palace, Salzburg	23 Apr 1775

* Works performed during his lifetime only

ENTERTAINMENT

On Stage

TOP 10 **LONGEST-RUNNING RODGERS & HAMMERSTEIN PRODUCTIONS ON BROADWAY**

SHOW / RUN	PERFORMANCES
1 Oklahoma! (31 Mar 1943–29 May 1948)	2,212
2 South Pacific (7 Apr 1949–16 Jan 1954)	1,925
3 The Sound of Music (16 Nov 1959–15 Jun 1963)	1,443
4 The King and I (29 Mar 1951–20 Mar 1954)	1,246
5 Carousel (19 Apr 1945–24 May 1947)	890
6 The King and I (11 Apr 1996–22 Feb 1998)	780
7 The King and I (2 May 1977–30 Dec 1978)	695
8 Flower Drum Song (1 Dec 1958–7 May 1960)	600
9 The Sound of Music (12 Mar 1998–20 Jun 1999)	533
10 Oklahoma! (21 Mar 2002–23 Feb 2003)	388

Dracula
Frank Langella took the title role in the long-running Broadway production of Dracula *and went on to reprise the part in the 1979 film version.*

Oklahoma!
The original 1943–48 Broadway production of Oklahoma! *broke theatre records before embarking on a 10-year tour.*

TOP 10 **LONGEST-RUNNING MYSTERIES AND THRILLERS ON BROADWAY**

SHOW / RUN	PERFORMANCES
1 Deathtrap (26 Feb 1978–13 Jul 1982)	1,793
2 Arsenic and Old Lace (10 Jan 1941–17 Jun 1944)	1,444
3 Angel Street (5 Dec 1941–30 Dec 1944)	1,295
4 Sleuth (12 Nov 1970–13 Oct 1973	1,222
5 The Bat (23 Aug 1920–Sep 1922)	867
6 Dracula (20 Oct 1977–6 Jan 1980)	925
7 Witness for the Prosecution (16 Dec 1954–30 Jun 1956)	645
8 Dial 'M' for Murder (29 Oct 1952–27 Feb 1954)	552
9 Sherlock Holmes (12 Nov 1974–4 Jan 1976)	471
10 An Inspector Calls (27 Apr 1994–28 May 1995)	454

Deathtrap by Ira Levin opened at the Music Box Theatre. Though nominated for four Tony Awards it failed to win any, but went on to achieve a record four-year run. Marian Seldes appeared in almost every one of its 1,793 performances. The film version of *Deathtrap*, released the year the play closed, starred Michael Caine – who also starred in *Sleuth*, also originally a long-running Broadway thriller.

TOP 10 **LONGEST-RUNNING COMEDIES IN THE UK**

SHOW	PERFORMANCES
1 No Sex, Please – We're British (1971–81; 1982–86; 1986–87)	6,761
2 The Complete Works of William Shakespeare (Abridged) (1996–2005)	4,266
3 Run for Your Wife (1983–91)	2,638
4 There's a Girl in My Soup (1966–69; 1969–72)	2,547
5 Pyjama Tops (1969–75)	2,498
6 Worm's Eye View (1945–51)	2,245
7 Boeing Boeing (1962–65; 1965–67)	2,035
8 Blithe Spirit (1941–42; 1942; 1942–46)	1,997
9 Dirty Linen (1976–80)	1,667
10 Reluctant Heroes (1950–54)	1,610

No Sex Please – We're British is the world's longest running comedy. It opened at the Strand Theatre, London, on 3 June 1971 and after transfers to the Garrick and Duchess Theatres finally closed on 5 September 1987. It fared less well on Broadway, opening at the Ritz Theatre, New York, on 20 February 1973, but closing after just 14 performances.

TOP 10 **MOST-PRODUCED PLAYS BY SHAKESPEARE, 1878–2008**

PLAY	PRODUCTIONS
1 As You Like It	81
2 = Hamlet	80
= Twelfth Night	80
4 The Taming of the Shrew	79
5 A Midsummer Night's Dream	76
6 Much Ado About Nothing	72
7 The Merchant of Venice	70
8 Macbeth	67
9 The Merry Wives of Windsor	62
10 Romeo and Juliet	61

Source: Shakespeare Centre

This list is based on an analysis of Shakespearean productions (rather than individual performances) from 31 December 1878 to 31 December 2008 at Stratford upon Avon and by the Royal Shakespeare Company in London and on tour.

TOP 10 **LONGEST-RUNNING MUSICALS IN THE UK**

SHOW / RUN	PERFORMANCES*
1 Les Misérables (8 Oct 1985–)	9,934#
2 Cats (11 May 1981–11 May 2002)	8,949
3 The Phantom of the Opera (9 Oct 1986–)	8,900#
4 Blood Brothers (27 Aug 1988–)	8,142#
5 Starlight Express (27 Mar 1984–12 Jan 2002)	7,406
6 Miss Saigon (20 Sep 1989–30 Oct 1999)	4,263
7 Mamma Mia! (23 Mar 1999–)	3,500+#
8 Jesus Christ, Superstar (9 Aug 1972–1980)	3,357
9 Evita (21 Jun 1978–8 Feb 1986)	2,900
10 Oliver! (30 Jun 1960–1966)	2,618

* Continuous runs only
# Still running, total as at 31 March 2008

Phantom phenomenon
The Phantom of the Opera *has become the third longest-running musical in the West End and longest on Broadway.*

Below: The play's the thing
David Tennant appeared in 2008–09 in the critically acclaimed title role of the much-performed Hamlet.

Box-office Blockbusters

TOP 10 **FILMS OF ALL TIME**

FILM / YEAR / TOTAL WORLD GROSS ($)

1
Titanic* 1997
1,848,813,795

2
**The Lord of the Rings:
The Return of the King**
2003
1,133,027,325

3
**Pirates of the Caribbean:
Dead Man's Chest** 2006
1,066,179,725

4
The Dark Knight 2008
1,001,842,429

5
**Harry Potter and the
Philosopher's Stone** 2001
985,817,659

6
**Pirates of the Caribbean:
At World's End** 2007
961,002,663

7
**Harry Potter and the
Order of the Phoenix**
2007
938,468,864

8
**The Lord of the Rings:
The Two Towers** 2002
926,287,400

9
**Star Wars: Episode I –
The Phantom Menace**
1999
924,317,554

10
Shrek 2# 2004
920,665,658

* Won Best Picture Oscar
# Animated

Only *Titanic* and *The Dark Knight* have
earned more than $500 million in the
USA alone.

Final role
Heath Ledger (The Joker) died before The Dark Knight *was released.*

TOP 10 **FILM BUDGETS**

	FILM	YEAR	ESTIMATED BUDGET ($)
1	Pirates of the Caribbean: At World's End	2007	300,000,000
2	Superman Returns	2006	270,000,000
3	Spider-Man 3	2007	258,000,000
4	= Pirates of the Caribbean: Dead Man's Chest	2006	225,000,000
	= Quantum of Solace	2008	225,000,000
6	X-Men: The Last Stand	2006	210,000,000
7	King Kong	2005	207,000,000
8	= Titanic	1997	200,000,000
	= Terminator 3: Rise of the Machines	2003	200,000,000
	= Spider-Man 2	2004	200,000,000
	= The Chronicles of Narnia: Prince Caspian	2008	200,000,000

FRANCHISE	NO. OF FILMS	YEARS	TOTAL WORLD GROSS ($)*
1 James Bond	22#	1963–2008	4,901,539,441
2 Harry Potter	5	2001–07	4,494,832,233
3 Star Wars†	6	1977–2005	4,309,312,004
4 The Lord of the Rings	3	2001–03	2,926,875,016
5 Pirates of the Caribbean	3	2003–07	2,681,446,403
6 Batman†	6	1989–2008	2,644,655,068
7 Spider-Man	3	2002–04	2,496,544,674
8 Indiana Jones	4	1981–2008	1,998,655,564
9 Shrek	2	2001–04	2,204,031,957
10 Jurassic Park	3	1993–2001	1,902,110,926

* Cumulative global earnings of the original film and all its sequels to 31 March 2009
\# Excluding 'unofficial' *Casino Royale* and *Never Say Never Again*
† Excluding animated versions

Bond begins
Sean Connery took the title role in six official James Bond films. With the release of the 22nd film, it has become the highest-earning series ever.

TOP 10 **SEQUELS**

FILM (YEAR)	US GROSS ($)	SEQUEL (YEAR)	US GROSS ($)	IMPROVEMENT (%)
1 Night of the Living Dead (1990)	5,835,247	Dawn of the Dead (2004)	59,020,957	911.5
2 The Terminator (1984)	38,371,200	Terminator 2: Judgment Day (1991)	204,843,345	433.8
3 Austin Powers: International Man of Mystery (1997)	53,883,989	Austin Powers: The Spy Who Shagged Me (1999)	206,040,086	282.4
4 First Blood (1982)	47,212,904	Rambo: First Blood Part II (1985)	150,415,432	218.6
5 Mad Max (1980)	8,750,000	Mad Max 2: The Road Warrior (1981)	23,667,907	170.5
6 Highlander (1986)	5,900,000	Highlander II: The Quickening (1991)	15,556,340	163.7
7 Batman Begins (2005)	205,343,774	The Dark Knight	533,345,358	159.7
8 The Evil Dead (1983)	2,400,000	Evil Dead 2 (1987)	5,923,044	146.8
9 Lethal Weapon (1987)	65,207,127	Lethal Weapon 2 (1989)	147,253,986	125.8
10 Bad Boys (1995)	65,807,024	Bad Boys II (2003)	138,608,444	110.6

FILM FLOPS

The Adventures of Pluto Nash (2002) is considered the greatest financial flop ever: its estimated budget was $100 million, but it earned only $7,103,972, a return of just 7.1 per cent. *Cutthroat Island* (1995) had a budget of $98 million but earned little more than $10 million on its US release. More recently, $100 million-plus budget films *Treasure Planet* (2002), *The Alamo* (2004), *Around the World in 80 Days* (2004) and *Stealth* (2005), incurred substantial losses, though reduced when foreign and video earnings are taken into account. *Waterworld* (1995), with a budget of $175 million, is often cited as a flop, but earned over $264 million globally.

Films of the Decades

TOP 10 **FILMS OF THE**
1920s

FILM	YEAR
1 The Big Parade	1925
2 The Four Horsemen of the Apocalypse	1921
3 Ben-Hur	1926
4 The Ten Commandments	1923
5 What Price Glory?	1926
6 The Covered Wagon	1923
7 Way Down East	1921
8 The Singing Fool	1928
9 Wings	1927
10 The Gold Rush	1925

The Birth of a Nation (1915) was the highest-earning film of the silent era.

Silent success
The Big Parade, *top 1920s film.*

TOP 10 **FILMS OF THE**
1930s

FILM	YEAR
1 Gone With the Wind*	1939
2 Snow White and the Seven Dwarfs	1937
3 King Kong	1933
4 The Wizard of Oz	1939
5 Frankenstein	1931
6 San Francisco	1936
7 = Hell's Angels	1930
= Lost Horizon	1937
= Mr Smith Goes to Washington	1939
10 Maytime	1937

* Winner of Best Picture Oscar

Gone With the Wind and *Snow White and the Seven Dwarfs* have generated more income than any pre-war film.

TOP 10 **FILMS OF THE**
1940s

FILM	YEAR
1 Bambi*	1942
2 Pinocchio*	1940
3 Fantasia*	1940
4 Song of the South#	1946
5 Mom and Dad	1944
6 Samson and Delilah	1949
7 The Best Years of Our Lives†	1946
8 The Bells of St Mary's	1945
9 Duel in the Sun	1946
10 This Is the Army	1943

* Animated
# Part animated/part live-action
† Winner of Best Picture Oscar

Four classic Disney cartoons offered colourful escapism during and after the austerity of the war years.

TOP 10 **FILMS OF THE**
1950s

FILM	YEAR
1 Lady and the Tramp*	1955
2 Peter Pan*	1953
3 Cinderella*	1950
4 The Ten Commandments	1956
5 Ben-Hur#	1959
6 Sleeping Beauty*	1959
7 Around the World in 80 Days	1956
8 This is Cinerama	1952
9 South Pacific	1958
10 The Robe	1953

* Animated
# Winner of Best Picture Oscar

As in the 1940s, feature-length animated films dominated the 1950s, along with popular biblical epics.

TOP 10 **FILMS OF THE**
1960s

FILM	YEAR
1 One Hundred and One Dalmatians*	1961
2 The Jungle Book*	1967
3 2001: A Space Odyssey	1968
4 The Sound of Music#	1965
5 Thunderball	1965
6 Goldfinger	1964
7 Doctor Zhivago	1965
8 You Only Live Twice	1967
9 The Graduate	1968
10 Butch Cassidy and the Sundance Kid	1969

* Animated
# Winner of Best Picture Oscar

For the first time, each of the Top 10 films earned more than $100 million around the world.

TOP 10 FILMS OF THE 1970s

FILM	YEAR
1 Star Wars*	1977
2 Jaws	1975
3 The Exorcist	1973
4 Grease	1978
5 Close Encounters of the Third Kind	1977
6 Superman	1978
7 Saturday Night Fever	1977
8 The Godfather	1972
9 Rocky	1976
10 Moonraker	1979

* Later retitled *Star Wars: Episode IV – A New Hope*

Blockbusters from Steven Spielberg and George Lucas hit the screens, with *Star Wars* once the all-time highest-earning.

TOP 10 FILMS OF THE 1980s

FILM	YEAR
1 E.T.: the Extra-Terrestrial	1982
2 Return of the Jedi*	1983
3 The Empire Strikes Back#	1980
4 Indiana Jones and the Last Crusade	1989
5 Rain Man†	1988
6 Batman	1989
7 Raiders of the Lost Ark	1981
8 Back to the Future	1985
9 Top Gun	1986
10 Indiana Jones and the Temple of Doom	1984

* Later retitled *Star Wars: Episode VI – Return of the Jedi*
# Later retitled *Star Wars: Episode V – The Empire Strikes Back*
† Winner of Best Picture Oscar

TOP 10 FILMS OF THE 1990s

FILM	YEAR
1 Titanic*	1997
2 Star Wars: Episode I – The Phantom Menace	1999
3 Jurassic Park	1993
4 Independence Day	1996
5 The Lion King#	1994
6 Forrest Gump*	1994
7 The Sixth Sense	1999
8 The Lost World: Jurassic Park	1997
9 Men in Black	1997
10 Armageddon	1998

* Winner of Best Picture Oscar
# Animated

A king's ransom
The Lord of the Rings: The Return of the King *became the second film to earn over $1 billion.*

TOP 10 FILMS OF THE 2000s *

FILM	YEAR
1 The Lord of the Rings: The Return of the King	2003
2 Pirates of the Caribbean: Dead Man's Chest	2006
3 The Dark Knight	2008
4 Harry Potter and the Philosopher's Stone	2001
5 Pirates of the Caribbean: At World's End	2007
6 Harry Potter and the Order of the Phoenix	2007
7 The Lord of the Rings: The Two Towers	2002
8 Shrek 2	2004
9 Harry Potter and the Goblet of Fire	2005
10 Spider-Man 3	2007

* As at 31 March 2009

AFI Hits

About AFI

Since 1998 the American Film Institute has been compiling its '100 Years of...' lists, selected by a panel of prominent individuals in the film community and presenting Top 100s in a variety of categories ('Thrills', 'Laughs', 'Songs', etc.). In 2008, the AFI identified its Top 10s in a range of genres. Among them, Steven Spielberg and Stanley Kubrick each directed three films, while Tom Hanks, Gene Hackman and Diane Keaton each appeared in (or, in the case of Hanks and the animated *Toy Story*, provided a voice for) a total of four of the films shown in these lists.

TOP 10 GANGSTER FILMS

	FILM	YEAR
1	The Godfather*	1972
2	Goodfellas	1990
3	The Godfather Part II*	1974
4	White Heat	1949
5	Bonnie and Clyde	1967
6	Scarface: The Shame of the Nation	1932
7	Pulp Fiction	1994
8	The Public Enemy	1931
9	Little Caesar	1931
10	Scarface	1983

* Won Best Picture Oscar

TOP 10 WESTERNS

	FILM	YEAR
1	The Searchers	1956
2	High Noon	1952
3	Shane	1953
4	Unforgiven*	1992
5	Red River	1948
6	The Wild Bunch	1969
7	Butch Cassidy and the Sundance Kid	1969
8	McCabe and Mrs Miller	1971
9	Stagecoach	1939
10	Cat Ballou	1965

* Won Best Picture Oscar

TOP 10 FANTASY FILMS

	FILM	YEAR
1	The Wizard of Oz	1939
2	The Lord of the Rings: The Fellowship of the Ring	2001
3	It's a Wonderful Life	1946
4	King Kong	1933
5	Miracle on 34th Street	1947
6	Field of Dreams	1989
7	Harvey	1950
8	Groundhog Day	1993
9	The Thief of Bagdad	1924
10	Big	1988

The Wizard of Oz
The film's 'Somewhere Over the Rainbow' previously topped the AFI '100 Years... 100 Songs' list.

TOP 10 **EPICS**

FILM	YEAR
1 Lawrence of Arabia*	1962
2 Ben-Hur*	1959
3 Schindler's List*	1993
4 Gone with the Wind*	1939
5 Spartacus	1960
6 Titanic*	1997
7 All Quiet on the Western Front*	1930
8 Saving Private Ryan*	1998
9 Reds	1981
10 The Ten Commandments	1956

* Won Best Picture Oscar

Lawrence of Arabia
Fifth on the AFI's '100 Years... 100 Movies', but here hailed as the all-time greatest epic.

TOP 10 **ROMANTIC COMEDIES**

FILM	YEAR
1 City Lights	1931
2 Annie Hall*	1977
3 It Happened One Night*	1934
4 Roman Holiday	1953
5 The Philadelphia Story	1940
6 When Harry Met Sally...	1989
7 Adam's Rib	1949
8 Moonstruck	1987
9 Harold and Maude	1971
10 Sleepless in Seattle	1993

* Won Best Picture Oscar

TOP 10 **SCIENCE-FICTION FILMS**

FILM	YEAR
1 2001: A Space Odyssey	1968
2 Star Wars: Episode IV – A New Hope	1977
3 E.T.: the Extra-Terrestrial	1982
4 A Clockwork Orange	1971
5 The Day the Earth Stood Still	1951
6 Blade Runner	1982
7 Alien	1979
8 Terminator 2: Judgment Day	1991
9 Invasion of the Body Snatchers	1956
10 Back to the Future	1985

TOP 10 **ANIMATED FILMS**

FILM	YEAR
1 Snow White and the Seven Dwarfs	1937
2 Pinocchio	1940
3 Bambi	1942
4 The Lion King	1994
5 Fantasia	1940
6 Toy Story	1995
7 Beauty and the Beast	1991
8 Shrek*	2001
9 Cinderella	1950
10 Finding Nemo	2003

* DreamWorks; all others Disney

Animated Hits

TOP 10 **ANIMATED FILMS IN THE UK**

FILM / YEAR / UK TOTAL GROSS (£)

1 Shrek 2* 2004
48,243,628

2 Toy Story 2# 2000
44,306,070

3 The Simpsons Movie 2007
38,312,694

4 Shrek the Third* 2007
38,079,462

5 Monsters, Inc.# 2002
37,907,451

6 Finding Nemo# 2003
37,364,251

7 The Incredibles# 2004
32,277,041

8 Wallace & Gromit: The Curse of
the Were-Rabbit* 2005
32,007,310

9 Chicken Run* 2000
29,514,237

10 Ice Age: The Meltdown† 2006
29,450,144

* DreamWorks
# Disney
† 20th Century Fox Animation

TOP 10 **ANIMATED FILMS**

FILM / YEAR / GROSS (US$)

Shrek 2*
2004
920,665,658

Finding Nemo#
2003
864,625,978

Shrek the Third*
2007
798,957,081

The Lion King#
1994
783,841,776

Ice Age: The Meltdown†
2006
651,564,512

Kung Fu Panda*
2008
631,908,951

The Incredibles#
2004
631,442,092

Ratatouille#
2007
621,426,008

Madagascar:
Escape 2 Africa*
2008
584,316,050

WALL-E#
2008
534,745,866

* DreamWorks
# Disney
† 20th Century Fox Animation

Just for kicks
Kung Fu Panda *had a production budget*
of $130 million, but earned almost five
times as much worldwide.

Animated automata
During the past decade, films such as Robots have benefited from advances in CGI.

TOP 10 ANIMATED FILMS BASED ON TV SERIES

FILM	TV SERIES*	FILM YEAR
1 The Simpsons Movie	1987	2007
2 Pokémon: The First Movie	1997	1999
3 The Rugrats Movie	1991	1998
4 The SpongeBob SquarePants Movie	1999	2004
5 Pokémon: The Movie 2000	1997	2000
6 Rugrats in Paris: The Movie - Rugrats II	1991	2000
7 TMNT	1987	2007
8 South Park: Bigger, Longer & Uncut	1997	1999
9 Beavis and Butthead Do America	1993	1996
10 Pokémon 3: The Movie	1997	2001

* Launched on TV in USA

Many TV animated series established substantial fan-bases before they hit the big screen. *The Simpsons Movie* has made over $527 million and the Top 10 a cumulative global total of over $1.5 billion.

Animated Film Budgets
Snow White and the Seven Dwarfs (1937) had a then-record animated film budget of $1.49 million. The $2.28 million of *Fantasia* (1940) was the biggest of the 1940s, and the $6 million of *Sleeping Beauty* (1959) the highest of the 1950s. Fifty years on, budgets of $100 million or more are common, with *WALL-E* (2008) setting a record of $180 million.

TOP 10 ANIMATED SCIENCE-FICTION FILMS

FILM	YEAR	WORLDWIDE TOTAL GROSS (US$)
1 WALL-E	2008	534,745,866
2 Lilo & Stitch	2002	273,144,470
3 Robots	2005	260,718,330
4 Atlantis: The Lost Empire	2001	186,053,745
5 Meet the Robinsons	2007	169,332,978
6 Pokémon: The First Movie	1999	163,644,662
7 Pokémon: The Movie 2000	2000	133,949,270
8 Treasure Planet	2002	109,578,115
9 Jimmy Neutron: Boy Genius	2001	102,992,536
10 Final Fantasy: The Spirits Within	2001	85,131,830

TOP 10 FILMS WITH CGI STARS*

FILM	YEAR	WORLDWIDE TOTAL GROSS (US$)
1 King Kong	2005	550,517,357
2 Godzilla	1998	379,014,294
3 Alvin and the Chipmunks	2007	359,656,974
4 Stuart Little	1999	300,235,367
5 Casper	1995	287,928,194
6 Scooby-Doo	2002	275,650,703
7 The Incredible Hulk	2008	263,427,064
8 Hulk	2003	245,360,480
9 Garfield: The Movie	2004	198,964,900
10 Scooby-Doo 2: Monsters Unleashed	2004	181,466,833

* Main or title-named character created by computer-generated imagery

Actors

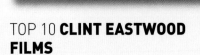

TOP 10 **HARRISON FORD FILMS**

FILM	YEAR
1 Indiana Jones and the Kingdom of the Crystal Skull	2008
2 Star Wars: Episode IV – A New Hope	1977
3 Star Wars: Episode VI – Return of the Jedi	1983
4 Star Wars: Episode V – The Empire Strikes Back	1980
5 Indiana Jones and the Last Crusade	1989
6 Raiders of the Lost Ark	1981
7 The Fugitive	1993
8 Indiana Jones and the Temple of Doom	1984
9 Air Force One	1997
10 What Lies Beneath	2000

TOP 10 **CLINT EASTWOOD FILMS**

FILM	YEAR
1 Million Dollar Baby*	2004
2 Gran Torino	2008
3 The Bridges of Madison County	1995
4 In the Line of Fire	1993
5 Unforgiven*	1992
6 A Perfect World	1993
7 Space Cowboys	2000
8 Every Which Way But Loose	1978
9 Absolute Power	1997
10 Any Which Way You Can	1980

* Won Best Director and Best Picture Oscars

Clint Eastwood
Unforgiven earned Clint Eastwood the first of two Best Director Oscars. His second was awarded for Best Picture Million Dollar Baby, which made over $200 million.

TOP 10 **PAUL NEWMAN FILMS**

FILM	YEAR
1 Road to Perdition	2002
2 The Sting	1973
3 Message in a Bottle	1999
4 The Towering Inferno	1974
5 Butch Cassidy and the Sundance Kid	1969
6 The Verdict	1982
7 The Color of Money*	1986
8 Nobody's Fool	1994
9 Absence of Malice	1981
10 Fort Apache the Bronx	1981

* Won Best Picture Oscar

In addition to the films in his Top 10, Paul Newman (1925–2008) appeared briefly as himself in *Silent Movie* (1976), which, if it were included, would be in ninth place. He also provided the voice of Doc Hudson in the animated film *Cars* (2006), which would appear first in his personal Top 10 by a considerable margin.

Whip-hand
Harrison Ford's Top 10 films – most notably the Indiana Jones and Star Wars series – have earned a total of almost $5 billion worldwide.

TOP 10 JOHNNY DEPP FILMS

FILM	YEAR
1 Pirates of the Caribbean: Dead Man's Chest	2006
2 Pirates of the Caribbean: At World's End	2007
3 Pirates of the Caribbean: The Curse of the Black Pearl	2003
4 Charlie and the Chocolate Factory	2004
5 Sleepy Hollow	1999
6 Platoon	1986
7 Chocolat	2000
8 Sweeney Todd: The Demon Barber of Fleet Street	2007
9 Donnie Brasco	1997
10 Finding Neverland	2004

All Johnny Depp's Top 10 films have earned more than $100 million each, his run of successes led – by a considerable margin – by the three *Pirates of the Caribbean* films, which have made $2.7 billion in total, with a fourth scheduled for release in 2012.

TOP 10 MATT DAMON FILMS

FILM	YEAR
1 Saving Private Ryan	1998
2 Ocean's Eleven	2001
3 The Bourne Ultimatum	2007
4 Ocean's Twelve	2004
5 Ocean's Thirteen	2006
6 The Departed	2006
7 The Bourne Supremacy	2004
8 Good Will Hunting	1997
9 The Bourne Identity	2002
10 The Talented Mr Ripley	1999

Pirate treasure
The three Pirates of the Caribbean *films to date head Johnny Depp's personal Top 10, having earned $2.7 billion globally.*

TOP 10 BRAD PITT FILMS

FILM	YEAR
1 Troy	2004
2 Mr & Mrs Smith	2005
3 Ocean's Eleven	2001
4 Ocean's Twelve	2004
5 Se7en	1995
6 The Curious Case of Benjamin Button	2008
7 Ocean's Thirteen	2007
8 Interview with the Vampire: The Vampire Chronicles	1994
9 Twelve Monkeys	1995
10 Sleepers	1996

Troy weight
Troy, *in which Brad Pitt took the role of Achilles, added to his run of box-office hits, making a world total of almost $500 million.*

Actresses

TOP 10 **MERYL STREEP FILMS**

	FILM	YEAR
1	Mamma Mia!	2008
2	The Devil Wears Prada	2006
3	Out of Africa	1985
4	Lemony Snicket's A Series of Unfortunate Events	2004
5	The Bridges of Madison County	1995
6	Death Becomes Her	1992
7	The Hours	2002
8	Kramer vs. Kramer	1979
9	The Manchurian Candidate	2004
10	The River Wild	1994

Meryl Streep has been nominated for Academy Awards on a total of 14 occasions, winning for her supporting role in *Kramer vs. Kramer*, and Best Actress for *Sophie's Choice* (1982), which falls outside her personal Top 10 in terms of box-office revenue. She provided the voice of the Blue Fairy in *A.I.: Artificial Intelligence* (2001) which, were it taken into account, would be in fourth place.

TOP 10 **SIGOURNEY WEAVER FILMS**

	FILM	YEAR
1	Ghostbusters	1984
2	The Village	2004
3	Ghostbusters II	1989
4	Aliens	1986
5	Alien: Resurrection	1997
6	Alien3	1992
7	Vantage Point	2008
8	Alien	1979
9	Galaxy Quest	1999
10	Holes	2003

Sigourney Weaver has made a speciality of playing vulnerable-but-tough parts, her roles in the two *Ghostbusters* and four *Alien(s)* films bringing her both fame and fortune. She provided the voice of the Ship's Computer in the animated film *WALL-E* (2008); if included it would rank first in her Top 10.

TOP 10 **TILDA SWINTON FILMS**

	FILM	YEAR
1	The Chronicles of Narnia: The Lion, the Witch and the Wardrobe	2005
2	The Chronicles of Narnia: Prince Caspian	2008
3	The Curious Case of Benjamin Button	2008
4	Constantine	2005
5	Vanilla Sky	2001
6	Burn After Reading	2008
7	The Beach	2000
8	Michael Clayton	2007
9	Adaptation.	2002
10	Broken Flowers	2005

British actress Tilda Swinton won a Best Supporting Actress Oscar for her role in *Michael Clayton*.

Fighting fit
Tilda Swinton took the role of the White Witch in the first two Narnia films, which have earned $1.2 billion worldwide.

TOP 10 **CATE BLANCHETT FILMS**

FILM	YEAR
1 The Lord of the Rings: The Return of the King	2003
2 The Lord of the Rings: The Two Towers	2002
3 The Lord of the Rings: The Fellowship of the Ring	2001
4 Indiana Jones and the Kingdom of the Crystal Skull	2008
5 The Curious Case of Benjamin Button	2008
6 The Aviator	2004
7 Babel	2006
8 The Talented Mr Ripley	1999
9 Elizabeth	1998
10 Elizabeth: The Golden Age	2007

TOP 10 **SCARLETT JOHANSSON FILMS**

FILM	YEAR
1 The Horse Whisperer	1998
2 The Island	2005
3 He's Just Not That Into You	2009
4 Lost in Translation	2003
5 The Prestige	2006
6 Vicky Cristina Barcelona	2008
7 Match Point	2005
8 Home Alone 3	1997
9 The Other Boleyn Girl	2008
10 Just Cause	1995

Shooting ahead
Sci-fi thriller The Island *is one of a number of high-earning Scarlett Johansson films.*

X-rated
Among Berry's highest-earning films, the three *X-Men* have earned a global total of $1.2 billion.

TOP 10 **HALLE BERRY FILMS**

FILM	YEAR
1 X-Men: The Last Stand	2006
2 Die Another Day	2002
3 X2: X-Men United	2003
4 The Flintstones	1994
5 X-Men	2000
6 Swordfish	2001
7 Gothika	2003
8 Boomerang	1992
9 Executive Decision	1996
10 Catwoman	2004

Oscar Stars & Directors

THE 10 LATEST STARS TO WIN TWO BEST ACTOR/ACTRESS OSCARS

	STAR	FIRST WIN	YEAR	SECOND WIN	YEAR
1	Sean Penn	Mystic River	2003	Milk	2008
2	Daniel Day-Lewis	My Left Foot	1989	There Will Be Blood	2007
3	Hilary Swank	Boys Don't Cry	1999	Million Dollar Baby*	2004
4	Jack Nicholson	One Flew over the Cuckoo's Nest*	1975	As Good as it Gets	1997
5	Tom Hanks	Philadelphia	1993	Forrest Gump*	1994
6	Jodie Foster	The Accused	1988	The Silence of the Lambs*	1991
7	Dustin Hoffman	Kramer vs. Kramer*	1979	Rain Man*	1988
8	Sally Field	Norma Rae	1979	Places in the Heart	1984
9	Katharine Hepburn	The Lion in Winter	1968	On Golden Pond	1981
10	Jane Fonda	Klute	1971	Coming Home	1978

* Film won Best Picture Oscar

Uniquely, Katharine Hepburn had already won two Best Actress Oscars, for *Morning Glory* in 1932/33 and *Guess Who's Coming to Dinner?* in 1967, which would also place her at No. 11 in this list.

Devil in disguise
Meryl Streep was nominated for a Best Actress Oscar for The Devil Wears Prada *(2006).*

TOP 10 ACTORS AND ACTRESSES WITH THE MOST OSCAR NOMINATIONS*

	ACTOR	WINS SUPPORTING	/ BEST	/ NOMINATIONS
1	Meryl Streep	1	1	15
2 =	Katharine Hepburn	0	4	12
=	Jack Nicholson	1	2	12
4 =	Bette Davis	0	2	10
=	Laurence Olivier	0	1	10
6 =	Paul Newman	0	1	9
=	Spencer Tracy	0	2	9
8 =	Marlon Brando	0	2	8
=	Jack Lemmon	1	1	8
=	Peter O'Toole	0	0	8
=	Al Pacino	0	1	8
=	Geraldine Page	0	1	8

* In all acting categories

THE 10 LATEST DIRECTORS TO WIN TWO BEST DIRECTOR OSCARS

	DIRECTOR	FIRST WIN	YEAR	SECOND WIN	YEAR
1	Clint Eastwood	Unforgiven	1992	Million Dollar Baby	2004
2	Steven Spielberg	Schindler's List	1993	Saving Private Ryan	1998
3	Oliver Stone	Platoon	1986	Born on the Fourth of July	1989
4	Milos Forman	One Flew Over the Cuckoo's Nest	1975	Amadeus	1984
5	Fred Zinnemann	From Here to Eternity	1953	A Man for All Seasons	1966
6	Robert Wise	West Side Story	1961	The Sound of Music	1965
7	David Lean	The Bridge on the River Kwai	1957	Lawrence of Arabia	1962
8	Billy Wilder	The Lost Weekend	1945	The Apartment	1960
9	George Stevens	A Place in the Sun	1951	Giant	1956
10	Elia Kazan	Gentleman's Agreement	1947	On the Waterfront	1954

John Ford is the only director to win four Best Director Oscars (from 1935 to 1952), while Frank Capra and William Wyler each reached a tally of three, with these the most recent of the relatively rare double winners.

Dream come true
Jennifer Hudson's debut Dreamgirls *won her the Best Supporting Actress Oscar.*

THE 10 **LATEST YEARS IN WHICH BEST PICTURE AND BEST DIRECTOR OSCARS WERE WON BY DIFFERENT FILMS**

	BEST PICTURE	BEST DIRECTOR FILM	YEAR
1	Crash	Brokeback Mountain	2005
2	Chicago	The Pianist	2002
3	Gladiator	Traffic	2000
4	Shakespeare in Love	Saving Private Ryan	1998
5	Driving Miss Daisy	Born on the Fourth of July	1989
6	Chariots of Fire	Reds	1981
7	The Godfather	Cabaret	1972
8	In the Heat of the Night	The Graduate	1967
9	Around the World in 80 Days	Giant	1956
10	The Greatest Show on Earth	The Quiet Man	1952

THE 10 **LATEST WINNERS OF AN OSCAR FOR THEIR DEBUT FILM** *

	ACTOR/ACTRESS	FILM	FILM YEAR
1	Jennifer Hudson#	Dreamgirls	2006
2	Anna Paquin#	The Piano	1993
3	Marlee Matlin†	Children of a Lesser God	1986
4	Haing S. Ngor#	The Killing Fields	1984
5	Timothy Hutton#	Ordinary People	1980
6	Tatum O'Neal#	Paper Moon	1973
7	Barbra Streisand†	Funny Girl	1968
8 =	Julie Andrews†	Mary Poppins	1964
=	Lila Kedrova#	Zorba the Greek	1964
10	Miyoshi Umeki#	Sayonara	1957

* In a film eligible for a Best or Best Supporting Actor/Actress Oscar win (hence excluding previous TV movies, etc.)
# Best Actor/Actress in a Supporting Role
† Best Actor/Actress in a Leading Role

Oscar Films & Studios

TOP 10 STUDIOS WITH THE MOST OSCAR* WINS IN ALL CATEGORIES

	STUDIO	WINS
1	MGM	191
2	20th Century Fox	187
3	Paramount	186
4	Warner Bros.	182
5	Columbia	155
6	United Artists	151
7	Universal	87
8	RKO Radio Pictures	56
9	Miramax	52
10	Buena Vista	47

* Oscar® is a Registered Trade Mark

THE 10 LATEST FILMS TO WIN THE BEST PICTURE OSCAR BUT NO OTHER MAJOR AWARD*

	FILM	YEAR
1	Crash	2005
2	Chariots of Fire	1981
3	Around the World in 80 Days	1956
4	The Greatest Show on Earth	1952
5	An American in Paris	1951
6	Rebecca	1940
7	Mutiny on the Bounty	1935
8	Grand Hotel	1932
9	Cimarron	1931
10	The Broadway Melody	1929

* In directing or acting categories

THE 10 FILMS WITH THE MOST NOMINATIONS WITHOUT A SINGLE WIN

	FILM	YEAR	NOMINATIONS
1 =	The Turning Point	1977	11
=	The Color Purple	1985	11
3	Gangs of New York	2002	10
4 =	The Little Foxes	1941	9
=	Peyton Place	1957	9
6 =	Quo Vadis	1951	8
=	The Nun's Story	1959	8
=	The Sand Pebbles	1966	8
=	The Elephant Man	1980	8
=	Ragtime	1981	8
=	The Remains of the Day	1993	8

TOP 10 STUDIOS WITH THE MOST BEST PICTURE OSCARS

STUDIO / WINS

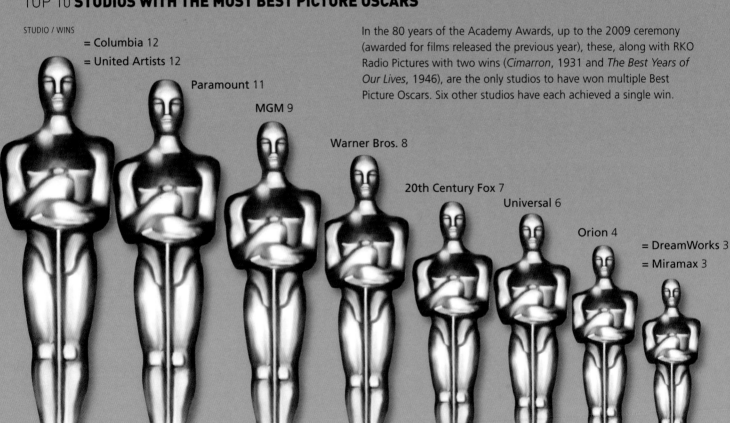

= Columbia 12
= United Artists 12
Paramount 11
MGM 9
Warner Bros. 8
20th Century Fox 7
Universal 6
Orion 4
= DreamWorks 3
= Miramax 3

In the 80 years of the Academy Awards, up to the 2009 ceremony (awarded for films released the previous year), these, along with RKO Radio Pictures with two wins (*Cimarron*, 1931 and *The Best Years of Our Lives*, 1946), are the only studios to have won multiple Best Picture Oscars. Six other studios have each achieved a single win.

Racing ahead
Ben-Hur's 11 Oscars, including Best Picture, Best Director and Best Actor for Charlton Heston, stood as a record for 38 years.

TOP 10 **FILMS TO WIN THE MOST OSCARS**

FILM	YEAR	NOMINATIONS	AWARDS
1 = Ben-Hur	1959	12	11
= Titanic	1997	14	11
= The Lord of the Rings: The Return of the King	2003	11	11
4 West Side Story	1961	11	10
5 = Gigi	1958	9	9
= The Last Emperor	1987	9	9
= The English Patient	1996	12	9
8 = Gone With the Wind	1939	13	8*
= From Here to Eternity	1953	13	8
= On the Waterfront	1954	12	8
= My Fair Lady	1964	12	8
= Cabaret#	1972	10	8
= Gandhi	1982	11	8
= Amadeus	1984	11	8
= Slumdog Millionaire	2008	10	8

* Plus two special awards
# Did not win Best Picture Oscar

TOP 10 **HIGHEST-EARNING BEST PICTURE OSCAR-WINNERS**

FILM	YEAR*	WORLD BOX OFFICE (US$)
1 Titanic	1997	1,848,813,795
2 The Lord of the Rings: The Return of the King	2003	1,129,219,252
3 Forrest Gump	1994	677,386,686
4 Gladiator	2000	457,640,427
5 Dances With Wolves	1990	424,208,842
6 Rain Man	1988	416,011,462
7 Gone With the Wind	1939	400,176,459
8 American Beauty	1999	356,296,601
9 Schindler's List	1993	321,267,179
10 A Beautiful Mind	2001	313,542,341

* Of release; Oscars are awarded the following year

Radio & TV

TOP 10 **NATIONAL RADIO STATIONS IN THE UK***

STATION / % SHARE OF TOTAL AUDIENCE

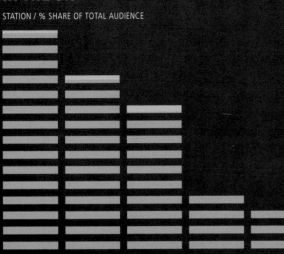

1	2	3	4	5	6	7	8	9	10
BBC Radio 2	BBC Radio 4	BBC Radio 1	BBC Radio 5 Live#	Classic FM	talk SPORT	Absolute Radio National†	BBC Radio 3	BBC World Service	= BBC 7 0.50
15.80	12.40	10.10	5.00	4.00	1.80	1.20	1.30	0.70	= Planet Rock 0.50

* Oct–Dec 2008   # Including Sports Extra   † Formerly Total Virgin Radio   Source: RAJAR

TOP 10 **LONGEST-RUNNING PROGRAMMES ON BBC RADIO**

PROGRAMME / FIRST BROADCAST

The Week's Good Cause 24 Jan 1926	The Shipping Forecast 26 Jan 1926	Choral Evensong 7 Oct 1926	Daily Service 2 Jan 1928*	The Week in Westminster 6 Nov 1929	Sunday Half Hour 14 Jul 1940

Desert Island Discs 29 Jan 1942	Saturday Night Theatre 3 Apr 1943	Composer of the Week# 2 Aug 1943	From Our Own Correspondent 4 Oct 1946

* Experimental broadcast; national transmission began December 1929
# Formerly *This Week's Composer*

TOP 10 **TELEVISION AUDIENCES IN THE USA**

	PROGRAMME	DATE	TOTAL	VIEWERS %
1	M*A*S*H Special	28 Feb 1983	50,150,000	60.2
2	Dallas	21 Nov 1980	41,470,000	53.3
3	Roots Part 8	30 Jan 1977	36,380,000	51.1
4	Super Bowl XVI	24 Jan 1982	40,020,000	49.1
5	Super Bowl XVII	30 Jan 1983	40,480,000	48.6
6	XVII Winter Olympics	23 Feb 1994	45,690,000	48.5
7	Super Bowl XX	26 Jan 1986	41,490,000	48.3
8	Gone With the Wind Pt.1	7 Nov 1976	33,960,000	47.7
9	Gone With the Wind Pt.2	8 Nov 1976	33,750,000	47.4
10	Super Bowl XII	15 Jan 1978	34,410,000	47.2

Source: Nielsen Media Research

In 2009 there were an estimated 114.5 million television households in the USA, so a single ratings point would represent one per cent, or 1,145,000 households, and so on. Historically, as more households acquired television sets, audiences generally increased, but the rise in channel choice and use of recording has checked this trend, and it is unlikely that such high percentages will ever again be attained. The two and a half hour feature-length 'Goodbye, Farewell, and Amen' episode of *M*A*S*H* was the last in a series that had run for more than 10 years. An estimated 50.15 million households, or almost 106 million individual viewers, tuned in, making it the most-watched broadcast of all time.

China watching
Boosted by the 2008 Beijing Olympics,
TV ownership in China now leads the world.

TOP 10 **TV COUNTRIES**

	COUNTRY	TV HOUSEHOLDS*
1	China	380,559,800
2	India	133,891,800
3	USA	118,035,600
4	Indonesia	55,665,400
5	Russia	51,272,700
6	Brazil	50,929,800
7	Japan	49,396,100
8	Germany	39,041,400
9	UK	26,819,500
10	Mexico	25,666,600

* Households with colour TVs, 2010 forecast

Source: Euromonitor International

TOP 10 **TELEVISION AUDIENCES IN THE UK**

	PROGRAMME	BROADCAST	AUDIENCE
1	1966 World Cup Final: England v West Germany	30 Jul 1966	32,300,000
2	Funeral of Diana, Princess of Wales	6 Sep 1997	32,100,000
3	The Royal Family documentary	21 Jun 1969	30,690,000
4	EastEnders Christmas episode (Den divorces Angie)	25 Dec 1986	30,150,000
5	Apollo 13 splashdown	17 Apr 1970	28,600,000
6	Cup Final Replay: Chelsea v. Leeds United	28 Apr 1970	28,490,000
7	Wedding of Prince Charles and Lady Diana Spencer	29 Jul 1981	28,400,000
8	Wedding of Princess Anne and Capt Mark Phillips	14 Nov 1973	27,600,000
9	Coronation Street (Alan Bradley killed by a tram)	19 Mar 1989	26,930,000
10	Only Fools and Horses (Batman and Robin episode)	29 Dec 1996	24,350,000

Source: British Film Institute

DVD & Film Downloads

TOP 10 **FILM GENRES ON DVD IN THE UK**

GENRE / SALES (%)

1. Comedy
22.3

2. Action/adventure
20.1

3. Drama
18.3

4. Children's/family
10.8

5. Thriller
9.4

6. Sci-Fi
6.8

7. Horror
5.6

8. Musical
3.3

9. War
2.2

10. Western
0.8

Source: British Video Association

TOP 10 **BESTSELLING DVDS OF ALL TIME IN THE UK**

1. Pirates of the Caribbean: The Curse of the Black Pearl

2. The Lord of the Rings: The Fellowship of the Ring

3. The Lord of The Rings: The Two Towers

4. Pirates of the Caribbean: Dead Man's Chest

5. The Lord of the Rings: The Return of the King

6. Shrek 2

7. The Shawshank Redemption

8. Gladiator

9. Casino Royale

10. Harry Potter and the Goblet of Fire

Source: British Video Association/ Official Charts Company

TOP 10 **MOST DOWNLOADED FILMS, 2007***

FILM / DOWNLOADS

1. Transformers
569,259

2. Knocked Up
509,314

3. Shooter
399,960

4. Pirates of the Caribbean: At World's End 379,749

5. Ratatouille
359,904

6. 300
358,226

7. Next
354,044

8. Hot Fuzz
352,905

9. The Bourne Ultimatum
336,326

10. Zodiac
334,699

* On Mininova

As at 3 October 2008, Netherlands-based torrent download site Mininova (founded 2005) recorded a total of 6,085,866,928 downloads (films and other categories) – equivalent to almost one for every person on the planet.

Prime mover
Transformers, *one of the bestselling DVDs and most downloaded films of 2007, is set to repeat its success with its 2009 sequel,* Transformers: Revenge of the Fallen.

TOP 10 **ONLINE DVD RENTALS IN THE UK, 2007**

DVD

1 Little Miss Sunshine
2 Children of Men
3 Casino Royale
4 Deja Vu
5 The Devil Wears Prada
6 The Last King of Scotland
7 The Queen
8 The Holiday
9 Hot Fuzz
10 Borat: Cultural Learnings of America for Make Benefit Glorious Nation of Kazakhstan

Source: MRIB/British Video Association

DVDs have been available for online rental via such companies as LoveFilm, Blockbuster and Amazon since 2004. In 2007, all the titles in the Top 10 were rented more than 100,000 times, with lead title *Little Miss Sunshine* renting 180,000 times.

TOP 10 **BESTSELLING SPORT VIDEOS* OF ALL TIME IN THE UK**

VIDEO

1 The Ashes: The Greatest Series
2 Rugby World Cup 2003: Official Review
3 Torvill & Dean: Face the Music
4 Nick Hancock: Football Nightmares
5 Manchester United: The Treble
6 Murray's Magic Moments
7 Danny Baker's Own Goals & Gaffs
8 Jeremy Clarkson's Motorsport Mayhem
9 England Rugby: Sweet Chariot
10 Very Best of Torvill & Dean

* All VHS and DVD formats

Source: British Video Association/ Official Charts Company

TOP 10 **BESTSELLING MUSIC VIDEOS* OF ALL TIME IN THE UK**

VIDEO

1 Riverdance
2 Lord of the Dance
3 Cats
4 Dream Cast: Les Misérables in Concert
5 Spice Girls: Official Video Vol. 1
6 Joseph & the Amazing Technicolor Dreamcoat
7 Three Tenors in Concert
8 Madonna: The Immaculate Collection
9 Queen: Greatest Flix 2
10 Robson & Jerome: So Far So Good

* All VHS and DVD formats

Source: British Video Association/Official Charts Company

THE COMMERCIAL WORLD

Men & Women at Work

TOP 10 COMPANIES WITH THE MOST EMPLOYEES

COMPANY / COUNTRY	INDUSTRY	EMPLOYEES
1 Wal-Mart Stores, USA	Retail	1,800,000
2 Indian Railways	Rail services	1,600,000
3 China National Petroleum, China	Oil and gas	1,090,232
4 State Grid, China	Electric power	844,031
5 US Postal Service, USA	Mail	803,000
6 Sinopec, China	Oil and gas	730,800
7 Deutsche Post, Germany	Post and courier	502,545
8 Agricultural Bank of China, China	Banking	478,895
9 UES (Unified Energy System), Russia	Electric power	461,200
10 Siemens, Germany	Electronics	461,000

Source: *Fortune Global 500 2008*

TOP 10 COUNTRIES WITH HIGHEST UNEMPLOYMENT

COUNTRY	ESTIMATED % LABOUR FORCE UNEMPLOYED
1 Nauru	90.0
2 Liberia	85.0
3 Zimbabwe	80.0
4 Burkina Faso	77.0
5 Turkmenistan	60.0
6 Djibouti	59.0
7 Zambia	50.0
8 Senegal	48.0
9 Nepal	46.0
10 Lesotho	45.0
UK	*5.5*
World average	*30.0*

Source: CIA, *World Factbook 2008*

Chinese workforce
China's predominantly rural (744.3 million) and urban (607.2 million) population includes a labour force of 807.7 million – those aged 15 to 64 currently employed and unemployed, but excluding unpaid groups such as students and retired people.

Woman's work
Garment manufacture is one of Cambodia's principal industries, traditionally employing a high proportion of women, making the country one of few where female employees outnumber male.

TOP 10 COUNTRIES WITH THE MOST WORKERS

	COUNTRY	WORKERS*
1	China	807,700,000
2	India	523,500,000
3	USA	155,200,000
4	Indonesia	112,000,000
5	Brazil	100,900,000
6	Russia	75,700,000
7	Bangladesh	70,860,000
8	Japan	66,150,000
9	Nigeria	51,040,000
10	Pakistan	50,580,000
	UK	*31,200,000*
	Top 10 total	*2,013,630,000*
	World total	*3,167,000,000*

* 2008 or latest year available; based on people aged 15–64 who are currently employed; excluding unpaid groups

Source: CIA, *World Factbook 2008*/International Labour Organization

As defined by the ILO, the 'labour force' includes people aged 15 to 64 currently employed and those who are unemployed, but excludes unpaid groups such as students, housewives and retired people.

Child labour
Despite legislation, issues of exploitation, health and safety, and depriving children of access to education, child workers continue to be employed in countries such as Nepal.

TOP 10 COUNTRIES WITH THE HIGHEST PROPORTION OF FEMALE WORKERS

	COUNTRY	LABOUR FORCE %*
1	Mozambique	53.4
2 =	Burundi	51.4
=	Rwanda	51.4
4	Cambodia	50.7
5	Malawi	50.0
6	Tanzania	49.7
7	Kazakhstan	49.4
8	Mali	49.2
9	Belarus	49.1
10	Lithuania	49.0
	UK	*44.1*
	World average	*39.9*

* Aged 15–64 who are currently employed; unpaid groups are not included

Source: World Bank, *World Development Indicators 2008*

TOP 10 COUNTRIES WITH THE HIGHEST PROPORTION OF CHILD WORKERS

	COUNTRY		7-14-YEAR OLDS AT WORK (%)*
1	Mali		70.9
2	Guinea-Bissau		67.5
3	Central African Republic		67.0
4	Sierra Leone		65.0
5	Chad	–	60.4
6	Ethiopia		56.0
7	Nepal		52.4
8	Cambodia		52.3
9	Burkina Faso		50.0
10	Guinea		48.3
	World average	*67,444*	*11.24*

* In latest year available; excludes unpaid work

Source: World Bank, *World Development Indicators 2008*/International Labour Organization

In Good Company

TOP 10 **GLOBAL COMPANIES MAKING THE GREATEST PROFIT PER SECOND**

PROFIT PER ANNUM/SECOND ($)

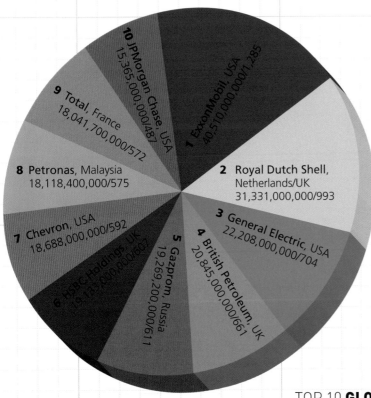

- **1** ExxonMobil, USA 40,510,000,000/1,285
- **2** Royal Dutch Shell, Netherlands/UK 31,331,000,000/993
- **3** General Electric, USA 22,208,000,000/704
- **4** British Petroleum, UK 20,845,000,000/661
- **5** Gazprom, Russia 19,269,200,000/611
- **6** HSBC Holdings, UK 19,133,000,000/607
- **7** Chevron, USA 18,688,000,000/592
- **8** Petronas, Malaysia 18,118,400,000/575
- **9** Total, France 18,041,700,000/572
- **10** JPMorgan Chase, USA 15,365,000,000/487

Macro Microsoft
In the 30 years since its founding, US software company Microsoft has grown to become the world's largest computer-technology corporation.

TOP 10 **GLOBAL COMPANIES BY REVENUE**

REVENUE 2008 40 = 400,000,000,000 ($)

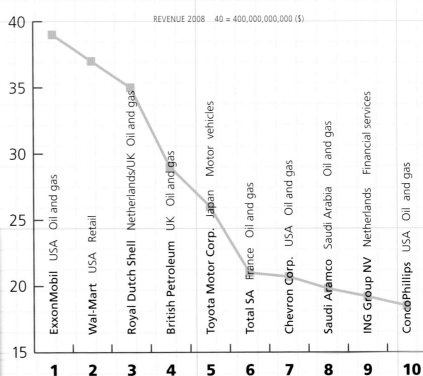

	1	2	3	4	5	6	7	8	9	10
	ExxonMobil USA Oil and gas	Wal-Mart USA Retail	Royal Dutch Shell Netherlands/UK Oil and gas	British Petroleum UK Oil and gas	Toyota Motor Corp. Japan Motor vehicles	Total SA France Oil and gas	Chevron Corp. USA Oil and gas	Saudi Aramco Saudi Arabia Oil and gas	ING Group NV Netherlands Financial services	ConocoPhillips USA Oil and gas

Gas giant
By various measures, oil and gas conglomerate ExxonMobil, created by the merger of Exxon and Mobil in 1999, is the world's biggest company.

TOP 10 **GLOBAL COMPANIES BY MARKET VALUE**

#	Company			Value
1	ExxonMobil	USA	Oil and gas	403,366,000,000
2	Petrochina	China	Oil and gas	325,320,000,000
3	General Electric	USA	Conglomerate	253,674,000,000
4	Microsoft	USA	Software	243,687,000,000
5	Wal-Mart	USA	Retail	235,605,000,000
6	Procter & Gamble	USA	Consumer goods	211,460,000,000
7	Industrial and Commercial Bank of China	China	Banking	208,397,000,000
8	Berkshire Hathaway	USA	Insurance	202,901,000,000
9	China Mobile	China	Telecommunications	198,558,000,000
10	Johnson & Johnson	USA	Healthcare	193,602,000,000

Wal-Mart, China
US retail leviathan Wal-Mart has over 7,000 stores in 14 countries. In 1996 it opened its first store in China, where it now has more than 100 outlets.

TOP 10 **COMPANIES IN THE UK BY REVENUE**

	COMPANY	SECTOR	REVENUE 2007 (£)
1	Royal Dutch/Shell Group	Oil, gas, chemicals	177,288,200,000
2	BP	Oil and gas	141,700,700,000
3	Tesco	Supermarkets	42,641,000,000
4	WPP Group	Media	31,665,000,000
5	Unilever	Food	31,650,800,000
6	Vodafone Group	Mobile telephones	31,104,000,000
7	GlaxoSmithKline plc	Pharmaceuticals	22,716,000,000
8	BT	Telecommunications	20,223,000,000
9	BHP Billiton	Mining	19,682,100,000
10	J. Sainsbury	Supermarkets	17,151,000,000

Source: *Financial Times UK 500 2008*

Rich Lists

TOP 10 RICHEST MEN*

NAME / COUNTRY (CITIZEN/ RESIDENCE, IF DIFFERENT)	SOURCE	NET WORTH ($)
1 William H. Gates III, USA	Microsoft (software)	40,000,000,000
2 Warren Edward Buffett, USA	Berkshire Hathaway (investments)	37,000,000,000
3 Carlos Slim Helu, Mexico	Communications	35,000,000,000
4 Lawrence Ellison, USA	Oracle (software)	22,500,000,000
5 Ingvar Kamprad, Sweden/Switzerland	Ikea (home furnishings)	22,000,000,000
6 Karl Albrecht, Germany	Aldi (supermarkets)	21,500,000,000
7 Mukesh Ambani, India	Reliance Industries (petrochemicals)	19,500,000,000
8 Lakshmi Mittal, India/UK	Mittal Steel	19,300,000,000
9 Theo Albrecht, Germany	Aldi (supermarkets)	18,800,000,000
10 Amancio Ortega, Spain	Zara (clothing)	18,300,000,000

* Excluding rulers and family fortunes

Source: Forbes magazine, The World's Billionaires 2009

Buffet buffeted
As a result of share price falls, Warren Buffet's fortune is $25 billion less than in 2008.

TOP 10 HIGHEST-EARNING CELEBRITIES

CELEBRITY*	PROFESSION	EARNINGS 2007–08 ($)
1 J. K. Rowling (UK)	Author	300,000,000
2 Oprah Winfrey	Talk-show host/ producer	275,000,000
3 50 Cent (Curtis James Jackson III)	Rap artist	150,000,000
4 Jerry Bruckheimer	Film and TV producer	145,000,000
5 Steven Spielberg	Film producer/director	130,000,000
6 Tyler Perry	Film and TV producer/director	125,000,000
7 Tiger Woods	Golfer	115,000,000
8 Jerry Seinfeld	Actor/comedian	85,000,000
9 Jay-Z (Shawn Corey Carter)	Rap artist	82,000,000
10 = Beyoncé Knowles	Singer/actress	80,000,000
= Will Smith	Film actor	80,000,000

* Individuals, excluding groups; all from the USA unless otherwise stated

Source: Forbes magazine, The Celebrity 100 2008

TOP 10 COUNTRIES WITH THE MOST DOLLAR BILLIONAIRES

COUNTRY*	$ BILLIONAIRES*
1 USA	318
2 Germany	54
3 China (including Hong Kong)	47
4 Russia	32
5 UK	25
6 India	24
7 Canada	20
8 Japan	17
9 Saudi Arabia	14
10 Turkey	13
World total	793

* Of residence, irrespective of citizenship

Source: Forbes magazine, The World's Billionaires 2009

TOP 10 **HIGHEST-EARNING DEAD CELEBRITIES**

	CELEBRITY*	EARNINGS PROFESSION	DEATH	2007–08 ($)
1	Elvis Presley	Rock star	16 Aug 1977	52,000,000
2	Charles Schultz	'Peanuts' cartoonist	12 Feb 2000	33,000,000
3	Heath Ledger (Australia)	Film actor	22 Jan 2008	20,000,000
4	Albert Einstein (Germany/USA)	Scientist	18 Apr 1955	18,000,000
5	Aaron Spelling	TV producer	23 Jun 2006	15,000,000
6	Theodor 'Dr Seuss' Geisel	Author	24 Sep 1991	12,000,000
7	= John Lennon (UK)	Rock star	8 Dec 1980	9,000,000
	= Andy Warhol	Artist	22 Feb 1987	9,000,000
9	Marilyn Monroe	Actress	5 Aug 1962	6,500,000
10	Steve McQueen	Actor	30 Nov 1980	6,000,000

* All from the USA unless otherwise stated

Source: *Forbes* magazine, *Top-Earning Dead Celebrities 2008*

Potter philanthropy
Harry Potter author J. K. Rowling has rocketed to pole position among celebrity earners, but has donated large sums to charities to aid children, families and medical research.

TOP 10 **HIGHEST-EARNING SPORTSMEN**

	SPORTSMAN / COUNTRY*	SPORT	ESTIMATED EARNINGS 2007–08
1	Tiger Woods	Golf	115,000,000
2	David Beckham (UK)	Football	50,000,000
3	Phil Mickelson	Golf	45,000,000
4	Kimi Raikkonen (Finland)	Motor racing	44,000,000
5	Kobe Bryant	Basketball	39,000,000
6	LeBron James	Basketball	38,000,000
7	Ronaldinho (Brazil)	Football	37,000,000
8	Roger Federer (Switzerland)	Tennis	35,000,000
9	Alex Rodriguez	Baseball	34,000,000
10	Fernando Alonso (Spain)	Motor racing	33,000,000

* All from the USA unless otherwise stated

Source: *Forbes* magazine, *The Celebrity 100 2008*

A league of his own
Football contracts and celebrity endorsements have propelled David Beckham into a wealth bracket unprecedented even in the heady world of professional football.

Energy

TOP 10 ENERGY-CONSUMING COUNTRIES

COUNTRY	OIL	GAS	ENERGY CONSUMPTION 2007* COAL	NUCLEAR	HEP#	TOTAL
1 USA	943.1	595.7	573.7	192.1	56.8	2,361.4
2 China†	384.9	63.3	1,318.4	14.2	109.3	1,890.1
3 Russia	125.9	394.9	94.5	36.2	40.5	692.0
4 Japan	228.9	81.2	125.3	63.1	18.9	517.4
5 India	128.5	36.2	208.0	4.0	27.7	404.4
6 Canada	102.3	84.6	30.4	21.1	83.3	321.7
7 Germany	112.5	74.5	86.0	31.8	6.2	311.0
8 France	91.3	37.7	12.0	99.7	14.4	255.1
9 South Korea	107.6	33.3	59.7	32.3	1.1	234.0
10 Brazil	96.5	19.8	13.6	2.8	84.1	216.8
UK	*78.2*	*82.3*	*39.2*	*14.1*	*2.1*	*215.9*
World total	*3,952.8*	*2,637.7*	*3,177.5*	*622.0*	*709.2*	*11,099.2*

* Millions of tonnes of oil equivalent
\# Hydroelectric power
† Including Hong Kong

Source: *BP Statistical Review of World Energy 2008*

TOP 10 COUNTRIES WITH THE MOST NUCLEAR REACTORS

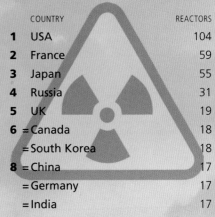

COUNTRY	REACTORS
1 USA	104
2 France	59
3 Japan	55
4 Russia	31
5 UK	19
6 = Canada	18
= South Korea	18
8 = China	17
= Germany	17
= India	17

Source: International Atomic Energy Agency

There are some 439 nuclear power stations in operation in a total of 30 countries around the world, with a further 41 under construction.

TOP 10 COUNTRIES WITH MOST RELIANCE ON NUCLEAR POWER

COUNTRY	NUCLEAR ELECTRICITY AS % OF TOTAL
1 France	76.9
2 Lithuania	64.4
3 Slovakia	54.3
4 Belgium	54.1
5 Ukraine	48.1
6 Sweden	46.1
7 Armenia	42.7
8 Slovenia	41.6
9 Switzerland	40.9
10 Hungary	36.8
UK	*15.1*

Source: International Atomic Energy Agency

Powering down
Prior to the planned 2009 closure of the Ignalina power station, Lithuania – one of 439 reactors in use worldwide – the country was one of the most nuclear-reliant.

TOP 10 **OIL-PRODUCING COUNTRIES**

	COUNTRY	% OF WORLD TOTAL	PRODUCTION 2007 (TONNES)
1	Saudi Arabia	12.6	493,100,000
2	Russia	12.6	491,300,000
3	USA	8.0	311,500,000
4	Iran	5.4	212,100,000
5	China	4.8	186,700,000
6	Mexico	4.4	173,000,000
7	Canada	4.1	158,900,000
8	United Arab Emirates	3.5	135,900,000
9	Venezuela	3.4	133,900,000
10	Kuwait	3.3	129,600,000
	UK	2.0	76,800,000
	Top 10 total	*62.1*	*2,426,000,000*
	World total	*100.0*	*3,905,900,000*

Source: *BP Statistical Review of World Energy 2008*

TOP 10 **NATURAL GAS-PRODUCING COUNTRIES**

	COUNTRY	% OF WORLD TOTAL	PRODUCTION 2007 (TONNES OF OIL EQUIVALENT)
1	Russia	20.6	546,700,000
2	USA	18.8	499,400,000
3	Canada	6.2	165,300,000
4	Iran	3.8	100,700,000
5	Norway	3.0	80,700,000
6	Algeria	2.8	74,700,000
7	Saudi Arabia	2.6	68,300,000
8	UK	2.5	65,200,000
9	China	2.4	62,400,000
10	Turkmenistan	2.3	60,700,000
	Top 10 total	*65.0*	*1,724,100,000*
	World total	*100.0*	*2,654,100,000*

Source: *BP Statistical Review of World Energy 2008*

TOP 10 **WIND-POWER COUNTRIES**

COUNTRY / % OF WORLD TOTAL / CAPACITY 2007 (MEGAWATTS)

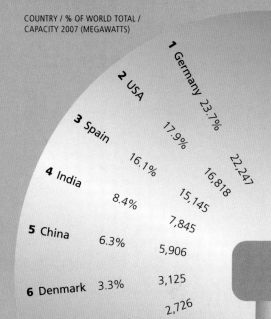

	COUNTRY	% OF WORLD TOTAL	CAPACITY 2007 (MEGAWATTS)
1	Germany	23.7%	22,247
2	USA	17.9%	16,818
3	Spain	16.1%	15,145
4	India	8.4%	7,845
5	China	6.3%	5,906
6	Denmark	3.3%	3,125
7	Italy	2.9%	2,726
8	France	2.6%	2,454
9	UK	2.5%	2,389
10	Portugal	2.3%	2,150

Source: Global Wind Energy Council, *Global Wind 2007 Report*, 2008

Wind power
The Tehachapi Pass Wind Farm, California: it has been proposed that by 2030 wind power will provide 20 per cent of the USA's electricity.

Environment

High score
Based on a range of 16 factors that include air quality, water resources, biodiversity and habitat, and sustainable energy, Switzerland tops the world Environmental Performance Index.

TOP 10 ENVIRONMENTAL PERFORMANCE INDEX COUNTRIES

	COUNTRY	EPI SCORE*
1	Switzerland	95.5
2 =	Norway	93.1
=	Sweden	93.1
4	Finland	91.4
5	Costa Rica	90.5
6	Austria	89.4
7	New Zealand	88.9
8	Latvia	88.8
9	Colombia	88.3
10	France	87.8
	UK	*86.3*

* Environmental Performance Index score out of 100

Source: Environmental Performance Index 2008

THE 10 WORST ENVIRONMENTAL PERFORMANCE INDEX COUNTRIES

	COUNTRY	EPI SCORE*
1	Niger	39.1
2	Angola	39.5
3	Sierra Leone	40.0
4	Mauritania	44.2
5 =	Burkina Faso	44.3
=	Mali	44.3
7	Chad	45.9
8	Dem. Rep. of Congo	47.3
9 =	Guinea-Bissau	49.7
=	Yemen	49.7

*Environmental Performance Index score out of 100

Source: Environmental Performance Index

THE 10 WORST OIL TANKER SPILLS

TANKER / LOCATION	DATE	APPROX. SPILLAGE (TONNES)
1 Atlantic Empress and Aegean Captain, Trinidad	19 Jul 1979	273,875
2 Castillio de Bellver, Cape Town, South Africa	6 Aug 1983	255,125
3 Olympic Bravery, Ushant, France	24 Jan 1976	250,000
4 Amoco Cadiz, Finistère, France	16 Mar 1978	223,275
5 Odyssey, Atlantic, off Canada	10 Nov 1988	140,075
6 Haven, off Genoa, Italy	11 Apr 1991	136,500
7 Torrey Canyon, Scilly Isles, UK	18 Mar 1967	124,150
8 Sea Star, Gulf of Oman	19 Dec 1972	123,175
9 Irenes Serenade, Pilos, Greece	23 Feb 1980	118,950
10 Texaco Denmark, North Sea, off Belgium	7 Dec 1971	102,375

Source: Environmental Technology Center, *Oil Spill Intelligence Report*

In addition to these, it is estimated that around two million tonnes of oil spills into the seas every year. The *Exxon Valdez* disaster in Alaska on 24 March 1989 ranks outside the 10 worst at about 35,000 tonnes, but resulted in major ecological damage.

On tap
India's huge population and the demands of its agricultural economy make it the world's top water consumer.

TOP 10 **FRESHWATER-CONSUMING COUNTRIES**

COUNTRY	ANNUAL FRESHWATER WITHDRAWALS* PER CAPITA (CU M)	TOTAL (CU KM)
1 India	585	645.84
2 China	415	549.76
3 USA	1,600	477.00
4 Pakistan	1,072	169.39
5 Japan	690	88.43
6 Indonesia	372	82.78
7 Thailand	1,288	82.75
8 Bangladesh	560	79.40
9 Mexico	731	78.22
10 Russia	535	76.68
UK	*197*	*11.75*

* In latest year for which data available

Source: World Resources Institute

TOP 10 **ENVIRONMENTAL CONCERNS IN THE UK**

CONCERN	% OF PEOPLE CONCERNED*
1 Disposal of hazardous waste	66
2 Effects of livestock methods (BSE, etc.)	59
3 Pollution of lakes, rivers and seas	55
4 =Pollution of bathing waters and beaches	52
=Traffic exhaust fumes	52
6 Loss of plants and animals in the UK	50
7 Depletion of the ozone layer	49
8 Tropical forest destruction	48
9 =Global warming/climate change	46
=Loss of trees and hedgerows	46

* Survey respondents who said they were 'very worried'

Source: Department of the Environment, Farming and Rural Affairs, *Survey of Public Attitudes to Quality of Life and to the Environment*, 2007

TOP 10 **CARBON DIOXIDE-EMITTING COUNTRIES**

COUNTRY	CO_2 EMISSIONS 2007 (TONNES OF CARBON)
1 China	1,801,931,966
2 USA	1,586,212,500
3 Russia	432,485,549
4 India	429,601,050
5 Japan	337,363,549
6 Germany	209,624,474
7 Canada	144,738,203
8 UK	144,726,159
9 South Korea	130,071,952
10 Italy	121,081,684
Top 10 total	*5,337,837,086*
World total	*8,470,854,977*

Source: Carbon Dioxide Information Analysis Center (CDIAC)

Shopping Lists

-50%

TOP 10 RETAILERS IN THE UK

	STORE GROUP	ANNUAL SALES (£)*
1	Tesco	42,641,000,000
2	J. Sainsbury	17,151,000,000
3	W.M. Morrison	12,969,000,000
4	Kingfisher (B&Q, etc.)	8,675,900,000
5	Marks & Spencer	8,581,100,000
6	DSG (Dixons)	7,929,700,000
7	Boots	6,848,000,000
8	John Lewis Partnership	6,762,800,000
9	Inchcape (automotive)	6,056,800,000
10	Home Retail (Argos, Homebase)	5,606,700,000

* 2008 or latest accounting period

TOP 10 NON-STORE* SHOPPING COUNTRIES

	COUNTRY	TOTAL	SPENDING £ PER CAPITA (2008)#
1	Qatar	406,100,000	474.50
2	Monaco	14,200,000	432.90
3	USA	127,978,500,000	420.30
4	Japan	51,715,400,000	405.00
5	UK	24,415,400,000	400.20
6	Germany	27,564,300,000	335.30
7	South Korea	12,689,600,000	264.20
8	Norway	1,233,700,000	262.40
9	Finland	1,378,500,000	260.20
10	Switzerland	1,786,000,000	237.20
	World	*331,186,900,000*	*49.30*

* Includes vending, home shopping, Internet retailing and direct selling
# Retail value excluding sales taxes

Source: Euromonitor International

TOP 10 GLOBAL RETAILERS

	COMPANY / BASE	RETAIL SALES 2007* ($)
1	Wal-Mart Stores, Inc., USA	374,526,000,000
2	Carrefour, France	112,604,000,000
3	Tesco plc, UK	94,740,000,000
4	Metro AG, Germany	87,586,000,000
5	Home Depot, Inc., USA	77,349,000,000
6	Kroger Co., USA	70,235,000,000
7	Schwarz Unternehmens Treuhand KG, Germany	69,346,000,000
8	Target Corp., USA	63,267,000,000
9	Costco Wholesale Corp., USA	63,088,000,000
10	Aldi GmbH, Germany	58,487,000,000

* Financial year

Source: Deloitte, *2009 Global Powers of Retailing*

Free!

TOP 10 OLDEST-ESTABLISHED DEPARTMENT STORES IN THE UK

	STORE / LOCATION*	FOUNDED
1	**Fortnum & Mason**, London	1707
2	**Boswells**, Oxford	1738
3	**Debenhams**#, London	1778
4	**Browns**, Chester	1780
5	**Joplings**, Sunderland	1804
6	**Heals**, London	1810
7	**Harvey Nichols**, London	1813
8	**Jarrolds**, Norwich	1823
9	**Austins**, Derry, Northern Ireland	1830
10	**Kendals**, Manchester	1832

* Original store, excluding branches
# Founded as Flint & Clark; Clark & Debenham 1813; Debenham & Freebody 1851

Save!

TOP 10 INTERNET SHOPS IN THE UK*

SHOP

1 Amazon UK
2 Argos
3 Play.com
4 Tesco.com
5 Marks & Spencer
6 Amazon.com
7 Next
8 Dell
9 Tesco Direct
10 Ticketmaster

* Based on visits to online retailers of goods and services; excluding eBay and price-comparison sites

Source: MRG-Hitwise Hot Shops

Top of the shops
Toronto's Eaton Centre shopping mall attracts a million visitors a week, making it one of North America's foremost retail locations.

TOP 10 IN-STORE SHOPPING COUNTRIES

	COUNTRY	TOTAL	SPENDING £ PER CAPITA (2008)*
1	Norway	27,818,000,000	5,917.10
2	Qatar	4,957,300,000	5,791.90
3	Switzerland	43,149,900,000	5,730.30
4	Ireland	24,531,900,000	5,603.00
5	Denmark	26,968,700,000	4,937.90
6	Austria	39,090,200,000	4,680.50
7	Monaco	152,900,000	4,658.70
8	Belgium	49,237,000,000	4,636.90
9	Canada	153,098,700,000	4,615.60
10	Finland	24,081,800,000	4,546.10
	UK	*270,108,700,000*	*4,426.90*
	World	*5,305,487,000,000*	*789.80*

* Retail value excluding sales taxes

Source: Euromonitor International

Food Favourites

TOP 10 **VEGETABLE CONSUMERS**

COUNTRY	AVERAGE CONSUMPTION PER CAPITA (2008)		
	KG	LB	OZ
1 Greece	257.0	566	9
2 South Korea	249.8	550	11
3 Turkey	237.9	524	8
4 Jordan	215.5	475	2
5 China	212.5	468	8
6 Portugal	202.8	447	2
7 Israel	194.4	528	9
8 Romania	189.7	418	4
9 Egypt	185.7	409	6
10 United Arab Emirates	173.5	382	8
UK	*71.4*	*157*	*7*
World average	*95.3*	*210*	*2*

Source: Euromonitor International

TOP 10 **MEAT CONSUMERS**

COUNTRY	AVERAGE CONSUMPTION PER CAPITA (2008)		
	KG	LB	OZ
1 Nauru	122.2	269	6
2 Argentina	116.1	255	15
3 Australia	106.1	233	15
4 Portugal	103.5	228	3
5 New Zealand	103.2	227	8
6 Austria	101.8	224	7
7 Greece	99.6	219	9
8 Monaco	97.0	213	14
9 USA	88.3	194	11
10 Ireland	79.7	175	11
UK	*44.9*	*99*	*0*
World average	*35.7*	*78*	*11*

Source: Euromonitor International

Meaty Measure

In 2008, the world devoured a total of 238,663,700 tonnes of beef, veal, lamb, mutton, goat, pork, poultry and other meat.

TOP 10 **EGG CONSUMERS**

COUNTRY	TOTAL TONNES	CONSUMPTION (2008) PER CAPITA		
		KG	LB	OZ
1 China	28,609,000	21.6	47	10
2 Japan	2,567,200	20.1	44	5
3 Monaco	600	18.8	41	7
4 Antigua & Barbuda	1,600	18.2	40	2
5 = Czech Republic	185,900	18.0	39	11
= Saint Kitts & Nevis	900	18.0	39	11
7 Mexico	1,953,300	17.8	39	4
8 Bulgaria	123,500	16.3	35	15
9 France	1,000,900	16.2	35	11
10 Luxembourg	7,600	15.9	35	1
UK	*707,700*	*11.6*	*25*	*9*
World	*61,875,900*	*9.3*	*20*	*8*

Source: Euromonitor International

TOP 10 **FISH AND SHELLFISH CONSUMERS**

COUNTRY	TOTAL TONNES	CONSUMPTION (2008) PER CAPITA		
		KG	LB	OZ
1 Portugal	856,300	80.5	177	8
2 Singapore	280,500	60.5	133	6
3 Malaysia	1,523,500	55.2	121	11
4 South Korea	2,410,500	50.2	110	11
5 Brunei	16,600	42.1	92	13
6 Iceland	12,200	40.9	90	3
7 Japan	4,860,200	38.1	84	0
8 Norway	168,100	35.8	78	15
9 Myanmar	1,852,500	35.6	78	8
10 China	45,527,900	34.4	75	13
UK	*894,900*	*14.7*	*32*	*7*
World	*104,376,900*	*15.6*	*34*	*6*

Source: Euromonitor International

TOP 10 **CRISP AND CHIP CONSUMERS**

	COUNTRY	TOTAL TONNES	CONSUMPTION (2008) PER CAPITA KG	LB	OZ
1	Ireland	19,700	4.5	9	15
2	Norway	17,800	3.8	8	6
3	Nauru	50	3.6	7	15
4	Iceland	1,100	3.5	7	12
5	UK	191,300	3.1	6	13
6 =	Canada	93,100	2.8	6	3
=	Netherlands	45,900	2.8	6	3
8	Spain	121,800	2.7	5	15
9	Andorra	200	2.4	5	5
10	USA	806,200	2.3	5	1
	World	*2,390,100*	*0.4*	*0*	*14*

Source: Euromonitor International

Potato head
Fast food world leader USA is out-eaten by other countries in per capita crisp and chip consumption.

TOP 10 **FAST FOOD COUNTRIES***

	COUNTRY	TOTAL (£)	PER CAPITA (£)
1	USA	89,629,900,000	297.0
2	Canada	9,051,000,000	275.4
3	Ireland	1,129,400,000	262.7
4	UK	13,385,700,000	220.5
5	Australia	4,312,500,000	209.6
6	New Zealand	629,200,000	154.4
7	Iceland	44,800,000	148.7
8	Denmark	727,000,000	133.5
9	Japan	16,686,900,000	130.6
10	Norway	572,700,000	122.6
	World total	*221,390,700,000*	*33.4*

* Ranked by per capita consumption, 2007

Source: Euromonitor International

Beverage Report

TOP 10 WINE CONSUMERS

	COUNTRY	CONSUMPTION PER CAPITA (2008)	
		LITRES	PINTS
1	Luxembourg	62.6	110.2
2	Italy	45.7	80.4
3	Portugal	45.5	80.1
4	France	40.9	72.0
5	Monaco	39.2	69.0
6	Switzerland	37.9	66.7
7	Slovenia	36.6	64.4
8	Austria	36.5	64.2
9	Liechtenstein	36.4	64.0
10	Greece	35.3	62.1
	UK	22.6	39.8
	World average	4.0	7.0

TOP 10 COFFEE DRINKERS

	COUNTRY	CONSUMPTION PER CAPITA (2008)			
		KG	LB	OZ	CUPS*
1	Finland	10.0	22	1	1,500
2	Norway	8.4	18	8	1,260
3	Sweden	8.2	18	1	1,230
4	Denmark	7.9	17	7	1,185
5	Switzerland	5.9	13	0	885
6	Netherlands	5.6	12	6	840
7	Germany	5.4	11	14	810
8	Belgium	5.3	11	11	795
9	= Estonia	5.2	11	7	780
	= Iceland	5.2	11	7	780
	UK	1.4	3	1	210
	World average	0.8	1	12	120

* Based on average of 150 cups per kg (2 lb 3 oz)

TOP 10 FRUIT AND VEGETABLE DRINK CONSUMERS

	COUNTRY	CONSUMPTION PER CAPITA (2008)	
		LITRES	PINTS
1	Canada	49.1	86.4
2	Netherlands	43.7	76.9
3	Poland	41.7	73.4
4	Germany	40.8	71.8
5	Slovenia	38.1	67.0
6	UK	38.0	66.9
7	Ireland	36.9	64.9
8	USA	36.0	63.4
9	Australia	35.8	63.0
10	Norway	34.5	60.7
	World average	9.3	16.4

Source: Euromonitor International (all lists)

The world drank an estimated 61,922,200,000 litres (108,967,772,216 pints) of fruit and vegetable juice in 2008.

TOP 10 **COLA DRINK CONSUMERS**

	COUNTRY	CONSUMPTION PER CAPITA (2008) LITRES	PINTS
1	Mexico	105.9	186.4

	COUNTRY	LITRES	PINTS
2 =	Norway	99.5	175.1
=	USA	99.5	175.1
4	St Vincent and the Grenadines	87.9	154.7
5	Chile	78.2	137.6
6	Belize	76.2	134.1
7	Dominica	75.9	133.6
8	St Lucia	74.5	131.1
9	United Arab Emirates	73.5	129.3
10	Belgium	69.9	123.0
	UK	*57.3*	*100.8*
	World average	*17.4*	*30.6*

TOP 10 **TEA DRINKERS**

	COUNTRY	CONSUMPTION PER CAPITA (2008) KG	LB	OZ	CUPS*
1	Turkey	2.8	6	3	1,232
2	Ireland	2.6	5	12	1,144
3	Uzbekistan	2.4	5	5	1,056
4	UK	2.1	4	10	924
5 =	Kazakhstan	1.7	3	12	748
=	Turkmenistan	1.7	3	12	748
7	Iran	1.4	3	1	616
8 =	Poland	1.3	2	14	572
=	Russia	1.3	2	14	572
10 =	Japan	1.1	2	7	484
=	Pakistan	1.1	2	7	484
	World average	*0.4*	*0*	*14*	*176*

* Based on average 440 cups per kg (2 lb 3 oz)

As well as a major tea consumer, Turkey is the sixth largest producer, growing over 190,000 tonnes a year out of a world total of 3.9 million tonnes. In the UK, once the quintessential bastion of the 'cuppa', the consumption of traditional tea has declined as herbal and other flavours and coffee have gained ground.

TOP 10 **ALCOHOLIC DRINK CONSUMERS**

	COUNTRY	CONSUMPTION PER CAPITA (2008) LITRES	PINTS
1	Czech Republic	191.3	336.6
2	Ireland	166.2	292.5
3	Luxembourg	161.2	283.6
4	Austria	148.5	261.3
5 =	Estonia	145.9	256.7
=	Germany	145.9	256.7
7	Slovenia	139.7	245.8
8	Australia	131.0	230.5
9	UK	126.3	222.3
10	Slovakia	125.5	220.8
	World average	*35.2*	*61.9*

Prost!
Germany hosts the world's largest beer festival, the Munich Oktoberfest, its many breweries and beer halls further emphasizing the importance of alcohol in the country's culture.

Sweet Treats

TOP 10 **SUGAR AND SWEETENER CONSUMERS**

COUNTRY		CONSUMPTION PER CAPITA (2008) KG	LB
1	United Arab Emirates	70.9	156.3
2	USA	64.3	141.8
3	Hungary	63.9	140.9
4	New Zealand	61.6	135.8
5	Luxembourg	59.4	131.0
6	Sri Lanka	58.9	129.9
7	Brazil	57.4	126.5
8	Iceland	57.3	126.3
9	Belgium	56.7	125.0
10	Switzerland	56.2	123.9
	UK	*40.2*	*88.6*
	World average	*2.7*	*59.5*

Source (all lists): Euromonitor International

TOP 10 **CHOCOLATE CONSUMERS**

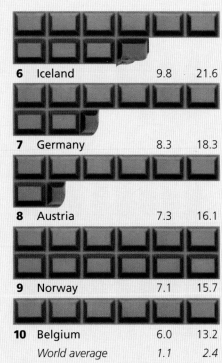

COUNTRY		CONSUMPTION PER CAPITA (2008) KG	LB
1	UK	11.5	25.4
2	Liechtenstein	10.9	24.0
3	Luxembourg	10.1	22.3
4	= Ireland	9.9	21.8
	= Switzerland	9.9	21.8
6	Iceland	9.8	21.6
7	Germany	8.3	18.3
8	Austria	7.3	16.1
9	Norway	7.1	15.7
10	Belgium	6.0	13.2
	World average	*1.1*	*2.4*

TOP 10 **ICE-CREAM CONSUMERS**

COUNTRY / CONSUMPTION PER CAPITA (2008) LITRES / PINTS

1 Australia 18.0 / 31.7

2 USA 14.8 / 26.0

3 Nauru 14.4 / 25.3

4 New Zealand 13.3 / 23.4

TOP 10 JAM AND PRESERVE CONSUMERS

	COUNTRY	CONSUMPTION PER CAPITA (2008)		
		KG	LB	OZ
1	Norway	4.2	9	4
2	Sweden	3.3	7	4
3	Denmark	3.0	6	10
4	Luxembourg	2.9	6	6
5	Iceland	2.8	6	3
6	= Belgium	2.3	5	1
	= France	2.3	5	1
8	= Germany	1.9	4	3
	= Monaco	1.9	4	3
10	USA	1.8	4	0
	UK	*1.3*	*2*	*14*
	World average	*0.3*	*0*	*11*

TOP 10 BISCUIT CONSUMERS

	COUNTRY	CONSUMPTION PER CAPITA (2008)	
		KG	LB
1	Netherlands	10.7	23.6
2	Argentina	9.7	21.4
3	UK	8.8	19.4
4	Portugal	8.5	18.7
5	= Chile	8.0	17.6
	= New Zealand	8.0	17.6
7	= Belgium	7.8	17.2
	= USA	7.8	17.2
9	= Australia	7.4	16.3
	= Italy	7.4	16.3
	World average	*2.2*	*4.9*

TOP 10 GUM CONSUMERS

COUNTRY / TOTAL CONSUMPTION 2008 (TONNES)

1 USA 218,500 **2** China 157,300
3 = Brazil = Mexico 60,000 **5** Japan 52,700
6 UK 31,100 **7** Iran 27,600 **8** Italy 26,100
9 Russia 25,700 **10** Germany 23,100
Top 10 total 682,100 World total 1,056,900

5 Canada 12.9 / 22.7

6 Norway 12.7 / 22.3

7 Finland 11.9 / 20.9

8 Sweden 11.6 / 20.4

9 = Iceland 10.5 / 18.5
= Italy 10.5 / 18.5

UK 9.0 / 15.8
World average 2.6 / 4.6

Keeping in Touch

TOP 10 **MOBILE PHONE CALLS**

COUNTRY / MINUTES PER CAPITA (2008)

1 Cuba
2,827.6

2 Finland
1,615.7

3 Italy
1,336.0

4 Maldives
1,332.7

5 Austria
1,160.5

6 Norway
1,129.3

Source: Euromonitor
International

TOP 10 **COUNTRIES FOR INTERNATIONAL PHONE CALLS**

COUNTRY	MINUTES PER CAPITA (2008)
1 Bermuda	2,787.4
2 Andorra	989.7
3 United Arab Emirates	956.4
4 Luxembourg	916.8
5 Singapore	879.1
6 Liechtenstein	795.5
7 Barbados	692.1
8 Aruba	556.9
9 Cyprus	316.5
10 USA	308.8
UK	*87.1*
World average	*32.7*

Source: Euromonitor International

7 Japan
1,067.3

8 UK
1,006.0

9 Portugal
998.8

10 Nigeria
983.3

TOP 10 **MOBILE PHONE COUNTRIES**

COUNTRY	% POPULATION	SUBSCRIBERS TOTAL (2008)
1 China	49.0	649,700,000
2 India	32.7	376,120,000
3 USA	85.7	260,000,000
4 Russia	121.2	172,000,000
5 Brazil	79.7	151,900,000
6 Indonesia	49.9	115,600,000
7 Japan	79.6	102,980,000
8 Germany	123.5	101,500,000
9 Pakistan	56.8	91,442,341
10 UK	116.0	70,000,000
World total	*60.6*	*4,100,000,000*

Source: CIA, *The World Factbook 2008*

Especially in countries that previously had an undeveloped landline system, the rapid increase in mobile-phone usage has seen China and India take the lead. In high-uptake countries where people regularly update their phones without cancelling their older contracts, the anomalous situation arises where there are more phones than people.

TOP 10 **COUNTRIES WITH THE MOST POST OFFICES**

	COUNTRY	AVERAGE NO. OF PEOPLE SERVED PER OFFICE	POST OFFICES (2007)*
1	India	7,432	155,204
2	China	22,186	59,886
3	Russia	3,519	40,489
4	USA	7,471	36,721
5	Mexico	3,599	29,600
6	Japan	5,318	24,064
7	Indonesia	11,627	19,922
8	France	3,612	17,066
9	Ukraine	3,004	15,379
10	Italy	4,263	13,811
	UK	*4,418*	*13,756*

* Or latest year and in those countries for which data available

Source: Universal Postal Union

TOP 10 **COUNTRIES WITH THE MOST LETTER BOXES**

	COUNTRY	LETTER BOXES (2007)*
1	India	661,887
2	USA	351,000
3	China	195,336#
4	Japan	192,300
5	France	156,000
6	Russia	153,487
7	UK	116,000
8	Germany	108,000
9	Italy	61,500
10	Poland	55,138

* Or latest year and in those countries for which data available
\# Situated on streets only

Source: Universal Postal Union

Japanese mail
Despite its high-tech communications, the traditional postal system remains important in Japan.

TOP 10 **SOCIAL NETWORKS IN THE WORLD**

	NETWORK	UNIQUE VISITS*
1	Blogger	221,503,000
2	Facebook	200,189,000
3	MySpace	126,168,000
4	Wordpress	113,661,000
5	Windows Live Spaces	86,760,000
6	Yahoo Geocities	69,159,000
7	Flickr	63,866,000
8	hi5	58,069,000
9	Orkut	46,446,000
10	Six Apart	45,606,000
	Total Internet audience	*996,304,000*
	Total social network audience	*681,249,000*

* During November 2008

Source: comScore.com

TOP 10 **SOCIAL NETWORKS IN THE USA**

	NETWORK	% BY INTERNET VISITS*
1	MySpace	39.37
2	Facebook	17.54
3	YouTube	10.39
4	Tagged	1.55
5	Yahoo! Answers	1.36
6	myYearbook	1.09
7	Yahoo! Groups	0.96
8	Meebo	0.64
9	Yahoo! Member Directory	0.53
10	Bebo	0.49

* During December 2008

Source: Marketingcharts.com

TOP 10 **SOCIAL NETWORKS IN THE UK**

	NETWORK	% BY INTERNET VISITS*
1	Facebook	39.82
2	YouTube	16.57
3	Bebo	8.56
4	MySpace	4.49
5	Yahoo! Answers	1.03
6	Nasza Klasa	0.73
7	Twitter	0.66
8	Tagged	0.65
9	BBC h2g2	0.64
10	Gumtree.com	0.61

* During February 2009

World Tourism

TOP 10 **TOURIST DESTINATIONS**

	COUNTRY	INTERNATIONAL VISITORS (2007)
1	France	81,900,000
2	Spain	59,193,000
3	USA	55,986,000
4	China	54,720,000
5	Italy	43,654,000
6	UK	30,677,000
7	Germany	24,420,000
8	Ukraine	23,122,000
9	Turkey	22,248,000
10	Mexico	21,424,000
	Top 10 total	417,344,000
	World total	903,300,000

Source: World Tourism Organization

Textes : Goscinny · Dessins : Sempé
Le Petit Nicolas®
Imav éditions - contact@imaveditions.com
www.petitnicolas.net
Distribution · Éditions du Désastre · www.desastre.com
Printed in France
© Imav éditions 2006
NP 016

TOP 10 **TOURIST EARNING COUNTRIES**

	COUNTRY	INTERNATIONAL TOURISM RECEIPTS, 2007 ($)
1	USA	97,712,000,000
2	Spain	57,795,000,000
3	France	54,228,000,000
4	Italy	42,651,000,000
5	China	41,919,000,000
6	UK	37,617,000,000
7	Germany	36,029,000,000
8	Australia	22,244,000,000
9	Austria	18,887,000,000
10	Turkey	18,487,000,000
	Top 10 total	427,569,000,000
	World total	856,000,000,000

Source: World Tourism Organization

TOP 10 **TOURISM SPENDING COUNTRIES**

	COUNTRY	INTERNATIONAL TOURISM EXPENDITURE, 2007 ($)
1	Germany	82,900,000,000
2	USA	76,200,000,000
3	UK	72,300,000,000
4	France	36,700,000,000
5	China	29,800,000,000
6	Italy	27,300,000,000
7	Japan	26,500,000,000
8	Canada	24,800,000,000
9	Russia	22,300,000,000
10	South Korea	20,900,000,000
	Top 10 total	419,700,000,000
	World total	856,000,000,000

Source: World Tourism Organization

French leave
Along with the appeal of its food and culture, France's cities, resorts and rural retreats have established it as the world's foremost tourist venue.

Park and ride
The former hunting park of Austrian emperors, the Vienna Prater opened as a public park on 7 April 1766.

TOP 10 **AMUSEMENT AND THEME PARKS**

PARK / LOCATION	EST. ATTENDANCE (2008)
1 The Magic Kingdom at Walt Disney World, Lake Buena Vista, Florida, USA	17,063,000
2 Disneyland, Anaheim, California, USA	14,721,000
3 Tokyo Disneyland, Tokyo, Japan	14,293,000
4 Disneyland Paris, Marne-La-Vallée, France	12,688,000
5 Tokyo Disneysea, Tokyo, Japan	12,498,000
6 Epcot at Walt Disney World, Lake Buena Vista, Florida, USA	10,935,000
7 Disney's Hollywood Studios at Walt Disney World, Lake Buena Vista, Florida, USA	9,608,000
8 Disney's Animal Kingdom at Walt Disney World, Lake Buena Vista, Florida, USA	9,540,000
9 Universal Studios Japan, Osaka, Japan	8,300,000
10 Everland, Kyonggi-Do, South Korea	7,200,000

Source: Park World

Magic kingdom
The original Disneyland opened in Anaheim, California, in 1955 and has been replicated in Florida, Japan, France and Hong Kong.

TOP 10 **OLDEST AMUSEMENT PARKS***

PARK / LOCATION	YEAR OPENED
1 Bakken, Klampenborg, Denmark	1583
2 The Prater, Vienna, Austria	1766
3 Widam Park, Budapest, Hungary	1838
4 Blackgang Chine Cliff Top Theme Park, Ventnor, Isle of Wight, UK	1842
5 Tivoli Gardens, Copenhagen, Denmark	1843
6 Lake Compounce Amusement Park, Bristol, Connecticut, USA	1846
7 Hanayashiki, Tokyo, Japan	1853
8 Grand Pier, Teignmouth, UK	1867
9 Blackpool Central Pier, Blackpool, UK	1868
10 Cedar Point, Sandusky, Ohio, USA	1870

* In same location

Source: National Amusement Park Historical Association

TOP 10 **MOST-VISTED NATIONAL TRUST PROPERTIES**

PROPERTY / LOCATION	VISITORS (2007–08)
1 Wakehurst Place Garden, West Sussex	477,173
2 Waddesdon Manor, Buckinghamshire	386,544
3 Stourhead, Wiltshire	382,271
4 Fountains Abbey & Studley Royal, North Yorkshire	348,725
5 Polesden Lacey, Surrey	258,310
6 Carrick-a-Rede Rope Bridge, County Antrim, Northern Ireland	222,613
7 Penrhyn Castle, Gwynedd, Wales	212,727
8 Belton House, Lincolnshire	212,256
9 St Michael's Mount, Cornwall	203,798
10 Sheffield Park Garden, East Sussex	202,940

Source: National Trust

Big Wheel

One of the Vienna Prater park's most famous features, the Riesenrad Ferris wheel, opened on 21 June 1897. Invented by George Gale Ferris in 1893, this surviving example was designed by British engineer Walter Bassett, previously responsible for wheels in Blackpool and Earls Court, UK. The Riesenrad has been featured in films, most notably *The Third Man* (1949) and James Bond film *The Living Daylights* (1987).

ON THE MOVE

Road Transport

TOP 10 **MOTOR-VEHICLE MANUFACTURING COUNTRIES, 2007**

COUNTRY	CARS	COMMERCIAL VEHICLES	TOTAL
1 Japan	9,944,637	1,651,690	11,596,327
2 USA	3,924,268	6,856,461	10,780,729
3 China	6,381,116	2,501,340	8,882,456
4 Germany	5,709,139	504,321	6,213,460
5 South Korea	3,723,482	362,826	4,086,308
6 France	2,550,869	464,985	3,015,854
7 Brazil	2,388,402	582,416	2,970,818
8 Spain	2,195,780	693,923	2,889,703
9 Canada	1,342,133	1,236,105	2,578,238
10 India	1,707,839	598,929	2,306,768
UK	*1,534,567*	*215,686*	*1,750,253*
World	*53,049,391*	*20,103,305*	*73,152,696*

Source: OICA Statistics Committee

TOP 10 **COUNTRIES DRIVING ON THE LEFT**

COUNTRY	TOTAL VEHICLES REGISTERED (2006)
1 Japan	74,252,134
2 UK	34,974,500
3 Australia	13,410,000
4 India	12,950,000
5 Thailand	9,500,000
6 Malaysia	7,857,500
7 Indonesia	7,350,000
8 South Africa	7,180,000
9 New Zealand	2,760,000
10 Ireland	2,051,000

Source: *Ward's Motor Vehicle Facts & Figures 2008*

Some 75 countries and territories drive on the left. Where countries with different rules meet, such as China and Pakistan, drivers have to change sides as they cross the border.

TOP 10 **MOTOR-VEHICLE MANUFACTURERS, 2007**

COUNTRY / CARS / COMMERCIAL VEHICLES / TOTAL

General Motors (USA)
6,259,520
3,090,298
9,349,818

Toyota (Japan)
7,211,474
1,323,216
8,534,690

Volkswagen group
(Germany)
5,964,004
303,887
6,267,891

Ford (USA)
3,565,626
2,681,880
6,247,506

World
56,301,121
15,877,355
72,178,476

Source: OICA
Statistics Committee

Production line
Japan's motor vehicle production leads the world.

TOP 10 **BESTSELLING CARS OF ALL TIME**

MANUFACTURER/MODEL	YEARS IN PRODUCTION	APPROX. SALES*
1 Toyota Corolla	1966–	35,000,000
2 Volkswagen Golf	1974–	25,000,000
3 Volkswagen Beetle	1937–2003#	21,529,464
4 Ford Escort/Orion	1968–2003	20,000,000
5 Ford Model T	1908–27	16,536,075
6 Honda Civic	1972–	16,500,000
7 Nissan Sunny/Sentra/Pulsar	1966–	16,000,000
8 Volkswagen Passat	1973–	15,000,000
9 Lada Riva	1980–	13,500,000
10 Chevrolet Impala/Caprice	1958–	13,000,000

* To 2008, except where otherwise indicated
\# Produced in Mexico 1978–2003

TOP 10 **MOTOR VEHICLE-OWNING COUNTRIES**

COUNTRY	CARS	VEHICLES	COMMERCIAL TOTAL (2006)
1 USA	135,046,706	108,975,048	244,021,754
2 Japan	57,521,043	16,731,091	74,252,134
3 Germany	46,569,657	3,172,042	49,741,699
4 Italy	35,297,600	4,579,600	39,877,200
5 France	30,400,000	6,261,000	36,661,000
6 China	11,000,000	24,000,000	35,000,000
7 UK	30,920,000	4,054,500	34,974,500
8 Russia	26,800,000	5,890,000	32,690,000
9 Spain	20,908,700	5,146,400	26,055,100
10 Brazil	19,446,000	4,823,200	24,269,200
World	*635,284,155*	*255,477,307*	*890,761,462*

Source: *Ward's Motor Vehicle Facts & Figures 2008*

Honda (Japan)
3,868,546
43,268
3,911,814

PSA Peugeot Citroën (France)
3,024,863
432,522
3,457,385

Nissan (Japan)
2,650,813
780,585
3,431,398

Fiat (Italy)
1,990,715
688,736
2,679,451

Renault-Dacia-Samsung (France)
2,276,044
392,996
2,669,040

Hyundai (South Korea)
2,292,075
325,650
2,617,725

Rail Transport

THE 10 FIRST UNDERGROUND RAILWAY SYSTEMS

CITY / FIRST LINE ESTABLISHED

1 London, UK
10 Jan 1863

2 Budapest, Hungary
2 May 1896

3 Glasgow, UK
14 Dec 1896

4 Boston, USA
1 Sep 1897

5 Paris, France
19 Jul 1900

6 Berlin, Germany
15 Feb 1902

TOP 10 LONGEST UNDERGROUND RAILWAY NETWORKS

CITY / OPENED / STATIONS / TOTAL TRACK LENGTH (KM/MILES)

2 New York
USA 1904
422 stations
368 / 229

3 Madrid
Spain 1919
231 stations
294 / 183

4 Moscow
Russia 1935
142 stations
293 / 182

5 Seoul
South Korea 1974
266 stations
287 / 179

1 London
UK 1863
268 stations
408 / 254

TOP 10 LONGEST RAIL NETWORKS

LOCATION / TOTAL RAIL LENGTH (KM/MILES)

1 USA
226,656 / 141,367

2 Russia
87,157 / 54,156

3 China
75,438 / 47,051

4 India
63,221 / 39,431

5 Germany
48,215 / 30,072

6 Canada
48,068 / 29,980

7 Australia
38,550 / 24,044

8 Argentina
31,902 / 19,897

9 France
29,370 / 18,318

10 Brazil
29,295 / 18,271

UK 16,567 / 10,333
World 1,370,782 / 854,971

Source: CIA, *The World Factbook 2008*

The total length of the world rail networks today is equivalent to some 34 times round the Earth at the Equator.

TOP 10 BUSIEST UNDERGROUND RAILWAY NETWORKS

CITY	PASSENGERS PER ANNUM (2008)*
1 Tokyo, Japan	2,916,000,000
2 Moscow, Russia	2,529,000,000
3 Seoul, South Korea	2,047,000,000
4 New York, USA	1,563,000,000
5 Mexico City, Mexico	1,417,000,000
6 Paris, France	1,388,000,000
7 Hong Kong, China	1,309,000,000
8 Beijing, China	1,200,000,000
9 London, UK	1,197,000,000
10 Shanghai, China	1,122,000,000

* Or latest year for which figures available

Russian rush hour
One of the world's busiest systems, the Moscow Metro is noted for the elegance of its stations.

⑩ Buenos Aires, Argentina
1 Dec 1913

⑦ New York, USA
27 Oct 1904

⑧ Philadelphia, USA
4 Mar 1907

⑨ Hamburg, Germany
15 Feb 1912

Egypt
40,840,000,000 ⑩

⑥ Shanghai
China 1995
162 stations
228 / 142

⑦ Paris
France 1900
300 stations
214 / 133

⑧ Tokyo
Japan 1927
168 stations
203 / 126

⑨ Beijing
China 1969
123 stations
200 / 120

⑩ Mexico City
Mexico 1969
147 stations
177 / 110

⑨ Italy
46,440,000,000

⑤ France
78,460,000,000

⑥ Germany
74,730,000,000

⑦ Ukraine
53,230,000,000

⑧ UK
46,760,000,000

④ Russia
173,000,000,000

③ Japan
254,000,000,000

② India
696,000,000,000

① China
722,800,000,000

TOP 10 **FASTEST RAIL JOURNEYS**

JOURNEY*	TRAIN	DISTANCE		SPEED	
		KM	MILES	KM/H	MPH
1 Lorraine–Champagne, France	TGV 5422	167.6	104.1	279.3	173.6
2 Okayama–Hiroshima, Japan	Nozomi 1	144.9	90.0	255.7	158.9
3 Taichung–Zuoying, Taiwan	7 trains	179.5	111.5	244.7	152.0
4 Brussels, Belgium–Valence, France	Thalys Soleil	831.7	516.8	244.6	152.0
5 Frankfurt–Siegburg/Bonn, Germany	ICE 10	143.3	89.04	232.4	144.4
6 Madrid–Zaragoza, Spain	7 AVE trains	307.2	190.9	227.6	141.4
7 Shenyang–Qinhuangdao, China	D24 & D28	404.0	251.0	197.1	122.5
8 Seoul–Seodaejeon, South Korea	KTX 410 & 411	161.0	100.0	193.2	120.0
9 London–York, UK	1 IC255	303.2	188.4	173.3	107.7
10 Alvesta–Hässleholm, Sweden	X2000 543	98.0	60.9	172.9	107.4

* Fastest journey for each country; all those in the Top 10 have other equally or similarly fast services

Source: *Railway Gazette International*, 2007 World Speed Survey

Train à Grande Vitesse
The French TGV holds the record for fastest scheduled journey.

TOP 10 **BUSIEST RAIL NETWORKS**

LOCATION / PASSENGER KM PER ANNUM*

* Number of passengers multiplied by distance carried in 2008 or latest year for which figures available; totals include national and local services where applicable

Source: UIC Railisa Database

Water Transport

TOP 10 LONGEST SHIP CANALS

CANAL / COUNTRY
OPENED
LENGTH (KM/MILES)

1

Grand Canal, China
AD 283*
1,795 / 1,114

2

Erie Canal, USA
1825
584 / 363

3

Göta Canal, Sweden
1832
360 / 240

4

St Lawrence Seaway,
Canada/USA
1959
290 / 180

5

Canal du Midi, France
1692
240 / 190

6

Main-Danube, Germany
1992
171 / 106

7

Suez, Egypt
1869
162 / 101

8

Albert, Belgium
1939
130 / 81

9

Moscow (formerly
Moscow-Volga, Russia
1937
129 / 80

10

Volga-Don, Russia
1952
101 / 63

* Extended from AD 605–10
and rebuilt between 1958–72

Connecting Hang Zhou in the
south to Beijing in the north,
China's Grand Canal was largely
built by manual labour alone,
long before the invention of the
mechanized digging used in the
construction of the other major
artificial waterways. The Panama
Canal, opened in 1914 (82 km/
51 miles), just fails to find
a place in the Top 10.

TOP 10 LONGEST CANALS IN THE UK

CANAL / YEAR COMPLETED	LOCKS	TUNNELS	LENGTH KM	MILES
1 Grand Union (main line) (1814)	166	2	220.5	137.0
2 Leeds and Liverpool (1816)	93	2	204.4	127.0
3 Trent and Mersey (1777)	73	4	149.7	93.0
4 Kennet and Avon (1810)	106	1	139.2	86.5
5 Oxford (1790)	43	1	123.9	77.0
6 Shropshire Union (1805)	47	0	107.0	66.5
7 Caledonian (1822)	29	0	96.6	60.0
8 Staffordshire and Worcestershire (1772)	45	0	74.2	46.1
9 Llangollen (1805)	21	2	74.0	46.0
10 Lancaster (1799)	0	0	68.4	42.5

Source: British Waterways

TOP 10 MERCHANT SHIPPING COUNTRIES

Grand Canal
Suzhou's location
on both the Yangtze
river and the Grand
Canal makes it one
of China's most
important trade hubs.

COUNTRY	SHIPS
1 Panama	6,323
2 Liberia	2,204
3 China	1,826
4 Malta	1,438
5 Singapore	1,292
6 Bahamas	1,223
7 Antigua and Barbuda	1,146
8 Hong Kong*	1,114
9 Russia	1,074
10 Marshall Islands	1,049
UK	*518*

* Special Administrative Region of China

Source: *CIA World Factbook 2008*

TOP 10 **LONGEST SAILING VESSELS** *

Tall ship
The five-masted cruise ship Royal Clipper *has 42 sails with a total area of 5,202 sq m (55,994 sq ft). She carries 228 passengers and a crew of 105.*

	SHIP / COUNTRY BUILT	YEAR	LENGTH M	LENGTH FT
1	Wind Surf (France)	1990	187	617
2	Wind Star (France)	1986	134	440
3	Royal Clipper (Poland)	2000	134	439
4	Moshulu (UK)	1904	121	396
5	Sea Cloud II (Spain)	2001	117	384
6	Peking (Germany)	1911	115	378
7	Kruzenshtern (Germany)	1926	114	376
8	= Juan Sebastián Elcano (Spain)	1927	113	370
	= Esmerelda (Spain)	1953	113	370
10	Dar Młodzieży (Poland)	1982	111	363

* Currently afloat

TOP 10 **PORTS IN THE UK**

PORT	TOTAL TRAFFIC 2007 (TONNES)
1 Grimsby & Immingham	66,200,000
2 London	52,700,000
3 Tees & Hartlepool	49,800,000
4 Southampton	43,300,000
5 Forth	36,700,000
5 Milford Haven	35,500,000
6 Liverpool	32,300,000
8 Felixtowe	25,700,000
9 Dover	25,100,000
10 Sullom Voe	16,600,000
All UK ports	*581,100,000*
Top 10 total	*383,900,000*

Source: Department for Transport, *Transport Statistics Bulletin: Provisional Port Statistics 2007*

TOP 10 **BUSIEST PORTS**

PORT / COUNTRY	CARGO 2007 (TONNES)
1 Shanghai, China	561,450,000
2 Singapore, Singapore	483,616,000
3 Rotterdam, Netherlands	401,181,000
4 Ningbo, China	344,000,000
5 Guangzhou, China	343,250,000
6 Tianjin, China	309,460,000
7 Qingdao, China	265,020,000
8 Qinhuangdao, China	248,930,000
9 Hong Kong, China	245,433,000
10 Busan, South Korea	243,564,000
Top 10 total	*3,445,904,000*

Source: American Association of Port Authorities

Shangai
The world's busiest port, Shanghai, handles over 26 million containers a year, a total of 1.5 million tonnes of goods a day.

The First to Fly

THE 10 FIRST COUNTRIES TO HAVE BALLOON FLIGHTS*

1 France   21 Nov 1783

The Montgolfier brothers, Joseph and Etienne, tested their first unmanned hot-air balloon in the French town of Annonay on 5 June 1783. On 21 November 1783 François Laurent, Marquis d'Arlandes and Jean-François Pilâtre de Rozier took off from the Bois de Boulogne, Paris, in a Montgolfier hot-air balloon. This first manned flight covered a distance of about 9 km (5.5 miles) in 23 minutes, landing safely near Gentilly.

2 Italy   25 Feb 1784

Chevalier Paolo Andreani and the brothers Augustino and Carlo Giuseppe Gerli (the builders of the balloon) made the first flight outside France, at Moncucco near Milan, Italy.

3 Austria   6 Jul 1784

Johann Georg Stuwer made the first Austrian flight from the Prater, Vienna.

4 Scotland   27 Aug 1784

James Tytler (known as 'Balloon Tytler'), a doctor and newspaper editor, took off from Comely Gardens, Edinburgh, in a hot air balloon, achieving an altitude of 107 m (350 ft) in a 0.8 km (0.5-mile) hop in a homemade balloon.

5 England   15 Sep 1784

Watched by a crowd of 200,000, Italian balloonist Vincenzo Lunardi ascended from the Artillery Company Ground, Moorfields, London, flying to Standon near Ware in Hertfordshire. On 4 October 1784 James Sadler flew a Montgolfier balloon at Oxford, thereby becoming the first English-born pilot.

6 Ireland   19 Jan 1785

Although there are earlier claims, it is likely that Richard Crosbie's hydrogen-balloon flight from Ranelagh Gardens, Dublin, was the first in Ireland.

7 Holland   11 Jul 1785

French balloon pioneer Jean-Pierre Blanchard, took off from The Hague in a hydrogen balloon.

8 Germany   3 Oct 1785

Blanchard made the first flight in Germany from Frankfurt.

9 Belgium   20 Oct 1785

Blanchard flew his hydrogen balloon from Ghent.

10 Switzerland   5 May 1788

Blanchard flew from Basel. As well as flights from other European cities, Blanchard made the first in the USA, from Philadelphia, on 9 January 1793, watched by George Washington.

* Several of the balloonists listed also made subsequent flights, but in each instance only their first flight in each country is included

THE 10 FIRST ROCKET AND JET AIRCRAFT

	AIRCRAFT	COUNTRY	FIRST FLIGHT
1	Heinkel He 176*	Germany	20 Jun 1939
2	Heinkel He 178	Germany	27 Aug 1939
3	DFS 194*	Germany	Aug 1940#
4	Caproni-Campini N-1	Italy	28 Aug 1940
5	Heinkel He 280V-1	Germany	2 Apr 1941
6	Gloster E.28/39	UK	15 May 1941
7	Messerschmitt Me 163 Komet*	Germany	13 Aug 1941
8	Messerschmitt Me 262V-3	Germany	18 Jul 1942
9	Bell XP-59A Airacomet	USA	2 Oct 1942
10	Gloster Meteor F Mk 1	UK	5 Mar 1943

* Rocket-powered
# Precise date unknown

Prototypes of the rocket-powered Heinkel 176 and the turbojet Heinkel 178 first flew prior to the outbreak of World War II. The first operational jets were developed in the early years of the war, with the Messerschmitt Me 262 the first jet fighter in service. The German Arado Ar 234V-1 Blitz ('Lightning'), which first flew on 15 June 1943, was the world's first jet bomber.

Jet fighter
The Gloster Meteor was the only Allied jet fighter of World War II.

THE 10 **FIRST ROUND-THE-WORLD FLIGHTS**

	PILOT(S) / AIRCRAFT	ROUTE (START/ END LOCATION)	TOTAL DISTANCE		DATES
			KM	MILES	
1	Lt Lowell H. Smith/Lt Leslie P. Arnold (USA), Douglas World Cruiser, Chicago	Seattle, Washington, USA	42,398	26,345	6 Apr–28 Sep 1924
2	Lt Erik H. Nelson/Lt John Harding Jr (USA), Douglas World Cruiser, New Orleans	Seattle, Washington, USA	44,342	27,553	6 Apr–28 Sep 1924
3	Dr Hugo Eckener, Ernst Lehmann and crew (Germany), Airship, Graf Zeppelin	Lakehurst, New Jersey, USA	37,787	20,373	8–29 Apr 1929
4	Wiley Post and Harold Gatty (USA), Lockheed Vega Winne Mae York, USA	Roosevelt Field, Long Island, New	24,903	15,474	23 Jun–1 Jul 1931
5	Wolfgang von Gronau, Ghert von Roth, Franz Hack, Fritz Albrecht (Germany), Dornier seaplane, Grönland-Wal D-2053	List, Germany	44,000	27,240	22 Jul–23 Nov 1932
6	Wiley Post (USA), Lockheed Vega Winne Mae (first solo)	Floyd Bennett Field, New York, USA	25,093	15,596	15–22 Jul 1933
7	Howard Hughes, Lt Thomas Thurlow, Henry P. McClean Conner, Richard Stoddart, Eddie Lund (USA), Lockheed 14, New York World's Fair 1939	Floyd Bennett Field, New York, USA	23,612	14,672	10–14 Jul 1938
8 =	Clifford Evans (USA), Piper PA-12, City of Washington	Teterboro, New, Jersey, USA	40,494	25,162	9 Aug–10 Dec 1947
=	George Truman (USA), Piper PA-12, City of the Angels	Teterboro, New Jersey, USA	40,493	25,162	9 Aug–10 Dec 1947
10	Capt James Gallagher and crew of 13 (USA), Boeing B-50A, Lucky Lady II (first non-stop circumnavigation with in-flight refuelling)	Fort Worth, Texas, USA	37,742	23,452	26 Feb–2 Mar 1949

Homecoming
Circumnavigators Wiley Post and Harold Gatty are welcomed home by a New York ticker-tape parade (1931).

Air Travel

TOP 10 BUSIEST INTERNATIONAL ROUTES FROM LONDON HEATHROW

DESTINATION AIRPORT	PASSENGERS (2007)
1 John F. Kennedy, New York, USA	2,839,221
2 Dublin, Ireland	1,974,169
3 Amsterdam, Netherlands	1,799,214
4 Paris-Charles de Gaulle, France	1,789,538
5 O'Hare, Chicago, Illinois, USA	1,604,770
6 Dubai	1,571,472
7 Hong Kong, China	1,453,229
8 Frankfurt, Germany	1,449,577
9 Los Angeles, California, USA	1,405,694
10 Madrid, Spain	1,180,326

In 2007, 25 per cent of Heathrow's 67,852,000 passengers flew to or from one of the Top 10 airports.

TOP 10 AIRLINES WITH THE MOST AIRCRAFT

1 symbol = 100 airplanes

* USA unless otherwise stated
\# 2008 or latest available year

AIRLINE / COUNTRY*	MAIN FLEET SIZE#
1 American Airlines	616
2 Southwest Airlines	539
3 Delta Air Lines	457
4 United Airlines	407
5 Continental Airlines	380
6 US Airways	361
7 Lufthansa, Germany	344
8 Northwest Airlines	336
9 Air Canada, Canada	334
10 China Southern Airlines, China	299
British Airways, UK	*245*

TOP 10 AIRLINES WITH THE MOST PASSENGERS

AIRLINE / COUNTRY / PASSENGERS CARRIED (2007)*

1 Southwest Airlines
USA
101,911,000

2 American Airlines
USA
98,162,000

3 Air France-KLM
France
94,795,000

4 Delta Air Lines
USA
72,900,000

Russian giant
Capable of carrying a load of over 250 tonnes, only two Antonov An-225s have been built.

TOP 10 **LONGEST AIRCRAFT**

AIRCRAFT	WEIGHT (LB)	M	LENGTH FT	IN
1 Ekranoplan KM Caspian Sea Monster	1,080,000	106.1	348	0
2 Antonov An-225 Cossack	1,322,750	84.0	275	7
3 Lockheed C-5 Galaxy	840,000	75.5	247	10
4 Airbus A340-600	807,400	75.3	246	11
5 Boeing 777-300ER	775,000	73.9	242	4
6 Lun Ekranoplan	882,000	73.2	240	0
7 Airbus A380F	1,305,000	72.9	239	3
8 Boeing 747	875,000	70.7	231	10
9 Antonov An-124 Condor	892,872	69.1	226	9
10 H-4 Hercules ('Spruce Goose')	400,000	66.6	218	6

The 1,080,000-lb (540-tonne) Ekranoplan KM Caspian Sea Monster, designed to skim above the surface of water or land, thereby evading radar detection, is as long as a football pitch.

TOP 10 **BUSIEST AIRPORTS**

AIRPORT	LOCATION	PASSENGERS (2007)
1 Atlanta Hartsfield International	Atlanta, USA	89,379,287
2 Chicago O'Hare	Chicago, USA	76,177,855
3 London Heathrow	London, UK	68,068,304
4 Tokyo International	Tokyo, Japan	66,823,414
5 Los Angeles International	Los Angeles, USA	61,896,075
6 Charles De Gaulle	Paris, France	59,922,177
7 DFW International	Dallas/Fort Worth, USA	59,786,476
8 Frankfurt	Frankfurt, Germany	54,161,856
9 Beijing	Beijing, China	53,583,664
10 Madrid	Madrid, Spain	52,122,702

Source: Airports Council International

* Total of international and domestic

Source: International Air Transport Association

5 United Airlines
USA
68,400,000

6 Lufthansa
Germany
62,900,000

7 China Southern Airlines China
56,900,000

8 Northwest Airlines
USA
53,700,000

9 Japan Airlines International Japan
50,442,000

10 All Nippon Airways
Japan
50,384,000

Transport Disasters

THE 10 **WORST AIR DISASTERS**

LOCATION / DATE / INCIDENT   NO. KILLED

 New York, USA, 11 Sep 2001   c. 1,622
Following a hijacking by terrorists, an American Airlines
Boeing 767 was deliberately flown into the North Tower of
the World Trade Center, killing all 81 passengers (including
five hijackers), 11 crew on board and an estimated 1,530.

 New York, USA, 11 Sep 2001   c. 677
As part of the coordinated attack, hijackers commandeered
a second Boeing 767 and crashed it into the South Tower
of the World Trade Center, killing all 56 passengers and
nine crew on board and approximately 612 on the ground.

 Tenerife, Canary Islands, 27 Mar 1977   583
Two Boeing 747s (PanAm and KLM, carrying 380
passengers and 16 crew and 234 passengers and 14
crew respectively) collided and caught fire on the runway.

 Mt Ogura, Japan, 12 Aug 1985   520
A JAL Boeing 747 on an internal flight from Tokyo to Osaka
crashed, killing all but four of the 509 passengers and all
15 crew on board.

 Charkhi Dadri, India, 12 Nov 1996   349
A Saudi Arabian Airlines Boeing 747 collided with a Kazakh
Airlines Ilyushin IL 76 cargo aircraft and exploded, killing all
312 on the Boeing and all 37 on the Ilyushin.

 Paris, France, 3 Mar 1974   346
Immediately after take-off for London, a Turkish Airlines
DC-10 suffered an explosive decompression when a door
burst open and crashed killing all on board.

 Off the Irish coast, 23 Jun 1985   329
An Air India Boeing 747 on a flight from Vancouver to
Delhi exploded in mid-air, probably as a result of a terrorist
bomb, killing all 307 passengers and 22 crew.

 Riyadh, Saudi Arabia, 19 Aug 1980   301
Following an emergency landing a Saudia (Saudi Arabian)
Airlines Lockheed TriStar caught fire. The crew were unable
to open the doors and all on board died from smoke.

 Off the Iranian coast, 3 Jul 1988   290
An Iran Air A300 airbus was shot down in error by a missile
fired by the USS Vincennes, resulting in the deaths of all
274 passengers and 16 crew.

 Sirach Mountain, Iran, 19 Feb 2003   275
An Ilyushin 76 crashed into the mountain in poor
weather. It was carrying 257 Revolutionary Guards
and a crew of 18, none of whom survived.

THE 10 **WORST PEACETIME MARINE DISASTERS**

SHIP / DATE / LOCATION / INCIDENT   ESTIMATED NO. KILLED

 Doña Paz 21 Dec 1987   <3,000
Tabias Strait, Philippines
The ferry *Doña Paz* was struck by oil tanker MT *Vector*.
Some sources claim a total of 4,341 victims.

 SS Kiangya 4 Dec 1948   2,750–3,920
Off Shanghai, China
The overloaded passenger steamship is believed to have
struck a Japanese mine.

 MV Le Joola 26 Sep 2002   >1,863
Off The Gambia
The overcrowded Senegalese ferry capsized in a storm.

 Tek Sing 6 Feb 1822   1,600
Gaspar Strait, Indonesia
The large Chinese junk laden with migrant Chinese
workers ran aground and sank.

 Sultana 27 Apr 1865   1,547
Mississippi River, USA
A boiler on the Mississippi paddleboat Sultana exploded
and the vessel sank.

 RMS Titanic 15 Apr 1912   1,517
North Atlantic
The *Titanic*, the world's largest liner, sank on her maiden
voyage after striking an iceberg.

 Toya Maru 26 Sep 1954   1,159
Tsugaru Strait, Japan
The Japanese ferry between Hokkaido and Honshu sank
in a typhoon, with an estimated 150 rescued.

 General Slocum 15 Jun 1904   1,021
New York, USA,
The excursion steamship caught fire in the East River,
New York, with many victims burned or drowned.

 MS al-Salam Boccaccio 98 3 Feb 2006   1,018
Red Sea
The Egyptian car ferry sank following a fire on board.

 RMS Empress of Ireland 29 May 1914   1,012
Saint Lawrence River, Canada
The Royal Mail ship was struck by Norwegian
collier SS *Storstad*, resulting in Canada's worst-ever
marine disaster.

THE 10 **WORST BRIDGE COLLAPSES**

BRIDGE / LOCATION / DATE / INCIDENT   APPROX. NO. KILLED

Angers, France, 16 Apr 1850   226
The bridge began to vibrate and collapsed as 478 soldiers marched across it.

Tangiwai New Zealand, 24 Dec 1953   151
Volcanic lava engulfed the bridge over the Walouru river as a passenger train crossed; some victims were carried 48 km (30 miles) by the force of the flow.

Makahali, Nepal, 26 Nov 1974   140
A suspension bridge over a river collapsed in the Baitadi district.

Liziyida, China, 9 Jul 1981   130
The bridge was destroyed by a mud-flow, resulting in a train derailment.

Munnar, India, 8 Nov 1984   125
A rope bridge collapsed over a swollen stream; the victims were mostly schoolchildren.

Hyatt Regency Skywalks,
Kansas City, USA, 17 Jul 1981   114
The collapse of two aerial footbridges occurred during a dance at the hotel.

Mahububnagar, India, 2 Sep 1956   112
A narrow-gauge train fell into the river when the bridge collapsed.

Colgante, Naga City, Philippines,
16 Sep 1972   100
Many pilgrims jumped into the river as the wooden bridge collapsed.

Ashtabula, Ohio, USA, 29 Dec 1876   92
The bridge collapsed in heavy snow, causing a train to plunge into the valley where it caught fire; at the time, this was America's worst railway disaster.

Yarmouth, Norfolk, UK, 2 May 1845   79
As a crowd of people on the bridge watched a performer in the river below, their weight caused its suspension chains to snap.

* Those where the collapse caused the disaster; excluding those where a ship, train or other impact resulted in the collapse

THE 10 **WORST MOTOR VEHICLE AND ROAD DISASTERS**

LOCATION / DATE / INCIDENT   NO. KILLED

Afghanistan, 3 Nov 1982   >2,000
Following a collision with a Soviet army truck, a petrol tanker exploded in the 2.7-km (1.7-mile) Salang Tunnel. Some authorities have put the death toll from the explosion, fire and fumes as high as 3,000.

Colombia, 7 Aug 1956   1,200
Seven army ammunition trucks exploded at night in the centre of Cali, destroying eight city blocks, including a barracks where 500 soldiers were sleeping.

Spain, 11 July 1978   217
A liquid gas tanker exploded in Los Alfaques, a camping site at San Carlos de la Rapita.

Thailand, 15 Feb 1991   171
A dynamite truck exploded in Phang Nga.

Nigeria, 5 Nov 2000   150–200
A petrol tanker collided with a line of parked cars on the Ile-Ife-Ibadan Expressway, exploding and burning many to death. Some 96 bodies were recovered, but some estimates put the final toll as high as 200.

Nepal, 26 Nov 1974   148
Hindu pilgrims were killed when a suspension bridge over the River Mahakali collapsed.

Egypt, 9 Aug 1973   127
A bus drove into an irrigation canal.

Togo, 6 Dec 1965   >125
Two lorries collided with dancers during a festival at Sotouboua.

South Korea, 28 Apr 1995   110
An underground explosion destroyed vehicles and caused about 100 cars and buses to plunge into the pit it created.

The Gambia, 12 Nov 1992   100
After brake failure, a bus ferrying passengers to a dock plunged into a river.

10

SPORT & LEISURE

Olympic Countries

TOP 10 **MEDAL-WINNING COUNTRIES AT THE SUMMER PARALYMPICS***

COUNTRY	GOLD	MEDALS SILVER	BRONZE	TOTAL
1 USA	701	604	635	1,940
2 UK	512	497	485	1,494
3 Canada	464	285	315	1,064
4 France	338	321	302	961
5 Australia	315	335	299	949
6 West Germany	303	253	242	798
7 Holland	243	210	176	629
8 Poland	209	221	180	610
9 Spain	191	187	204	582
10 Sweden	211	206	149	566

* Up to and including the 2008 Beijing Games

The first Paralympics to take place at the same venue as the Olympic Games was in Rome in 1960; they are held every four years.

Paralympic power
British Paralympic champion David Weir adds a gold to his overall Olympic tally of two gold, two silver and two bronze medals.

THE 10 **LATEST CITIES TO HOST THE SUMMER OLYMPICS**

CITY / COUNTRY
MOST GOLDS / COMPETING COUNTRIES
DATES

9 Montreal, Canada
USSR, 125 / 92
17 Jul–1 Aug 1976

Munich, West Germany
USSR, 99 / 121
26 Aug–10 Sep 1972

10

8 Moscow, USSR
USSR, 195 / 80
19 Jul–3 Aug 1980

Beijing, China
China, 51 / 204
8–24 Aug 2008

1

7 Los Angeles, USA
USA, 174 / 140
28 Jul–12 Aug 1984

4 Atlanta, USA
USA, 101 / 197
20 Jul–4 Aug 1996

5

Barcelona, Spain
Unified Team, 112 / 169
25 Jul–9 Aug 1992

2 Athens, Greece
USA, 103 / 202
13–29 Aug 2004

6 Seoul, South Korea
USSR, 132 / 159
17 Sep–2 Oct 1988

All but one of the 205 IOC countries competed in the Beijing Games, Brunei being the only absentee. Three countries made their Olympic debut in 2008: the Marshall Islands, Montenegro and Tuvalu.

Sydney, Australia
USA, 97 / 199
15 Sep–1 Oct 2000 **3**

Olympic spectacle
The opening ceremony of the 2008 Beijing Summer Olympics. A total of 11,028 athletes competed in 302 events. Of the 204 competing nations, 87 of them won at least one of the 958 medals on offer.

TOP 10 **MEDAL-WINNING NATIONS AT THE SUMMER OLYMPICS***

COUNTRY	GOLD	MEDALS SILVER	BRONZE	TOTAL
1 USA	930	730	638	2,298
2 USSR#	395	319	296	1,010
3 Great Britain†	207	255	253	715
4 France	191	212	233	636
5 Germany§	163	163	203	529
6 Italy	190	158	174	522
7 Sweden	142	160	173	475
8 Hungary	159	140	159	458
9 Australia	131	137	164	432
10 East Germany	153	129	127	409

* Totals for all Summer Olympics, 1896–2008, excluding the 1906 Intercalated Games in Athens
# USSR totals for Summer Olympics, 1952–88; Unified Team figures for 1992 are excluded
† Great Britain totals include those won by athletes from Great Britain and Ireland, 1896–1920
§ Germany totals for 1896–1952 and 1992–2008; totals for West Germany (1968–88), East Germany (1968–88) and United Germany (1956–64) are excluded

TOP 10 **MEDAL-WINNING COUNTRIES AT THE 2008 BEIJING OLYMPICS**

COUNTRY	GOLD	MEDALS SILVER	BRONZE	TOTAL
1 USA	36	38	36	110
2 China	51	21	28	100
3 Russia	23	21	28	72
4 Great Britain	19	13	15	47
5 Australia	14	15	17	46
6 Germany	16	10	15	41
7 France	7	16	17	40
8 South Korea	13	10	8	31
9 Italy	8	10	10	28
10 Ukraine	7	5	15	27

This list is based on medal totals. The IOC ranks countries in order of gold medals won: by this reckoning, Japan would figure at No. 8, with nine golds, six silvers and 10 bronze medals; just outside the Top 10, Cuba – which would be in 28th place with just two golds – achieved a creditable 11 silvers and 11 bronzes, 24 medals in all, 16 of them in boxing, judo, wrestling and Taekwondo.

Great Olympians

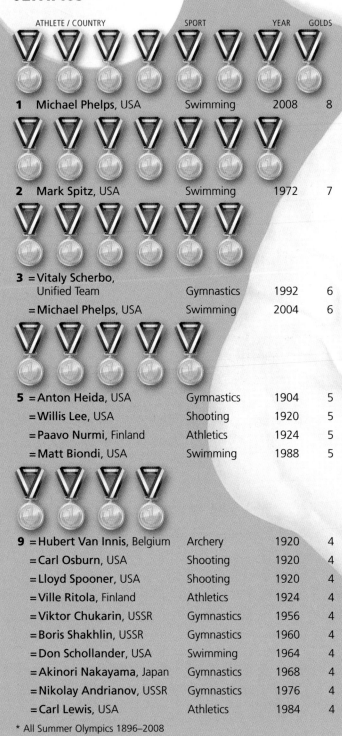

	ATHLETE / COUNTRY	SPORT	YEAR	GOLDS
1	Michael Phelps, USA	Swimming	2008	8
2	Mark Spitz, USA	Swimming	1972	7
3 =	Vitaly Scherbo, Unified Team	Gymnastics	1992	6
=	Michael Phelps, USA	Swimming	2004	6
5 =	Anton Heida, USA	Gymnastics	1904	5
=	Willis Lee, USA	Shooting	1920	5
=	Paavo Nurmi, Finland	Athletics	1924	5
=	Matt Biondi, USA	Swimming	1988	5
9 =	Hubert Van Innis, Belgium	Archery	1920	4
=	Carl Osburn, USA	Shooting	1920	4
=	Lloyd Spooner, USA	Shooting	1920	4
=	Ville Ritola, Finland	Athletics	1924	4
=	Viktor Chukarin, USSR	Gymnastics	1956	4
=	Boris Shakhlin, USSR	Gymnastics	1960	4
=	Don Schollander, USA	Swimming	1964	4
=	Akinori Nakayama, Japan	Gymnastics	1968	4
=	Nikolay Andrianov, USSR	Gymnastics	1976	4
=	Carl Lewis, USA	Athletics	1984	4

* All Summer Olympics 1896–2008

Seven of Michael Phelps' eight gold medals in 2008 were in world-record times and one in a new Olympic-record time.

TOP 10 **MOST SUMMER OLYMPIC GOLD MEDALS***

	ATHLETE / COUNTRY	SPORT	YEARS	GOLDS
1	Michael Phelps, USA	Swimming	2004–08	14
2 =	Paavo Nurmi, Finland	Athletics	1920–28	9
=	Larissa Latynina, USSR	Gymnastics	1956–64	9
=	Mark Spitz, USA	Swimming	1968–72	9
=	Carl Lewis, USA	Athletics	1984–96	9
6 =	Sawao Kato, Japan	Gymnastics	1968–76	8
=	Birgit Fischer-Schmidt, East Germany/Germany	Canoeing	1980–2004	8
=	Matt Biondi, USA	Swimming	1984–92	8
=	Jenny Thompson, USA	Swimming	1992–2004	8
10 =	Aladár Gerevich, Hungary	Fencing	1932–60	7
=	Viktor Chukarin, USSR	Gymnastics	1952–56	7
=	Boris Shakhlin, USSR	Gymnastics	1956–64	7
=	Vera Caslavska, Czechoslovakia	Gymnastics	1960–68	7
=	Nikolay Andrianov, USSR	Gymnastics	1972–80	7

* All Summer Olympics 1896–2008

THE 10 **FIRST ATHLETES TO WIN MEDALS AT FIVE OR MORE SUMMER OLYMPICS**

	ATHLETE / COUNTRY	SPORT	YEARS
1	Heikki Ilmari Savolainen, Finland	Gymnastics	1928–52
2	Aladár Gerevich, Hungary	Fencing	1932–60
3 =	Pál Kovács, Hungary	Fencing	1936–60
=	Edoardo Mangiarotti, Italy	Fencing	1936–60
5	Gustav Fischer, Switzerland	Dressage	1952–68
6	Hans Günther Winkler, United Germany/West Germany	Show-jumping	1956–76
7	Ildikó Ságiné–Rejtö née Uljaki-Rejtö, Hungary	Fencing	1960–76
8	John Michael Plumb, USA	Three-Day Event	1964–84
9	Reiner Klimke, United Germany/West Germany	Dressage	1964–88
10 =	Birgit Fischer-Schmidt, East Germany/Germany	Canoeing	1980–2004
=	Teresa Edwards, USA	Basketball	1984–2000
=	Stephen Redgrave, Great Britain	Rowing	1984–2000

Michael Phelps
Phelps beat Mark Spitz's 36-year Olympic record with eight golds in 2008.

TOP 10 **MOST MEDALS IN A SUMMER OLYMPICS CAREER (MEN)***

	ATHLETE / COUNTRY / SPORT	YEARS	GOLD	SILVER	BRONZE	TOTAL
1	Michael Phelps, USA Swimming	2004–08	14	0	2	16
2	Nikolai Andrianov, USSR Gymnastics	1972–80	7	5	3	15
3 =	Edoardo Mangiarotti, Italy Fencing	1936–60	6	5	2	13
=	Takashi Ono, Japan Gymnastics	1952–64	5	4	4	13
=	Boris Shakhlin, USSR Gymnastics	1956–64	7	4	2	13
6 =	Paavo Nurmi, Finland Athletics	1920–28	9	3	0	12
=	Sawao Kato, Japan Gymnastics	1968–76	8	3	1	12
=	Alexei Nemov, Russia Gymnastics	1996–2000	4	2	6	12
9 =	Carl Osburn, USA Shooting	1912–24	5	4	2	11
=	Viktor Chukarin, USSR Gymnastics	1952–56	7	3	1	11
=	Mark Spitz, USA Swimming	1968–72	9	1	1	11
=	Matt Biondi, USA Swimming	1984–92	8	2	1	11

* All Summer Olympics 1896–2008

TOP 10 **MOST MEDALS IN A SUMMER OLYMPICS CAREER (WOMEN)***

	ATHLETE / COUNTRY / SPORT	YEARS	GOLD	SILVER	BRONZE	TOTAL
1	Larissa Latynina, USSR Gymnastics	1956–64	9	5	4	18
2 =	Birgit Fischer-Schmidt, East Germany/Germany Canoeing	1980–2004	8	4	0	12
=	Dara Torres, USA Swimming	1984–2008	4	4	4	12
=	Jenny Thompson, USA Swimming	1992–2000	8	3	1	12
5 =	Vera Cáslavská, Czechoslovakia Gymnastics	1960–68	7	4	0	11
=	Natalie Coughlin, USA Swimming	2004–08	3	4	4	11
7 =	Agnes Keleti, Hungary Gymnastics	1952–56	5	3	2	10
=	Polina Astakhova, USSR Gymnastics	1956–64	5	2	3	10
9 =	Lyudmila Tourischeva, USSR Gymnastics	1968–76	4	3	2	9
=	Nadia Comaneci, Romania Gymnastics	1976–80	5	3	1	9

* All Summer Olympics 1896–2008

Athletics

TOP 10 MEDAL-WINNING COUNTRIES IN TRACK AND FIELD EVENTS AT THE 2008 BEIJING OLYMPICS

	COUNTRY	GOLD	SILVER	BRONZE	TOTAL
1	USA	7	9	7	23
2	Russia	6	5	7	18
3	Kenya	5	5	4	14
4	Jamaica	6	3	2	11
5	=Belarus	1	3	3	7
	=Ethiopia	4	1	2	7
7	=Cuba	1	2	2	5
	=Ukraine	1	1	3	5
9	=Australia	1	2	1	4
	=Great Britain	1	2	1	4

100-m Records

When Usain Bolt set a new world record in the 2008 100-m final at the Beijing Olympics, he broke his own world record of 9.72 seconds, which he had set at New York on 31 May 2008. The women's 100 m world record is 10.49 seconds, set by Florence Griffith-Joyner (USA) at Indianapolis on 16 July 1988.

TOP 10 FASTEST MEN OVER 100 METRES*

	ATHLETE / COUNTRY / VENUE	DATE	TIME (SECS)
1	Usain Bolt, Jamaica Beijing, China	16 Aug 2008	9.69
2	Asafa Powell, Jamaica Rieti, Italy	9 Sep 2007	9.74
3	Tyson Gay, USA Eugene, Oregon, USA	28 Jun 2008	9.77
4	Maurice Greene, USA Athens, Greece	16 Jun 1999	9.79
5	=Donovan Bailey, Canada Atlanta, Georgia, USA	27 Jul 1996	9.84
	=Bruny Surin, Canada Seville, Spain	22 Aug 1999	9.84
7	=Leroy Burrell, USA Lausanne, Switzerland	6 Jul 1994	9.85
	=Justin Gatlin, USA Athens, Greece	22 Aug 2004	9.85
	=Olusoji A. Fasuba, Nigeria Doha, Qatar	12 May 2006	9.85
10	=Carl Lewis, USA Tokyo, Japan	25 Aug 1991	9.86
	=Frank Fredericks, Namibia Lausanne, Switzerland	03 Jul 1996	9.86
	=Ato Boldon, Trinidad Walnut, California, USA	19 Apr 1998	9.86
	=Francis Obikwelu, Portugal Athens, Greece	22 Aug 2004	9.86

* Based on the fastest time ever achieved by each

Source: IAAF

Lightning Bolt
Jamaican athlete Usain Bolt won three gold medals at the 2008 Olympics, setting a new world record for the 100 m.

TOP 10 FASTEST MARATHONS*

ATHLETE / COUNTRY / VENUE/DATE / TIME (HR:MIN:SECS)

10 Paul Tergat,
Kenya
London, 14 Apr 2002
2:05:48

9 Khalid Khannouchi,
USA
Chicago, 24 Oct 1999
2:05:42

8 Khalid Khannouchi,
USA
London, 14 Apr 2002
2:05:38

7 Abderrahim Goumri,
Morocco
London, 13 Apr 2008
2:05:30

6 Samuel Kamau Wanjiru,
Kenya
London, 13 Apr 2008
2:05:24

* As at 1 January 2009

Source: IAAF

TOP 10 **LONGEST LONG JUMPS***

	ATHLETE[#]	VENUE	DATE	DISTANCE (M)
1	Mike Powell	Tokyo, Japan	30 Aug 1991	8.95
2	Bob Beamon	Mexico City	18 Oct1968	8.90
3	Carl Lewis	Tokyo, Japan	30 Aug 1991	8.87
4	Robert Emmiyan, Russia	Tsakhkadzor, Armenia	22 May 1987	8.86
5	Carl Lewis	Indianapolis, USA	19 Jun 1983	8.79
6 =	Carl Lewis	Indianapolis, USA	24 Jul 1982	8.76
=	Carl Lewis	Indianapolis, USA	18 Jul 1988	8.76
8	Carl Lewis	Indianapolis, USA	16 Aug 1987	8.75
9 =	Larry Myricks	Indianapolis, USA	18 Jul 1988	8.74
=	Erick Walder	El Paso, USA	2 Apr 1994	8.74

* As at 1 January 2009
\# All USA unless otherwise stated

Source: IAAF

The longest jump by a British athlete is 8.27 metres by Chris Tomlinson at Tallahassee, Florida, on 13 April 2002. The longest jump in the twenty-first century is 8.73 metres by Irving Saladino (Panama) at Hengelo, the Netherlands, on 24 May 2008. He equalled that mark in winning the gold medal at the Beijing Olympics. The women's world record is 7.52 metres, set by Galina Chistyakova (Russia) at Leningrad on 11 June 1988.

The fastest women's marathon is 2 hours 15 minutes 25 seconds by Paula Radcliffe (GB) in winning the London Marathon on 13 April 2003. The fastest marathon by a British male athlete is 2 hours 7 minutes 13 seconds by Steve Jones, when he won the Chicago Marathon on 20 October 1985.

3 Paul Tergat, Kenya
Berlin, 28 Sep 2003
2:04:55

1 Haile Gebrselassie, Ethiopia
Berlin, 30 Sep 2007
2:04:26

5 Martin Lel, Kenya
London, 13 Apr 2008
2:05:15

4 Sammy Korir, Kenya
Berlin, 28 Sep 2003
2:04:56

2 Haile Gebrselassie, Ethiopia
Dubai, 28 Sep 2003
2:04:53

Cricket

TOP 10 BEST BOWLING FIGURES IN A TEST INNINGS*

	PLAYER	COUNTRY / OPPONENTS	VENUE	DATE	FIGURES
1	Jim Laker	England v Australia	Manchester	26 Jul 1956	10–53
2	Anil Kumble	India v Pakistan	Delhi	4 Feb 1999	10–74
3	George Lohmann	England v South Africa	Johannesburg	2 Mar 1896	9–28
4	Jim Laker	England v Australia	Manchester	26 Jul 1956	9–37
5	Muttiah Muralitharan	Sri Lanka v Zimbabwe	Kandy	4 Jan 2002	9–51
6	Richard Hadlee	New Zealand v Australia	Brisbane	8 Nov 1985	9–52
7	Abdul Qadir	Pakistan v England	Lahore	25 Nov 1987	9–56
8	Devon Malcolm	England v South Africa	The Oval	18 Aug 1994	9–57
9	Muttiah Muralitharan	Sri Lanka v England	The Oval	27 Aug 1998	9–65
10	Jasubhai Patel	India v Australia	Kanpur	19 Dec 1959	9–69

* As at 1 January 2009; date indicates start of each Test match

TOP 10 HIGHEST TEAM TOTALS IN FIRST-CLASS CRICKET*

	TEAM / OPPONENTS	VENUE	SEASON	TOTAL
1	Victoria v New South Wales	Melbourne	1926–27	1,107
2	Victoria v Tasmania	Melbourne	1922–23	1,059
3	Sri Lanka v India	Colombo	1997–98	952–6 dec
4	Sind v Baluchistan	Karachi	1973–74	951–7 dec
5	Hyderabad v Andhra Pradesh	Hyderabad	1993–94	944–6 dec
6	New South Wales v South Australia	Sydney	1900–01	918
7 =	Holkar v Mysore	Indore	1945–46	912–8 dec
=	Tamil Nadu# v Goa	Panjim	1988–89	912–6 dec
9	Railways v Dera Ismail Khan	Lahore	1964–65	910–6 dec
10	England v Australia	The Oval	1938	903–7 dec

* As at 1 January 2009; dec = declared
# Tamil Nadu's total included 52 penalty runs from their opponents' failure to meet the required bowling rate

TOP 10 HIGHEST TEAM TOTALS IN TWENTY20 CRICKET*

	TEAM / OPPONENTS	VENUE	DATE	TOTAL
1	Sri Lanka v Kenya	Johannesburg	14 Sep 2007	260–6
2	Somerset v Gloucestershire	Taunton	27 Jun 2006	250–3
3	Nondescripts v Sri Lanka Air Force Sports Club	Colombo	16 Oct 2005	245–4
4	Essex v Sussex	Chelmsford	24 Jun 2008	242–3
5	Chennai v Punjab	Mohali	19 Apr 2008	240–5
6	Ragama v Saracens	Colombo	4 Mar 2007	237–6
7	Lahore Lions v Leopards	Karachi	27 Feb 2006	234–4
8	Victoria v New South Wales	Sydney	21 Jan 2006	233–7
9 =	Karachi Dolphins v Lahore Lions	Lahore	25 Apr 2005	228–7
=	Somerset v Gloucestershire	Taunton	6 Jul 2005	228–5

* As at 1 January 2009

Run records
Mohammad Yousuf's 1,788 runs in 2006, a match average of 99.33, broke Sir Viv Richards' 30-year-old record. He also set a new record by scoring nine centuries in a calendar year.

TOP 10 **MOST WICKETS IN FIRST-CLASS CRICKET***

	PLAYER	YEARS	MATCHES	WICKETS
1	Wilf Rhodes	1898–1930	1,110	4,204
2	A. P. 'Titch' Freeman	1914–1936	592	3,776
3	Charlie Parker	1903–1935	635	3,278
4	Jack Hearne	1888–1923	639	3,061
5	Tom Goddard	1922–1952	593	2,979
6	Alex Kennedy	1907–1936	677	2,874
7	Derek Shackleton	1948–1969	647	2,857
8	Tony Lock	1946–1971	654	2,844
9	Fred Titmus	1949–1982	792	2,830
10	W. G. Grace	1865–1908	870	2,809

* As at 1 January 2009; all players from England

TOP 10 **MOST TEST RUNS IN A CALENDAR YEAR***

	PLAYER / COUNTRY	YEAR	MATCHES	INNINGS	RUNS
1	Mohammad Yousuf, Pakistan	2006	11	19	1,788
2	Viv Richards, West Indies	1976	11	19	1,710
3	Graeme Smith, South Africa	2008	15	25	1,656
4	Ricky Ponting, Australia	2005	15	28	1,544
5	Ricky Ponting, Australia	2003	11	18	1,503
6	= Michael Vaughan, England	2002	14	26	1,481
	= Justin Langer, Australa	2004	14	27	1,481
8	= Sunil Gavaskar, India	1979	17	26	1,407
	= Virender Sehwag, India	2008	14	27	1,407
10	Sachin Tendulkar, India	2002	16	26	1,392

* As at 1 January 2009

Ball Games

Above: Hurling
Cork v Waterford in the 2007 Championship.
Between them they have 32 hurling titles.

Right: Norm Duke
Norm Duke became the first professional bowler
to win three consecutive major tournaments.

TOP 10 MOST ALL-IRELAND GAELIC FOOTBALL TITLES*

	TEAM	WINS FIRST	LAST	TOTAL
1	Kerry	1903	2007	35
2	Dublin	1891	1995	22
3	Galway	1925	2001	9
4	Meath	1949	1999	7
5	Cork	1890	1990	6
6	=Down	1960	1994	5
	=Cavan	1933	1952	5
	=Wexford	1893	1918	5
9	=Kildare	1905	1928	4
	=Tipperary	1889	1920	4

* All-Ireland Senior Football Championship
1887–2008

The senior final is played at Croke Park,
Dublin, on either the third or fourth
Sunday each September. The winners
receive the Sam Maguire trophy.

TOP 10 MOST ALL-IRELAND HURLING TITLES*

	TEAM	TITLES FIRST	LAST	TOTAL
1	Kilkenny	1904	2008	31
2	Cork	1890	2005	30
3	Tipperary	1887	2001	25
4	Limerick	1897	1973	7
5	=Dublin	1889	1938	6
	=Wexford	1910	1996	6
7	=Galway	1923	1988	4
	=Offaly	1981	1998	4
9	Clare	1914	1997	3
10	Waterford	1948	1959	2

* The All-Ireland Senior Hurling Championship
from 1887–2008

The senior final is played at Dublin's Croke
Park on the first or second Sunday each
September. The winning team receives the
Liam McCarthy Cup.

TOP 10 MOST PROFESSIONAL BOWLERS ASSOCIATION (PBA) TITLES

	BOWLER* / TOTAL WINS#
1	Walter Ray Williams Jr 45
2	Earl Anthony 43
3	=Mark Roth 34
	=Pete Weber 34
5	Parker Bohn III 32
6	=Norm Duke 30
	=Dick Weber 30
8	Mike Aulby 29
9	Don Johnson 26
10	Brian Voss 24

* All bowlers from the USA
# As at 1 January 2009

TOP 10 MOST WOMEN'S MAJOR FAST-PITCH SOFTBALL TITLES*

		TITLES		
	TEAM / LOCATION	FIRST	LAST	TOTAL
1	Raybestos/Stratford Brakettes, Stratford, Connecticut	1958	2007	26
2	Orange Lionettes, California	1950	1970	9
3	Jax Maids, New Orleans, Louisiana	1942	1947	5
4	California Commotion, Woodland Hills, California	1996	1999	4
5	= Arizona Ramblers, Phoenix, Arizona	1940	1949	3
	= Redding Rebels, California	1993	1995	3
7	= National Screw & Manufacturing, Cleveland, Ohio	1936	1937	2
	= J.J. Krieg's, Alameda, California	1938	1939	2
	= Hi-Ho Brakettes, Stratford, Connecticut	1985	1988	2
	= Phoenix Storm, Phoenix, Arizona	2000	2001	2
	= Southern California Hurricanes, Lake Forest, California	2005	2008	2

* Amateur Softball Association of America (ASA) titles 1933–2008

TOP 10 MOST WORLD SNOOKER RANKING EVENT TITLES*

		TITLES		
	PLAYER / COUNTRY	FIRST	LAST	TOTAL
1	Stephen Hendry, Scotland	1987	2005	36
2	Steve Davis, England	1981	1995	28
3	Ronnie O'Sullivan, England	1993	2008	21
4	John Higgins, Scotland	1994	2008	19
5	Mark Williams, Wales	1996	2006	16
6	Jimmy White, England	1986	2004	10
7	John Parrott, England	1989	1996	9
8	Peter Ebdon, England	1993	2006	7
9	Ken Doherty, Ireland	1993	2006	6
10	Ray Reardon, Wales	1974	1982	5

* As at 1 January 2009

The World Professional Billiards and Snooker Association (WPBSA) introduced its ranking system in 1976, but positions were based solely on performances in the World Championship. Following the 1982 World Championship, two more events – the Jameson International and Professional Players Tournament – were designated as ranking tournaments. In the 2008–09 season, eight tournaments were classed as ranking events.

Ronnie O'Sullivan
Ronnie O'Sullivan capturing his third World Professional title against Ali Carter in 2008. On the way to the final, both men compiled maximum 147 breaks.

Basketball

TOP 10 MOST POINTS IN AN NBA CAREER

	PLAYER	YEARS	POINTS
1	Kareem Abdul-Jabbar	1969–89	38,387
2	Karl Malone	1985–2004	36,928
3	Michael Jordan	1984–2003	32,292
4	Wilt Chamberlain	1959–73	31,419
5	Moses Malone	1976–95	27,409
6	Elvin Hayes	1968–84	27,313
7	Hakeem Olajuwon	1984–2002	26,946
8	Oscar Robertson	1960–74	26,710
9	Dominique Wilkins	1982–99	26,668
10	John Havlicek	1962–78	26,395

Source: NBA

If figures from the American Basketball Association (ABA), which existed from 1967–76, were included then Julius Erving (30,026 points) and Dan Issel (27,482 points) would be added to the list; the total for Moses Malone would also increase to 29,580 points.

TOP 10 MOST CAREER POINTS IN NBA PLAYOFF GAMES

	PLAYER	YEARS	POINTS
1	Michael Jordan	1985–98	5,987
2	Kareem Abdul-Jabbar	1970–89	5,762
3	Shaquille O'Neal	1994–2008	5,121
4	Karl Malone	1986–2004	4,761
5	Jerry West	1961–74	4,457
6	Larry Bird	1980–92	3,897
7	John Havlicek	1963–77	3,776
8	Hakeem Olajuwon	1985–2002	3,755
9	Magic Johnson	1980–96	3,701
10	Kobe Bryant	1997–2008	3,686

Source: NBA

If his ABA (American Basketball Association) career playoff points were also included, Julius Erving would be on the list at No. 5 with 4,580 points.

TOP 10 MOST POINTS IN A SINGLE NBA GAME*

	PLAYER (TEAM)	OPPONENTS	DATE	POINTS
1	Wilt Chamberlain, Philadelphia Warriors	New York Knicks	2 Mar 1962	100
2	Kobe Bryant, Los Angeles Lakers	Toronto Raptors	22 Jan 2006	81
3	Wilt Chamberlain, Philadelphia Warriors	Los Angeles Lakers	8 Dec 1961#	78
4	= Wilt Chamberlain, Philadelphia Warriors	Chicago Packers	13 Jan 1962	73
	= Wilt Chamberlain, San Francisco Warriors	New York Knicks	16 Nov 1962	73
	= David Thompson, Denver Nuggets	Detroit Pistons	9 Apr 1978	73
7	Wilt Chamberlain, San Francisco Warriors	Los Angeles Lakers	3 Nov 1962	72
8	= Elgin Baylor, Los Angeles Lakers	New York Knicks	15 Nov 1960	71
	= David Robinson, San Antonio Spurs	Los Angeles Clippers	24 Apr 1994	71
10	Wilt Chamberlain, San Francisco Warriors	Syracuse Nationals	10 Mar 1963	70

* As at the end of the 2007–08 season
# Including three periods of overtime

The Birth of Basketball

The Aztecs' game of ollamalitzli, and similar ball and hoop games among other South American peoples, may have influenced the modern game of basketball, which was invented in December 1891 by Canadian physical education teacher Dr James A. Naismith at the International YMCA College at Springfield, Massachusetts. He set out to devise a game that could be played indoors during the winter. Peach baskets were originally used (players had to climb a ladder to retrieve the ball, until someone hit on the idea of removing the bottom!), but these were soon replaced by metal rings with netting.

TOP 10 **MOST THREE-POINT FIELD GOALS MADE IN AN NBA CAREER***

	PLAYER	YEARS	THREE-POINTERS MADE
1	Reggie Miller	1987–2005	2,560
2	Ray Allen	1996–2008	2,100
3	Dale Ellis	1983–2000	1,719
4	Glen Rice	1988–2004	1,559
5	Eddie Jones	1994–2008	1,546
6	Tim Hardaway	1989–2003	1,542
7	Nick Van Exel	1993–2006	1,528
8	Peja Stojakovic	1998–2008	1,426
9	Antoine Walker	1996–2008	1,386
10	Dan Majerle	1988–2002	1,360

* As at end of 2007–08 regular season

The three-point field goal had been tried many times since first tested in 1933, but it was not officially adopted by the NBA until the 1979–80 season.

THE 10 **MOST APPEARANCES IN THE NBA CHAMPIONSHIP FINALS***

	TEAM	TITLES	FINALS
1	Los Angeles Lakers/Minneapolis Lakers	15	29
2	Boston Celtics	16	20
3	Philadelphia 76ers/Syracuse Nationals	3	9
4	New York Knicks	2	8
5	Detroit Pistons	3	7
6 =	Chicago Bulls	6	6
=	Philadelphia Warriors/Golden State Warriors San Francisco Warriors	3	6
8 =	Baltimore Bullets/Washington Bullets	1	4
=	Houston Rockets	2	4
=	San Antonio Spurs	4	4
=	St Louis Hawks	1	4

* Up to and including the 2008 Championship

Miller thriller
Reggie Miller's 18-year career with the Indiana Pacers saw him achieve a total of 25,279 points, including 2,560 three-pointers and 4,141 assists. He was in the gold-medal winning US basketball team at the 1996 Olympics.

Combat Sports

TOP 10 OLYMPIC SHOOTING COUNTRIES*

COUNTRY# / MEDALS GOLD/SILVER/BRONZE/TOTAL

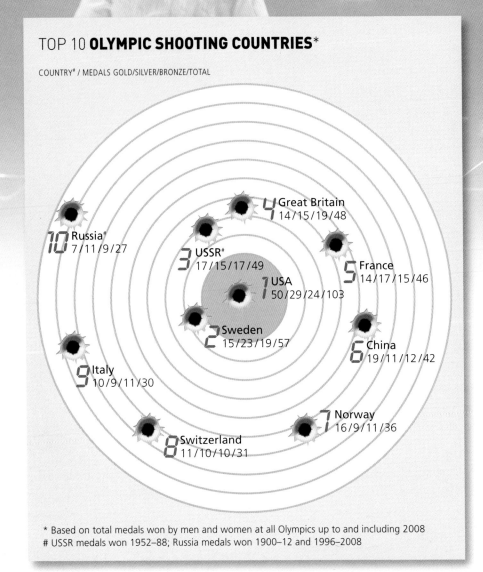

10 Russia#
7/11/9/27

4 Great Britain
14/15/19/48

3 USSR#
17/15/17/49

5 France
14/17/15/46

1 USA
50/29/24/103

2 Sweden
15/23/19/57

6 China
19/11/12/42

9 Italy
10/9/11/30

7 Norway
16/9/11/36

8 Switzerland
11/10/10/31

* Based on total medals won by men and women at all Olympics up to and including 2008
# USSR medals won 1952–88; Russia medals won 1900–12 and 1996–2008

TOP 10 OLYMPIC FENCING COUNTRIES*

	COUNTRY#	MEDALS		
		GOLD	SILVER	BRONZE	TOTAL
1	France	44	41	35	120
2	Italy	45	39	32	116
3	Hungary	34	22	27	83
4	USSR	18	15	16	49
5	USA	3	9	14	26
6	Germany	7	8	8	23
7	Poland	4	9	9	22
8 =	Russia	9	2	5	16
=	West Germany	7	8	1	16
10	Romania	3	4	7	14

* Based on total medals won by men and women at all Olympics up to and including 2008
# USSR medals won 1952–88; Russia medals won 1900–1912 and 1996–2008; Germany medals won 1896–1952 and 1992–2008; West Germany medals won 1968–88

TOP 10 OLYMPIC JUDO COUNTRIES*

	COUNTRY#	MEDALS		
		GOLD	SILVER	BRONZE	TOTAL
1	Japan	35	15	15	65
2 =	France	10	8	19	37
=	South Korea	9	14	14	37
4	Cuba	5	11	16	32
5	USSR	5	5	13	23
6	Netherlands	4	2	14	20
7	China	8	2	8	18
8	Great Britain	0	7	9	16
9	Brazil	2	3	10	15
10	Germany	3	0	10	13

* Based on total medals won by men and women at all Olympics up to and including 2008
# USSR medals won 1964–88; Germany medals won 1992–2008

Martial arts masters
Satoshi Ishii, one of Japan's judo gold medallists at Beijing 2008. The first of Japan's judo gold medallists was Takehide Nakatani in 1964.

THE 10 LAST UNDISPUTED WORLD HEAVYWEIGHT BOXING CHAMPIONS

	BOXER*	REIGN FROM	REIGN ENDED
1	Mike Tyson	1 Aug 1987	6 May 1989
2	Leon Spinks	15 Feb 1978	18 Mar 1978#
3	Muhammad Ali	30 Oct 1974	15 Feb 1978
4	George Foreman	22 Jan 1973	30 Oct 1974
5	Joe Frazier	16 Feb 1970	22 Jan 1973
6	Muhammad Ali	6 Feb 1967	29 Apr 1967†
7	Cassius Clay (later Muhammad Ali)	25 Feb 1964	19 Jun 1964§
8	Sonny Liston	25 Sep 1962	25 Feb 1964
9	Floyd Patterson	20 Jun 1960	25 Sep 1962
10	Ingemar Johansson (Sweden)	26 Jun 1959	20 Jun 1960

* As at 1 January 2009; all from the USA unless otherwise stated
# Spinks was stripped of his title by the WBC for refusing to fight the No. 1 contender Ken Norton
† Ali was stripped of his title by the WBA and then WBC for failing to be drafted into the US army
§ The WBA withdrew recognition of Ali after his refusal to participate in a re-match with Sonny Liston

Mike Tyson held the WBC, WBA and IBF titles from 1 August 1987 to 11 February 1990 and was generally acknowledged as the universal champion, despite the fact that a new body, the IBO, came into being in 1988 and had its first heavyweight champion (Francesco Damiani of Italy) in May 1989.

TOP 10 LONGEST REIGNS AS WWE (WORLD WRESTLING ENTERTAINMENT) WORLD HEAVYWEIGHT CHAMPION*

	WRESTLER	REIGN FROM	REIGN ENDED	DAYS
1	Batista	3 Apr 2005	10 Jan 2006	282
2	Triple H	15 Dec 2002	21 Sep 2003	280
3	Chris Benoit	14 Mar 2004	15 Aug 2004	154
4 =	King Booker	23 Jul 2006	26 Nov 2006	126
=	Batista	26 Nov 2006	1 Apr 2007	126
6	Rey Mysterio	2 Apr 2006	23 Jul 2006	112
7	Edge	16 Dec 2007	30 Mar 2008	105
8 =	Triple H	14 Dec 2003	14 Mar 2004	91
=	Batista	16 Sep 2007	16 Dec 2007	91
10	Triple H	12 Sep 2004	6 Dec 2004	85

* As at 1 January 2009

Paul Michael Levesque, better known as Triple H (formerly Hunter Hearst Helmsley), has held the title for a record 616 days over a total of five reigns. The World Heavyweight Championship on the Raw brand of the WWE was launched in 2002, with Triple H winning the first title.

Have an Edge
Edge knocked down Chris Benoit at Wrestlemania 21 before getting hold of the Money in the Bank briefcase to win the match.

On Two Wheels

A close-run thing
The 23 seconds that separated winner Contador (left) and Evans (right) in the 2007 Tour de France was the closest of the 21st century.

THE 10 **CLOSEST TOURS DE FRANCE***

	WINNER / COUNTRY	RUNNER-UP / COUNTRY	YEAR	WINNING MARGIN MIN	SEC
1	Greg LeMond, USA	Laurent Fignon, France	1989	0	8
2	Alberto Contador, Spain	Cadel Evans, Australia	2007	0	23
3	Oscar Pereiro, Spain	Andreas Klöden, Germany	2006	0	32
4	Jan Janssen, Netherlands	Herman Van Springel, Belgium	1968	0	38
5	Tony Roche, Ireland	Pedro Delgado, Spain	1987	0	40
6	Bernard Thévenet, France	Hennie Kuiper, Netherlands	1977	0	48
7	Jacques Anquetil, France	Raymond Poulidor, France	1964	0	55
8	Carlos Sastre, Spain	Cadel Evans, Australia	2008	0	58
9	Lance Armstrong, USA	Jan Ullrich, Germany	2003	1	1
10	Lucien Almar, France	Jan Janssen, Netherlands	1966	1	7

* Based on difference between the winner's time and that of the runner-up; up to and including the 2008 race

TOP 10 **COUNTRIES WITH THE MOST WINNERS OF THE UCI WORLD ROAD RACE CHAMPIONSHIPS***

	COUNTRY	MEN	WOMEN	TOTAL
1	Belgium	25	6	31
2	Italy	19	2	21
3	France	8	9	17
4	Netherlands	7	7	14
5 =	Great Britain	1	4	5
=	Spain	5	0	5
=	Switzerland	3	2	5
=	USA	3	2	5
9	West Germany	2	2	4
10 =	Germany	1	2	3
=	Lithuania	0	3	3
=	Soviet Union	0	3	3

* Up to and including 2008

TOP 10 MOTORCYCLE MANUFACTURERS WITH THE MOST WORLD TITLES*

	MANUFACTURER / COUNTRY	MOTOGP	500CC	350CC	250CC	125CC	80CC	50CC	TOTAL
1	Honda, Japan	4	13	6	19	15	0	2	59
2	MV Agusta, Italy	0	16	9	5	7	0	0	37
3	Yamaha, Japan	2	9	5	14	4	0	0	34
4	Aprilia, Italy	0	0	0	8	8	0	0	16
5	Suzuki, Japan	0	7	0	0	3	0	5	15
6	Kawasaki, Japan	0	0	4	4	1	0	0	9
7 =	Derbi, Spain	0	0	0	0	3	3	2	8
=	Kreidler, Germany	0	0	0	0	0	0	8	8
9	Moto Guzzi, Italy	0	0	4	3	0	0	0	7
10	Gilera, Italy	0	5	1	0	0	0	0	6

* Solo classes only up to and including 2008

TOP 10 COUNTRIES PROVIDING THE MOST WORLD MOTORCYCLE CHAMPIONS*

	COUNTRY	500CC/ MOTOGP	350CC	250CC	125CC	50/80CC	TOTAL
1	Italy	19	8	21	23	2	73
2	UK	17	13	9	4	1	44
3	Spain	1	0	6	12	12	31
4	USA	15	0	2	0	0	17
5	West Germany	0	2	7	2	4	15
6	Australia	7	1	1	3	0	12
7 =	Rhodesia	1	5	2	0	0	8
=	Switzerland	0	0	0	4	4	8
9	Japan	0	1	2	4	0	7
10 =	France	0	0	3	2	0	5
=	South Africa	0	3	2	0	0	5

* Solo classes only up to and including 2008

TOP 10 RIDERS WITH THE MOST MOTOGP RACE WINS*

	RIDER / COUNTRY / YEARS	WINS
1	Valentino Rossi Italy, 2000–08	71
2	Giacomo Agostini Italy, 1965–76	68
3	Mick Doohan Australia, 1990–98	54
4	Mike Hailwood UK, 1961–67	37
5	Eddie Lawson USA, 1984–92	31
6	Kevin Schwantz USA, 1988–94	25
7	Wayne Rainey USA, 1988–93	24
8 =	Geoff Duke UK, 1950–59	22
=	John Surtees UK, 1956–60	22
=	Kenny Roberts USA, 1978–83	22

* 500cc 1949–2001; MotoGP 2002–08

Marco makes a mark
Marco Simoncelli's victory in the 2008 World 250cc Championship further increased his and Italy's commanding lead in the league table.

Football

TOP 10 TRANSFERS BETWEEN BRITISH CLUBS*

	PLAYER	FROM	TO	YEAR	FEE (£)
1	Dimitar Berbatov	Tottenham Hotspur	Manchester United	2008	30,750,000
2	Rio Ferdinand	Leeds United	Manchester United	2002	29,100,000
3	Shaun Wright-Phillips	Manchester City	Chelsea	2005	21,000,000
4	Wayne Rooney	Everton	Manchester United	2004	20,000,000
5	Robbie Keane	Tottenham Hotspur	Liverpool	2008	19,000,000
6	Rio Ferdinand	West Ham United	Leeds United	2000	18,000,000
7	Damien Duff	Blackburn Rovers	Chelsea	2003	17,000,000
8	Darren Bent	Charlton Athletic	Tottenham Hotspur	2007	15,500,000
9 =	Alan Shearer	Blackburn Rovers	Newcastle United	1996	15,000,000
=	Nicolas Anelka	Bolton Wanderers	Chelsea	2008	15,000,000
=	Jermain Defoe	Portsmouth	Tottenham Hotspur	2009	15,000,000

* As at the end of the 2009 January transfer window

TOP 10 MOST BARCLAYS PREMIER LEAGUE MANAGER OF THE MONTH AWARDS*

	MANAGER	CLUB(S)	FIRST AWARD	LATEST AWARD	TOTAL AWARDS
1	Alex Ferguson	Manchester United	Aug 1993	Mar 2008	21
2	Arsene Wenger	Arsenal	Mar 1998	Dec 2007	10
3	Bobby Robson	Newcastle United	Feb 2000	Oct 2003	6
4 =	Kevin Keegan	Newcastle United	Nov 1993	Sep 1995	5
=	Harry Redknapp	West Ham United, Portsmouth	Nov 1998	Apr 2006	5
=	Martin O'Neill	Leicester City, Aston Villa	Sep 1997	Nov 2007	5
7 =	Joe Kinnear	Wimbledon	Apr 1994	Sep 1996	4
=	Gordon Strachan	Coventry City, Southampton	Dec 1996	Dec 2002	4
=	Sam Allardyce	Bolton Wanderers	Aug 2001	Dec 2006	4
=	David Moyes	Everton	Nov 2002	Feb 2008	4
=	Rafael Benitez	Liverpool	Nov 2005	Oct 2008	4

* As at 1 January 2009

The award was first made in August 1993 and won by the Premier League's longest-serving manager, Sir Alex Ferguson. It was then known as the Carling Manager of the Month Award, and Ferguson received a trophy, a magnum of Champagne and a cheque for £750. Ferguson has won at least one award every season except 2001–02.

TOP 10 BARCLAYS PREMIER LEAGUE CLUBS' WAGE BILLS

	CLUB	ANNUAL WAGE BILL (£)*
1	Chelsea	132,800,000
2	Manchester United	92,300,000
3	Arsenal	89,700,000
4	Liverpool	77,600,000
5	Newcastle United	62,400,000
6	West Ham United	44,200,000
7	Tottenham Hotspur	43,800,000
8	Aston Villa	43,200,000
9	Everton	38,400,000
10	Middlesbrough	38,300,000

* 2006–07 season

Source: *The Deloitte Annual Review of Football Finance*

Ahead of the rest
Cristiano Ronaldo
scoring in the 2008
Champions League
final against Chelsea,
who equalized through
Frank Lampard –
they are two of the
highest-paid players
in British football.

TOP 10 **APPEARANCES IN THE BARCLAYS PREMIER LEAGUE***

PLAYER / CLUB(S)	APPEARANCES
1 Gary Speed Leeds United, Everton, Newcastle United, Bolton Wanderers	535
2 David James Liverpool, Aston Villa, West Ham United, Manchester City, Portsmouth	531
3 Ryan Giggs Manchester United	505
4 Sol Campbell Tottenham Hotspur, Arsenal, Portsmouth	466
5 Alan Shearer Blackburn Rovers, Newcastle United	441
6 Gareth Southgate Crystal Palace, Aston Villa, Middlesbrough	426
7 Emile Heskey Leicester City, Liverpool, Birmingham City, Wigan Athletic	420
8 Teddy Sheringham Nottingham Forest, Tottenham Hotspur, Manchester United, Portsmouth, West Ham United	418
9 Andy Cole Newcastle United, Manchester United, Blackburn Rovers Fulham, Manchester City, Portsmouth, Sunderland	413
10 Frank Lampard West Ham United, Chelsea	410

* As at 1 January 2009

Source: FA Premier League

TOP 10 **GOALSCORERS IN THE BARCLAYS PREMIER LEAGUE***

PLAYERS / CLUB(S)	GOALS
1 Alan Shearer Blackburn Rovers, Newcastle United	260
2 Andy Cole Newcastle United, Manchester United, Blackburn Rovers, Fulham, Manchester City, Portsmouth	187
3 Thierry Henry Arsenal	174
4 Robbie Fowler Liverpool, Leeds United, Manchester City	161
5 Les Ferdinand Queens Park Rangers, Newcastle United, Tottenham Hotspur, West Ham United, Leicester City, Bolton Wanderers	150
6 Teddy Sheringham Nottingham Forest, Tottenham Hotspur, Manchester United, Portsmouth, West Ham United	147
7 Michael Owen Liverpool, Newcastle United	143
8 Jimmy Floyd Hasselbaink Leeds United, Chelsea, Middlesbrough, Charlton Athletic	128
9 Dwight Yorke Aston Villa, Manchester United, Blackburn Rovers, Birmingham City, Sunderland	123
10 Ian Wright Arsenal, West Ham United	113

* As at 1 January 2009

Source: FA Premier League

Golf

	GOLFER	YEARS	US MASTERS	US OPEN	BRITISH OPEN	US PGA	TOTAL
1	Jack Nicklaus	1962–86	6	4	3	5	18
2	Tiger Woods	1997–2008	4	3	3	4	14
3	Walter Hagen	1914–29	0	2	4	5	11
4 =	Ben Hogan	1946–53	2	4	1	2	9
=	Gary Player, South Africa	1959–78	3	1	3	2	9
6	Tom Watson	1975–83	2	1	5	0	8
7 =	Harry Vardon, England	1896–1914	0	1	6	0	7
=	Gene Sarazen	1922–35	1	2	1	3	7
=	Bobby Jones	1923–30	0	4	3	0	7
=	Sam Snead	1942–54	3	0	1	3	7
=	Arnold Palmer	1958–64	4	1	2	0	7

* Professional Majors only, up to and including 2008; all golfers from the USA unless otherwise stated

In 1930, Bobby Jones achieved an unprecedented Grand Slam when he won the US and British Open titles as well as the Amateur titles of both countries. Nicklaus, Woods, Hogan, Player and Sarazen are the only golfers to have won all four Majors at least once.

Tiger Woods
Despite being in pain, Tiger Woods won the 2008 US Open. Shortly afterwards he had surgery on his troubled knee, which kept him out of the game for eight months.

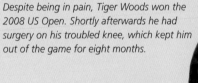

TOP 10 **MOST CAREER WINS ON THE US LPGA TOUR***

	GOLFER	YEARS	WINS
1	Kathy Whitworth	1962–85	88
2	Mickey Wright	1956–73	82
3	Annika Sörenstam	1995–2008	72
4	Patty Berg	1937–62	60
5	Louise Suggs	1946–62	58
6	Betsy Rawls	1951–72	55
7	Nancy Lopez	1978–97	48
8	JoAnne Carner	1969–85	43
9	Sandra Haynie	1962–82	42
10	Babe Zaharias	1940–55	41

* Up to and including the 2008 season; all golfers from the USA except Sörenstam (Sweden)

TOP 10 **MOST CAREER WINS ON THE US PGA TOUR***

	GOLFER	YEARS	WINS
1	Sam Snead	1936–65	82
2	Jack Nicklaus	1962–86	73
3	Tiger Woods	1996–2008	65
4	Ben Hogan	1938–59	64
5	Arnold Palmer	1955–73	62
6	Byron Nelson	1935–51	52
7	Billy Casper	1956–75	51
8	Walter Hagen	1916–36	44
9	Cary Middlecoff	1945–61	40
10 =	Gene Sarazen	1922–41	39
=	Tom Watson	1974–98	39

* Up to and including 2008; all golfers from the USA

TOP 10 **MOST WOMEN'S MAJORS IN A CAREER***

	GOLFER	YEARS	A	B	C	D	E	F	G	TOTAL
1	Patty Berg	1937–58	–	–	1	–	–	7	7	15
2	Mickey Wright	1958–66	–	4	4	–	–	2	3	13
3 =	Babe Zaharias	1940–54	–	–	3	–	–	3	4	10
=	Louise Suggs	1946–59	–	1	1	–	–	4	4	10
=	Annika Sörenstam, Sweden	1995–2006	3	3	3	1	–	–	–	10
6	Betsy Rawls	1951–69	–	2	4	–	–	–	2	8
7 =	Juli Inkster	1984–2002	2	2	2	–	1	–	–	7
=	Karrie Webb, Australia	1999–2006	2	1	2	1	1	–	–	7
9 =	Kathy Whitworth	1965–75	–	3	–	–	–	2	1	6
=	Pat Bradley	1980–86	1	1	1	–	3	–	–	6
=	Patty Sheehan	1983–96	1	3	2	–	–	–	–	6
=	Betsy King	1987–97	3	1	2	–	–	–	–	6

* As recognized by the Ladies Professional Golf Association (LPGA) up to and including 2008; all from the USA unless otherwise stated
A Kraft Nabisco Championship (previously Nabisco Dinah Shore, Nabisco Championship) 1983–2008
B LPGA Championship 1955–2008
C US Women's Open 1946–2008
D Women's British Open 2001–08
E du Maurier Classic 1979–2000
F Titleholders Championship 1937–42, 1946–66, 1972
G Western Open 1930–67

Nick Faldo
After playing in 46 Ryder Cup matches, Nick Faldo eventually received the honour of captaining the European team in 2008.

Karrie Webb
Australia's Karrie Webb, the last back-to-back winner of the US Women's Open, in 2000 and 2001.

TOP 10 **MOST MATCHES IN THE RYDER CUP***

	GOLFER / COUNTRY	TEAM(S)	YEARS	MATCHES
1	Nick Faldo, England	GB & I/Europe	1977–97	46
2	Bernhard Langer, Germany	Europe	1981–2002	42
3	Neil Coles, England	GB/GB & I	1961–77	40
4 =	Billy Casper, USA	USA	1961–75	37
=	Seve Ballesteros, Spain	Europe	1979–95	37
6 =	Christy O'Connor Snr, Ireland	GB/GB & I	1955–73	36
=	Colin Montgomerie, Scotland	Europe	1991–2006	36
8	Tony Jacklin, England	GB/GB & I/E	1967–79	35
9	Lanny Wadkins, USA	USA	1977–93	34
10	Arnold Palmer, USA	USA	1961–73	32

* Up to and including 2008

Great Britain (GB): 1921 to 1971; Great Britain & Ireland (GB & I): 1973 to 1977; Europe (E): 1979 to 2008

Rugby

Daisuke Ohata
When he scored three tries against Georgia in May 2006, Daisuke Ohata became the most prolific try-scorer in international rugby union.

TOP 10 **TRY-SCORERS IN INTERNATIONAL RUGBY***

	PLAYER / COUNTRY	YEARS	TESTS	TRIES#
1	Daisuke Ohata Japan	1996–2008	61	71
2	David Campese Australia	1982–96	101	64
3	Rory Underwood England/Lions	1984–06	91 (6)	50 (1)
4	Doug Howlett New Zealand	2000–07	62	49
5 =	Christian Cullen New Zealand	1996–2003	58	46
=	Shane Williams Wales/Lions	2000–08	67 (1)	46 (0)
7	Jeff Wilson New Zealand	1993–2001	60	44
8	Joe Rokocoko New Zealand	2003–08	52	43
9	Gareth Thomas Wales/Lions	1995–2007	103 (3)	41 (1)
10	Chris Latham Australia	1998–2007	78	40

* As at 2 April 2009
# Figures in brackets indicate the number of appearances for the British and Irish Lions

TOP 10 **TRY-SCORERS IN THE ENGAGE SUPER LEAGUE, 2008**

	PLAYER	CLUB	TRIES
1	Adrian Gardner	St Helens	26
2	Scott Donald	Leeds Rhinos	21
3	Luke Dorn	Castleford Tigers	19
4 =	Pat Richards	Wigan Warriors	17
=	Semi Tadulala	Bradford Bulls	17
6 =	Clint Greenshields	Catalans Dragons	16
=	Chris Hicks	Warrington Wolves	16
=	Kirk Yeaman	Hull FC	16
9 =	Paul Sykes	Bradford Bulls	15
=	Brent Webb	Leeds Rhinos	15

Source: Engage Super League

Nick Faldo
After playing in 46 Ryder Cup matches, Nick Faldo eventually received the honour of captaining the European team in 2008.

TOP 10 **MOST WOMEN'S MAJORS IN A CAREER***

GOLFER	YEARS	A	B	C	D	E	F	G	TOTAL
(1) Patty Berg	1937–58	–	–	1	–	–	7	7	15
(2) Mickey Wright	1958–66	–	4	4	–	–	2	3	13
(3) =Babe Zaharias	1940–54	–	–	3	–	–	3	4	10
=Louise Suggs	1946–59	–	1	1	–	–	4	4	10
=Annika Sörenstam, Sweden	1995–2006	3	3	3	1	–	–	–	10
(6) Betsy Rawls	1951–69	–	2	4	–	–	–	2	8
(7) =Juli Inkster	1984–2002	2	2	2	–	1	–	–	7
=Karrie Webb, Australia	1999–2006	2	1	2	1	1	–	–	7
(9) =Kathy Whitworth	1965–75	–	3	–	–	–	2	1	6
=Pat Bradley	1980–86	1	1	1	–	3	–	–	6
=Patty Sheehan	1983–96	1	3	2	–	–	–	–	6
=Betsy King	1987–97	3	1	2	–	–	–	–	6

* As recognized by the Ladies Professional Golf Association (LPGA) up to and including 2008; all from the USA unless otherwise stated
A Kraft Nabisco Championship (previously Nabisco Dinah Shore, Nabisco Championship) 1983–2008
B LPGA Championship 1955–2008
C US Women's Open 1946–2008
D Women's British Open 2001–08
E du Maurier Classic 1979–2000
F Titleholders Championship 1937–42, 1946–66, 1972
G Western Open 1930–67

Karrie Webb
Australia's Karrie Webb, the last back-to-back winner of the US Women's Open, in 2000 and 2001.

TOP 10 **MOST MATCHES IN THE RYDER CUP***

GOLFER / COUNTRY	TEAM(S)	YEARS	MATCHES
(1) Nick Faldo, England	GB & I/Europe	1977–97	46
(2) Bernhard Langer, Germany	Europe	1981–2002	42
(3) Neil Coles, England	GB/GB & I	1961–77	40
(4) =Billy Casper, USA	USA	1961–75	37
=Seve Ballesteros, Spain	Europe	1979–95	37
(6) =Christy O'Connor Snr, Ireland	GB/GB & I	1955–73	36
=Colin Montgomerie, Scotland	Europe	1991–2006	36
(8) Tony Jacklin, England	GB/GB & I/E	1967–79	35
(9) Lanny Wadkins, USA	USA	1977–93	34
(10) Arnold Palmer, USA	USA	1961–73	32

* Up to and including 2008

Great Britain (GB): 1921 to 1971; Great Britain & Ireland (GB & I): 1973 to 1977; Europe (E): 1979 to 2008

Horse Sports

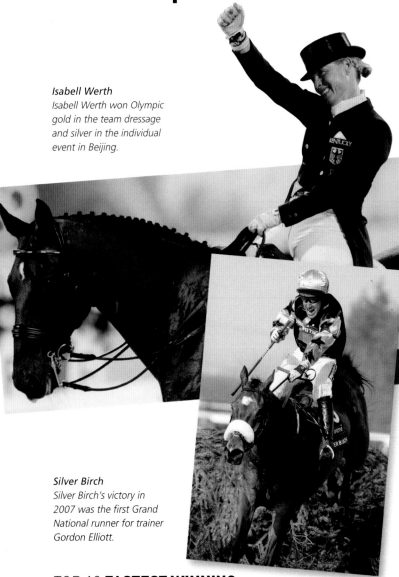

Isabell Werth
Isabell Werth won Olympic gold in the team dressage and silver in the individual event in Beijing.

Silver Birch
Silver Birch's victory in 2007 was the first Grand National runner for trainer Gordon Elliott.

TOP 10 **OLYMPIC EQUESTRIAN MEDALLISTS***

	RIDER / COUNTRY	YEARS	GOLD	SILVER	BRONZE	TOTAL
1	Reiner Klimke, West Germany	1964–88	7	0	2	9
2 =	Isabell Werth, Germany	1992–2008	5	3	0	8
=	Anky van Grunsven, Netherlands	1992–2008	3	5	0	8
4	Hans-Günther Winkler, West Germany	1956–76	5	1	1	7
5 =	Piero d'Inzeo, Italy	1956–72	0	2	4	6
=	Raimondo d'Inzeo, Italy	1956–72	1	2	3	6
=	Josef Neckermann, West Germany	1960–72	2	2	2	6
=	Michael Plumb, USA	1964–84	2	4	0	6
9 =	Earl Thomson, USA	1932–48	2	3	0	5
=	André Jousseaumé, France	1932–52	2	2	1	5
=	Henri Chammartin, Switzerland	1952–68	1	2	2	5
=	Gustav Fischer, Switzerland	1952–68	0	3	2	5
=	Liselott Linsenhoff, West Germany	1956–72	2	2	1	5
=	Christine Stückelberger, Switzerland	1976–88	1	3	1	5
=	Mark Todd, New Zealand	1984–2000	2	1	2	5

* Up to and including the 2008 Beijing Olympics

The Olympic equestrian events are divided into three separate disciplines: Dressage, Three-Day Eventing and Show Jumping. Both men and women compete together and medals are awarded separately for individual and team performances in each of the three disciplines.

TOP 10 **FASTEST WINNING TIMES OF THE AINTREE GRAND NATIONAL***

HORSE / YEAR / TIME (MINS:SECS)

10 Silver Birch
2007
9:13.6

9 Grittar
1982
9:12.6

8 Papillon
2000
9:09.7

7 Bindaree
2002
9:09.0

6 Party Politics
1992
9:06.3

* Up to and including 2008

The times of the substitute races held at Gatwick in the years 1916–18 are not included.

TOP 10 **JOCKEYS IN THE BREEDERS' CUP**

	JOCKEY	YEARS	WINS*
1	Jerry Bailey	1991–2005	15
2	Pat Day	1984–2001	12
3	Mike Smith	1992–2008	12
4	Chris McCarron	1985–2001	9
5	= Gary Stevens	1990–2000	8
	= Frankie Dettori	1994–2008	8
	= Garrett Gomez	2005–08	8
8	= Eddie Delahoussaye	1984–93	7
	= Laffit Pincay Jr.	1985–93	7
	= Jose Santos	1986–2002	7
	= Pat Valenzuela	1986–2003	7
	= Corey Nakatani	1996–2006	7
	= John Velazquez	1998–2006	7

* Up to and including 2008

Source: The Breeders' Cup

The 14 Breeders' Cup races in 2008 were worth $25.5 million in prize money, with the Breeders' Cup Classic offering $5 million.

Frankie Dettori takes the lead
Frankie Dettori rode the 2008 Breeders' Cup Classic winner and is the most successful European jockey in the Breeders' Cup.

TOP 10 **MOST FLAT RACING JOCKEYS TITLES IN THE UK***

			TITLES	
	JOCKEY	FIRST	LAST	TOTAL
1	Gordon Richards	1925	1953	26
2	George Fordham#	1855	1871	14
3	= Nat Flatman	1840	1852	13
	= Fred Archer	1874	1886	13
5	= Lester Piggott	1960	1982	11
	= Pat Eddery	1974	1996	11
7	Steve Donoghue#	1914	1923	10
8	= Morny Cannon	1891	1897	6
	= Kieren Fallon	1997	2003	6
10	= Doug Smith	1954	1959	5
	= Willie Carson	1972	1983	5

* Up to and including 2008
# Includes one shared title

5 Lord Gyllene
1997
9:05.8

4 Royal Athlete
1995
9:04.6

3 Red Rum
1973
9:01.9

2 Rough Quest
1996
9:00.8

1 Mr Frisk
1990
8:47.8

Motor Sport

TOP 10 **FASTEST WINNING SPEEDS OF THE INDIANAPOLIS 500***

	DRIVER	CAR	YEAR	SPEED KM/H	MPH
1	Arie Luyendyk, Netherlands	Lola-Chevrolet	1990	299.307	185.981
2	Rick Mears	Chevrolet-Lumina	1991	283.980	176.457
3	Bobby Rahal	March-Cosworth	1986	274.750	170.722
4	Juan Montoya, Colombia	G Force-Aurora	2000	269.730	167.607
5	Emerson Fittipaldi, Brazil	Penske-Chevrolet	1989	269.695	167.581
6	Helio Castroneves, Brazil	Dallara-Chevrolet	2002	267.954	166.499
7	Rick Mears	March-Cosworth	1984	263.308	163.612
8	Mark Donohue	McLaren-Offenhauser	1972	262.619	162.962
9	Al Unser	March-Cosworth	1987	260.995	162.175
10	Tom Sneva	March-Cosworth	1983	260.902	162.117

* Up to and including the 2008 race; all drivers from USA unless otherwise stated

TOP 10 **MOST NASCAR SPRINT CUP SERIES RACE WINS***

	DRIVER	WINS FIRST	LAST	TOTAL
1	Richard Petty	1960	1984	200
2	David Pearson	1961	1980	105
3 =	Bobby Allison	1966	1988	84
=	Darrell Waltrip	1975	1992	84
5	Cale Yarborough	1965	1985	83
6	Jeff Gordon#	1994	2007	81
7	Dale Earnhardt	1979	2000	76
8	Rusty Wallace	1986	2004	55
9	Lee Petty	1949	1961	54
10 =	Ned Jarrett	1955	1965	50
=	Junior Johnson	1955	1965	50

* Up to and including 2008
# Active in 2008

THE 10 **NEWEST GRANDS PRIX TO BE ADDED TO THE FORMULA ONE CALENDAR**

	RACE	FIRST HELD
1	Singapore GP*	28 Sep 2008
2	Turkish GP*	21 Aug 2005
3	Chinese GP*	26 Sep 2004
4	Bahrain GP*	4 Apr 2004
5	Malaysian GP*	17 Oct 1999
6	Luxembourg GP	28 Sep 1997
7	Pacific GP	17 Apr 1994
8	Hungarian GP*	10 Aug 1986
9	Australian GP*	3 Nov 1985
10	European GP*	25 Sep 1983

* Still part of Formula One schedule in 2009

The Luxembourg Grand Prix was discontinued in 1998 and the Pacific Grand Prix in 1995.

Below: Jeff Gordon
Jeff Gordon (No. 24) in action in his DuPont Chevrolet during the 2008 NASCAR Sprint Cup Series. He ended the season finishing seventh in the Series and amassing winnings of $4,650,649.

TOP 10 **MOST RACE WINS BY A DRIVER IN A FORMULA ONE CAREER***

	DRIVER / COUNTRY	YEARS	WINS
1	Michael Schumacher, Germany	1992–2006	91
2	Alain Prost, France	1981–93	51
3	Ayrton Senna, Brazil	1985–93	41
4	Nigel Mansell, UK	1985–94	31
5	Jackie Stewart, UK	1965–73	27
6	= Jim Clark, UK	1962–68	25
	= Niki Lauda, Austria	1974–85	25
8	Juan-Manuel Fangio, Argentina	1950–57	24
9	Nelson Piquet, Brazil	1980–91	23
10	Damon Hill, UK	1993–98	22

* Up to and including the 2008 season

TOP 10 **MOST FORMULA ONE GRAND PRIX RACE WINS BY A DRIVER IN A SEASON***

	DRIVER / COUNTRY	SEASON	WINS
1	Michael Schumacher, Germany	2004	13
2	Michael Schumacher	2002	11
3	= Nigel Mansell, UK	1992	9
	= Michael Schumacher	1995	9
	= Michael Schumacher	2000	9
	= Michael Schumacher	2001	9
7	= Ayrton Senna, Brazil	1988	8
	= Michael Schumacher	1994	8
	= Damon Hill, UK	1996	8
	= Mika Häkkinen, Finland	1998	8

* To the end of the 2008 season

Top: Singapore circuit
Spaniard Fernando Alonso won the first Formula
One Singapore Grand Prix in September 2008.

Above: Michael Schumacher
Michael Schumacher winning the 2006 European
GP, one of seven wins in his final season.

Rugby

Daisuke Ohata
When he scored three tries against Georgia in May 2006, Daisuke Ohata became the most prolific try-scorer in international rugby union.

TOP 10 **TRY-SCORERS IN INTERNATIONAL RUGBY***

	PLAYER / COUNTRY	YEARS	TESTS	TRIES#
1	Daisuke Ohata Japan	1996–2008	61	71
2	David Campese Australia	1982–96	101	64
3	Rory Underwood England/Lions	1984–06	91 (6)	50 (1)
4	Doug Howlett New Zealand	2000–07	62	49
5 =	Christian Cullen New Zealand	1996–2003	58	46
=	Shane Williams Wales/Lions	2000–08	67 (1)	46 (0)
7	Jeff Wilson New Zealand	1993–2001	60	44
8	Joe Rokocoko New Zealand	2003–08	52	43
9	Gareth Thomas Wales/Lions	1995–2007	103 (3)	41 (1)
10	Chris Latham Australia	1998–2007	78	40

* As at 2 April 2009
# Figures in brackets indicate the number of appearances for the British and Irish Lions

TOP 10 **TRY-SCORERS IN THE ENGAGE SUPER LEAGUE, 2008**

	PLAYER	CLUB	TRIES
1	Adrian Gardner	St Helens	26
2	Scott Donald	Leeds Rhinos	21
3	Luke Dorn	Castleford Tigers	19
4 =	Pat Richards	Wigan Warriors	17
=	Semi Tadulala	Bradford Bulls	17
6 =	Clint Greenshields	Catalans Dragons	16
=	Chris Hicks	Warrington Wolves	16
=	Kirk Yeaman	Hull FC	16
9 =	Paul Sykes	Bradford Bulls	15
=	Brent Webb	Leeds Rhinos	15

Source: Engage Super League

TOP 10 MOST WINS IN THE ENGAGE SUPER LEAGUE, 1996–2008

	TEAM	WINS
1	St Helens	254
2	Bradford Bulls	246
3	Leeds Rhinos	233
4	Wigan Warriors	230
5	Warrington Wolves	155
6	Hull FC	137
7	Castleford Tigers	118
8	London Broncos	116
9	Wakefield Trinity Wildcats	95
10	Huddersfield Giants/ Huddersfield-Sheffield Giants	86

The first season of Super League was in 1996 and was called the Stones Bitter Super League I. Twelve teams took part, and the first champions were St Helens, who beat Wigan Warriors by one point. Workington Town was the first team to be relegated from the Super League.

George Gregan
Australia's captain in the 2003 World Cup final defeat by England, George Gregan was born in Zambia, but played for Australia for 13 years.

TOP 10 MOST-CAPPED PLAYERS IN INTERNATIONAL RUGBY*

	PLAYER	COUNTRY	YEARS	TOTAL CAPS#
1	George Gregan	Australia	1994–2007	139
2	Jason Leonard	England/Lions	1990–2004	119 (5)
3	Fabien Pelous	France	1995–2007	118
4	Philippe Sella	France	1982–1995	111
5	Gareth Thomas	Wales/Lions	1995–2007	103 (3)
6	= Stephen Larkham	Australia	1996–2007	102
	= Percy Montgomery	South Africa	1997–2008	102
8	David Campese	Australia	1982–1996	101
9	Alessandro Troncon	Italy	1994–2007	100
10	Raphaël Ibanez	France	1996–2007	98

* As at 2 April 2009, among 'Big 10' nations (Australia, Argentina, England, France, Italy, Ireland, New Zealand, Scotland, South Africa and Wales)
# Figures in brackets indicate the number of appearances for the British and Irish Lions

TOP 10 BIGGEST WINS IN THE SIX NATIONS CHAMPIONSHIP*

	WINNER/LOSER	YEAR	VENUE	SCORE
1	England v Italy	2001	Twickenham	80–23
2	Ireland v Italy	2000	Lansdowne Road	60–13
3	England v Italy	2000	Rome	59–12
4	France v Italy	2005	Rome	56–13
5	Ireland v Wales	2002	Lansdowne Road	54–10
6	France v Italy	2003	Rome	53–27
7	Ireland v Italy	2007	Rome	51–24
8	= France v Italy	2008	Rome	50–8
	= England v Italy	2004	Rome	50–9
	= England v Wales	2002	Twickenham	50–10
	= England v Ireland	2000	Twickenham	50–18

* Since 2000, when Italy joined the competition, up to and including the 2009 Championship; based on the score of the winning team

Lawn Tennis

TOP 10 MOST WINS IN THE MASTERS SERIES*

PLAYER / COUNTRY	YEARS	WINS
(1) Andre Agassi, USA	1990–2004	17
(2) Roger Federer, Switzerland	2002–07	14
(3) Rafael Nadal, Spain	2005–08	12
(4) Pete Sampras, USA	1992–2000	11
(5) Thomas Muster, Austria	1990–97	8
(6) Michael Chang, USA	1990–97	7
(7) = Boris Becker, Germany	1990–96	5
= Jim Courier, USA	1991–93	5
= Gustavo Kuerten, Brazil	1999–2001	5
= Marcelo Rios, Chile	1997–99	5
= Marat Safin, Russia	2000–04	5

* As at the end of the 2008 Masters Series

The Association of Tennis Professionals (ATP) Masters Series was launched in 1990, its nine (eight in 2009) tournaments regarded as the most prestigious after the four Grand Slam events. In 2009 the series became known as the Masters 1000, because the winner of each tournament will receive 1000 ranking points.

TOP 10 MOST WEEKS SPENT AT THE TOP OF THE ATP RANKINGS*

PLAYER / COUNTRY	FIRST YEAR AT NO. 1	LAST YEAR AT NO. 1	WEEKS
(1) Pete Sampras, USA	1993	1999	286
(2) Ivan Lendl, Czechoslovakia	1983	1990	270
(3) Jimmy Connors, USA	1974	1983	268
(4) Roger Federer, Switzerland	2004	2008	237
(5) John McEnroe, USA	1980	1985	170
(6) Björn Borg, Sweden	1977	1981	109
(7) Andre Agassi, USA	1995	2003	101
(8) Lleyton Hewitt, Australia	2001	2003	80
(9) Stefan Edberg, Sweden	1990	1992	72
(10) Jim Courier, USA	1992	1993	58

* As at 1 January 2009

Source: ATP (Association of Tennis Professionals)

Federer's total were consecutive weeks and is the record for the most consecutive weeks at No. 1, beating the previous 160 of Jimmy Connors.

Mallorcan master
Rafael Nadal is one of two players from Mallorca to top the ATP rankings – Carlos Moya is the other.

TOP 10 **MOST CAREER TITLES (WOMEN)***

PLAYER / COUNTRY	YEARS	TITLES
(1) Martina Navratilova, Czechoslovakia/USA -	1974–94	167
(2) Chris Evert, USA	1971–88	154
(3) Steffi Graf, Germany	1986–99	107
(4) Margaret Court (née Smith), Australia	1968–76	92
(5) Evonne Cawley (née Goolagong), Australia	1970–80	68
(6) Billie Jean King, USA	1968–83	67
(7) = Lindsay Davenport, USA	1993–2008	55
= Virginia Wade, UK	1968–78	55
(9) Monica Seles, Yugoslavia/USA	1989–2002	53
(10) Martina Hingis, Switzerland	1996–2007	43

* In the Open era 1968–2008 as recognized by the WTA (women);
as at 1 January 2009

TOP 10 **MOST CAREER TITLES (MEN)***

PLAYER / COUNTRY	YEARS	TITLES
(1) Jimmy Connors, USA	1972–89	109
(2) Ivan Lendl, Czechoslovakia/USA	1980–93	94
(3) John McEnroe, USA	1978–91	77
(4) Pete Sampras, USA	1990–2002	64
(5) Björn Borg, Sweden	1974–81	63
(6) Guillermo Vilas, Argentina	1973–83	62
(7) Andre Agassi, USA	1987–2005	60
(8) = Ilie Nastase, Romania	1969–78	57
= Roger Federer, Switzerland	2001–08	57
(10) Boris Becker, Germany	1985–96	49

* In the Open era 1968-2008 as recognized by the ATP (men);
as at 1 January 2009

TOP 10 **MOST WEEKS SPENT AT THE TOP OF THE WTA RANKINGS**

PLAYER / COUNTRY	YEARS AT NO. 1 FIRST	LAST	WEEKS
(1) Steffi Graf, Germany	1987	1997	377
(2) Martina Navratilova, Czechoslovakia/USA	1978	1987	331
(3) Chris Evert, USA	1975	1985	260
(4) Martina Hingis, Switzerland	1997	2001	209
(5) Monica Seles, Yugoslavia/USA	1991	1996	178
(6) Justine Henin, Belgium	2003	2008	117
(7) Lindsay Davenport, USA	1998	2006	98
(8) Serena Williams, USA	2002	2008	61
(9) Amélie Mauresmo, France	2004	2006	39
(10) Tracy Austin, USA	1980 (Apr)	1980 (Nov)	22

* As at 1 January 2009

Source: WTA (Women's Tennis Association)

The most consecutive weeks at No. 1 is 186 by Steffi Graf between August 1987 and March 1991.

Justine Henin
Justine Henin first claimed the No. 1 spot in October 2003, displacing her fellow Belgian Kim Clijsters.

Titanic Victory

Swiss-born Richard Norris Williams (1891–1968) is the only survivor of the *Titanic* disaster to win an Olympic gold medal, as part of the US mixed doubles in Paris in 1924. Williams also won five US titles and one Wimbledon title.

Water Sports

TOP 10 **OLDEST CURRENT SWIMMING WORLD RECORDS***

	EVENT	SWIMMER / COUNTRY	TIME MINS:SECS	DATE SET
1	Women's 100 metres Butterfly	Inge de Bruijn, Netherlands	56.61	17 Sep 2000
2	Men's 1500 metres Freestyle	Grant Hackett, Australia	14:34.56	29 Jul 2001
3	Men's 400 metres Freestyle	Ian Thorpe, Australia	3:40.08	30 Jul 2002
4	Men's 50 metres Breaststroke	Oleg Lisogor, Ukraine	27.18	2 Aug 2002
5	Men's 50 metres Backstroke	Thomas Rupprath, Germany	24.80	27 Jul 2003
6	Men's 50 metres Butterfly	Roland Schoeman, South Africa	22.96	25 Jul 2005
7	Men's 800 metres Freestyle	Grant Hackett, Australia	7:38.65	27 Jul 2005
8	Men's 100 metres Butterfly	Ian Crocker, USA	50.40	30 Jul 2005
9	Women's 50 metres Breaststroke	Jade Edmistone, Australia	30.31	30 Jan 2006
10	Women's 100 metres Breaststroke	Leisel Jones, Australia	1:05.09	20 Mar 2006

* Long course swimming, as at 1 January 2009

TOP 10 **MEDAL-WINNING SWIMMING COUNTRIES AT THE COMMONWEALTH GAMES***

	COUNTRY	GOLD	SILVER	BRONZE	TOTAL
1	Australia	225	151	132	508
2	Canada	94	113	105	312
3	England	77	101	108	286
4	New Zealand	10	24	29	63
5	South Africa	14	23	15	52
6	Scotland	13	17	18	48
7	Wales	3	6	7	16
8	Jamaica	0	1	2	3
9	Malaysia	0	1	1	2
10 =	British Guiana	0	1	0	1
=	Papua New Guinea	1	0	0	1
=	Zimbabwe	1	0	0	1

* 1930–2006

Phelps' Records

Seven of Michael Phelps' record eight gold medals at the 2008 Beijing Olympics were set in new world record times. The eighth, the 100 metres butterfly, established a new Olympic record.

Swimming to victory
The United States is the leading nation in Olympic swimming events with 489 medals – 321 more than second-placed Australia.

TOP 10 **MEDAL-WINNING NATIONS IN AQUATIC EVENTS*** AT THE 2008 BEIJING OLYMPICS

	COUNTRY	GOLD	MEDALS SILVER	BRONZE	TOTAL
1	USA	12	11	10	33
2	Australia	7	7	9	23
3	China	8	4	6	18
4	Russia	3	4	4	11
5	=France	1	2	3	6
	=Japan	2	0	4	6
	=UK	2	2	2	6
8	Germany	2	1	2	5
9	=Hungary	1	3	0	4
	=Zimbabwe	1	3	0	4

* Swimming, synchronized swimming, diving and water polo

All but two of the USA's 33 medals were won in swimming events. The other two were both silver medals, and both in the water polo competition. Hungary beat the US 14–10 in the men's final and Netherlands won 9–8 in the women's final.

Alinghi
When Alinghi won the America's Cup for Switzerland in 2003, it was the first time a landlocked country had won the trophy.

THE 10 **LATEST WINNERS OF THE AMERICA'S CUP**

YEAR	VENUE	WINNER / COUNTRY	SKIPPER(S)
2007	Valencia, Spain	**Alinghi**, Switzerland	Brad Butterworth
2003	Auckland, New Zealand	**Alinghi**, Switzerland	Russell Coutts
2000	Auckland, New Zealand	**Team New Zealand**, New Zealand	Russell Coutts/ Dan Barker
1995	San Diego, USA	**Black Magic**, New Zealand	Russell Coutts
1992	San Diego, USA	**America3**, USA	Bill Koch/Buddy Melges
1988	San Diego, USA	**Stars & Stripes**, USA	Dennis Conner
1987	Fremantle, Australia	**Stars & Stripes**, USA	Dennis Conner
1983	Newport, USA	**Australia II**, Australia	John Bertrand
1980	Newport, USA	**Freedom**, USA	Dennis Conner
1977	Newport, USA	**Courageous**, USA	Ted Turner

There is uncertainty as to when the next America's Cup will be held. A court case in July 2008 ruled that it could take place sometime in 2009, but legal disputes have continued with no indication as to when they would be resolved.

Winter Sports

Canadian gold
Hayley Wickenheiser of Canada challenges Nanna Jansson of Sweden for the puck at the 2006 Turin Olympic Winter Games.

TOP 10 ICE-HOCKEY COUNTRIES AT THE OLYMPIC GAMES*

	COUNTRY	MEDALS: GOLD	SILVER	BRONZE	TOTAL
1	Canada	9	5	2	16
2	USA	3	8	2	13
3	Sweden	2	3	5	10
4	USSR#	7	1	1	9
5	Czechoslovakia†	0	4	4	8
6	Finland	0	2	3	5
7	= Czech Republic†	1	0	1	2
	= Great Britain	1	0	1	2
	= Russia#	0	1	1	2
	= Switzerland	0	0	2	2

* Up to and including the 2006 Turin Olympics
# Competed as the USSR 1956–88; Russia 1994–2006
† Competed as Czechoslovakia 1920–92; Czech Republic 1996–2006

Ice hockey was first contested at the Summer Olympics in 1920 and has featured at the Winter Olympics since 1924 for men and since 1998 for women.

TOP 10 FIS NORDIC COMBINED WORLD CUP TITLES*

	SKIER / COUNTRY	YEARS	TITLES
1	Hannu Manninen, Finland	2004–07	4
2	= Kenji Ogiwara, Japan	1993–95	3
	= Ronny Ackermann, Germany	2002–03, 2008	3
4	= Klaus Sulzenbacher, Austria	1988, 1990	2
	= Samppa Lajunen, Finland	1997, 2000	2
	= Bjarte Engen Vik, Norway	1998–99	2
7	= Tom Sandberg, Norway	1984	1
	= Geir Andersen, Norway	1985	1
	= Hermann Weinbuch, West Germany	1986	1
	= Torbjørn Løkken, Norway	1987	1
	= Trond-Arne Bredesen, Norway	1989	1
	= Fred Børre Lundberg, Norway	1991	1
	= Fabrice Guy, France	1992	1
	= Knut Tore Apeland, Norway	1996	1
	= Felix Gottwald, Austria	2001	1

* As at the end of the 2008–09 season

The FIS Nordic Combined World Cup was first held in the 1983–84 season, when it was won by Tom Sandberg of Norway.

TOP 10 MEDAL-WINNING COUNTRIES AT THE WINTER OLYMPICS*

	COUNTRY	MEDALS GOLD	SILVER	BRONZE	TOTAL
1	Norway	98	98	84	280
2	USA	78	80	58	216
3	USSR#	78	57	59	194
4	Austria	51	64	70	185
5	Germany†	60	59	41	160
6	Finland	41	57	52	150
7	Canada	38	38	43	119
8	Sweden	43	31	44	118
9	Switzerland	37	37	43	117
10	East Germany	39	36	35	110

* Up to and including the 2006 Turin Games, including medals won at figure skating and ice hockey included in the Summer Olympics prior to the inauguration of the Winter Games in 1924
# 1956–88
† 1928–32, 1952 and 1992–2006

TOP 10 MOST OVERALL ALPINE SKIING WORLD CUP TITLES (WOMEN)

	SKIER / COUNTRY	YEARS	TITLES
1	Annemarie Moser-Pröll, Austria	1971–75, 1979	6
2	= Vreni Schneider, Switzerland	1989, 1994–95	3
	= Petra Kronberger, Austria	1990–92	3
	= Janica Kostelic, Croatia	2001, 2003, 2006	3
5	= Nancy Greene, Canada	1967–68	2
	= Hanni Wenzel, Liechtenstein	1978, 1980	2
	= Erika Hess, Switzerland	1982, 1984	2
	= Michela Figini, Switzerland	1985, 1988	2
	= Maria Walliser, Switzerland	1986–87	2
	= Katja Seizinger, Germany	1996, 1998	2
	= Anja Pärson, Sweden	2004–05	2
	= Lindsey Vonn, USA	2008–09	2

* As at the end of the 2008–09 season

TOP 10 MOST OVERALL ALPINE SKIING WORLD CUP TITLES (MEN)

	SKIER / COUNTRY	YEARS	TITLES
1	Marc Girardelli, Luxembourg	1985–86, 1989, 1991, 1993	5
2	= Gustav Thöni, Italy	1971–73, 1975	4
	= Pirmin Zurbriggen, Switzerland	1984, 1987–88, 1990	4
	= Hermann Maier, Austria	1998, 2000–01, 2004	4
5	= Ingemar Stenmark, Sweden	1976–78	3
	= Phil Mahre, USA	1981–83	3
7	= Jean-Claude Killy, France	1967–68	2
	= Karl Schranz, Austria	1969–70	2
	= Lasse Kjus, Norway	1996, 1999	2
	= Stephan Eberharter, Austria	2002–03	2
	= Bode Miller, USA	2006, 2008	2
	= Aksel Lund Svindal, Norway	2007–09	2

* As at the end of the 2008–09 season

Alpine racer
In addition to his World Cup titles, Austrian champion Hermann Maier has won Olympic golds in the Super G and Giant slalom events and three World Championship golds.

Extreme Sports

TOP 10 **GOLD MEDALLISTS AT THE SUMMER X GAMES**

	ATHLETE* / COUNTRY	SPORT	YEARS	GOLDS
1	Dave Mirra, USA	BMX	1996–2005	13
2	Tony Hawk, USA	Skateboarding	1995–2003	9
3 =	Andy Macdonald, USA	Skateboarding	1996–2002	8
=	Travis Pastrana, USA	Moto X/Rally car racing	1999–2008	8
5	Fabiola da Silva*, Brazil	In-line skating	1996–2007	7
6	Bucky Lasek, USA	Skateboarding	1999–2006	6
7 =	Biker Sherlock, USA	Street luge	1996–98	5
=	Bob Burnquist, Brazil	Skateboarding	2001–08	5
9 =	Jamie Bestwick, England	BMX	2000–07	4
=	Ryan Nyquist, USA	BMX	2000–03	4
=	Pierre-Luc Gagnon, Canada	Skateboarding	2002-08	4
=	Dallas Friday*, USA	Water sports	2001–05	4
=	Danny Harf, USA	Water sports	2001–05	4
=	Elissa Steamer*, USA	Skateboarding	2004-08	4

* Female competitors; all others male

The first ESPN Extreme Games (now X Games) for 'alternative' sports were held in June–July 1995. The Games are held every year and since 1997 there has also been an annual Winter X Games. The current Summer X sports are: Freestyle BMX, MotoX (stunt motorcycling), Skateboarding and Rallying. Andy Macdonald holds the record with 15 X Games medals.

Pastrama (left)
All-round performer Travis Pastrana was also the 2000 AMA 125 cc National Motocross champion.

Pudzianowski (below)
Shortly after winning his record fifth Strongest Man title in 2008, Mariusz Pudzianowski announced his retirement.

THE 10 **LATEST WINNERS OF THE WORLD'S STRONGEST MAN CONTEST**

YEAR	STRONGMAN / COUNTRY
2008	Mariusz Pudzianowski, Poland
2007	Mariusz Pudzianowski, Poland
2006	Phil Pfister, USA
2005	Mariusz Pudzianowski, Poland
2004	Vasyl Virastyuk, Ukraine
2003	Mariusz Pudzianowski, Poland
2002	Mariusz Pudzianowski, Poland
2001	Svend Karlsen, Norway
2000	Janne Virtanen, Finland
1999	Jouko Ahola, Finland

The World's Strongest Man title has been contested since 1977. After the 2008 contest, staged in Charleston, West Virginia, USA, five times winner Mariusz Pudzianowski announced his retirement.

Chivas vs. Ghurkas
Chivas Regal (in yellow), four-times winners of the World Championship, in
action against the Ghurkas in the 26th annual competition – which they won.

TOP 10 **MOST ELEPHANT POLO WORLD TITLES**

	TEAM / COUNTRY	FIRST	WINS LAST	TOTAL
1	Tiger Tops Tuskers, Nepal	1983	2003	8
2	National Parks, Nepal	1986	1999	6
3	Chivas Regal, Scotland	2001	2005	4
4	=James Manclark Team, Scotland	1982	1982	1
	=Oberoi, India	1989	1989	1
	=Grindlays Maharajahs, Nepal	1990	1990	1
	=J&B Rare, International Team	1993	1993	1
	=International Distillers, Philippines	1995	1995	1
	=Tiger Mountain, India	1997	1997	1
	=Angus Estates, Scotland	2006	2006	1
	=Chopard, Hong Kong/China	2007	2007	1
	=Air Tusker, England	2008	2008	1

The first Elephant Polo World Championship was in 1982. The
Championship is now held at Meghauly near the Chitwan National
Park in Nepal each year.

TOP 10 **FASTEST WINNING TIMES FOR THE HAWAII IRONMAN**

	WINNER / COUNTRY	YEAR	TIME HRS:MINS:SECS
1	Luc Van Lierde, Belgium	1996	8:04:08
2	Mark Allen, USA	1993	8:07:45
3	Mark Allen	1992	8:09:08
4	Mark Allen	1989	8:09:15
5	Norman Stadler, Germany	2006	8:11:56
6	Faris Al-Sultan, Germany	2005	8:14:17
7	Chris McCormack, Australia	2007	8:15:34
8	Luc Van Lierde	1999	8:17:17
9	Chris Alexander, Australia	2008	8:17:45
10	Mark Allen	1991	8:18:32

Considered one of the most gruelling of all sporting contests,
competitors engage in a 3.86 km (2.4-mile) swim, a 180-km
(112-mile) cycle race, and full marathon (42.195 km/26 miles
385 yards). The first Hawaii Ironman was held at Waikiki Beach in
1978, but since 1981 the event's home has been at Kailua-Kona.

Leisure Pursuits

Interactive
Wii Music designer Shigeru Miyamoto demonstrates his creation. Over 50 million Nintendo Wii consoles have been sold.

TOP 10 **COUNTRIES SPENDING THE MOST ON VIDEO GAMES**

COUNTRY / SPEND PER CAPITA, 2008 (£)

1 UK	**2** Australia	**3** France	**4** Sweden	**5** USA
33.80	30.80	25.40	21.70	21.00

6 Netherlands	**7** Spain	**8** Canada	**9** Belgium	**10** Germany
17.20	15.50	15.30	13.30	9.30

World average 2.00 Source: Euromonitor International

TOP 10 **LEISURE ACTIVITIES* IN ENGLAND**

ACTIVITY*	%*
1 Watching television	84
2 Spending time with friends/family	75
3 Listening to music	70
4 Eating out at restaurants	59
5 Sport/exercise	58
6 = Days out	56
= Reading	56
8 Shopping	53
9 Going to pubs/bars/clubs	50
10 Internet/emailing	49

* Performed in free time, 2005–06

Source: Department of Culture, Media and Sport, *Taking Part: The National Survey of Culture, Leisure and Sport*

TOP 10 **COUNTRIES SPENDING THE MOST ON TOYS AND GAMES**

COUNTRY / SPEND PER CAPITA, 2008 (£)

UK	Australia	USA	France	Netherlands	Sweden
93.30	89.70	76.40	74.30	66.00	60.90

Belgium	Canada	Spain	Italy
57.30	53.40	47.10	43.20

World average 7.70

Source: Euromonitor International

TOP 10 MEDALS AT THE FLYING DISC WORLD CHAMPIONSHIPS*

	THROWER / COUNTRY	MALE/FEMALE	GOLD	SILVER	BRONZE	TOTAL

1	Harvey Brandt, USA	M	1	5	1	7

2	=Amy Bekken, USA	F	3	0	1	4
	=Christian Sandström, Sweden	M	3	0	1	4
	=Sune Wentzel, Norway	M	3	1	0	4
5	Conrad Damon, USA	M	0	2	1	3
6	=Tomas Burvall, Sweden	M	1	0	1	2
	=Amanda Carreiro, USA	F	2	0	0	2
	=Jennifer Griffin, USA	F	1	1	0	2
	=Mary Jorgenson, USA	F	0	2	0	2
	=Yukari Komatsu, Japan	F	1	1	0	2
	=Rick LeBeau, USA	M	0	1	1	2
	=Regina Olnils, Sweden	F	1	1	0	2
	=Snapper Pierson, USA	M	2	0	0	2
	=Judy Robbins, USA	F	1	0	1	2
	=Yumiko Tauchi, Japan	F	0	1	1	2

* In the overall competition, men and women, up to and including 2008

TOP 10 ACTIVE SPORT ACTIVITIES* IN THE UK

	ACTIVITY	%*
1	Swimming or diving (indoors)	14.5
2	Health, fitness, gym or conditioning activities	13.8
3	Cycling (health, recreation, training, competition)	10.0
4	Snooker, pool, billiards (excluding bar billiards)	7.7
5	Football (including 5-a-side) (outdoors)	7.6
6	Keep fit, aerobics, dance exercise	6.8
7	Jogging, cross-country, road running	6.2
8	Golf, pitch and putt, putting	5.5
9	Tenpin bowling	3.7
10	Swimming or diving (outdoors)	3.4

* Participated during previous four weeks 2006–07

Source: Department of Culture, Media and Sport, *Taking Part: The National Survey of Culture, Leisure and Sport*

THE 10 LATEST WINNERS OF THE BBC SPORTS PERSONALITY OF THE YEAR AWARD

YEAR	WINNER	SPORT
2008	Chris Hoy	Cycling
2007	Joe Calzaghe	Boxing
2006	Zara Phillips	Eventing
2005	Andrew Flintoff	Cricket
2004	Kelly Holmes	Athletics
2003	Jonny Wilkinson	Rugby Union
2002	Paula Radcliffe	Athletics
2001	David Beckham	Soccer
2000	Steve Redgrave	Rowing
1999	Lennox Lewis	Boxing

Source: BBC

Further Information

THE UNIVERSE & THE EARTH

Astronautics
www.astronautix.com
Spaceflight news and reference

Caves
www.caverbob.com
Lists of long and deep caves

Disasters
www.emdat.be
Emergency Events Database covering major
disasters since 1900

Islands
islands.unep.ch
Information on the world's islands

Mountains
peaklist.org
Lists of the world's tallest mountains

NASA
www.nasa.gov
The main website for the US space
programme

Oceans
www.oceansatlas.org
The UN's resource on oceanographic issues

Planets
www.nineplanets.org
A multimedia tour of the Solar System

Rivers
www.rev.net/~aloe/river
The River Systems of the World website

Space exploration
www.spacefacts.de
Manned spaceflight data

LIFE ON EARTH

Animals
animaldiversity.ummz.umich.edu
A wealth of animal data

Birds
www.bsc-eoc.org/avibase
A database on the world's birds

Conservation
iucn.org
The leading nature conservation site

Endangered
www.cites.org
Lists of endangered species of flora and fauna

Environment
www.unep.ch
Links to the UN's Earthwatch and other
programmes

Fish
www.fishbase.org
Global information on fishes

Food and Agriculture Organization
www.fao.org
Statistics from the UN's FAO website

Forests
www.fao.org/forestry
FAO's forestry website

Insects
ufbir.ifas.ufl.edu
The University of Florida Book of Insect Records

Sharks
www.flmnh.ufl.edu/fish/sharks
The Florida Museum of Natural History's shark
data files

THE HUMAN WORLD

Crime, UK
www.homeoffice.gov.uk
Home Office crime and prison population figures

Leaders
www.terra.es/personal2/monolith/00index.htm
Facts about world leaders since 1945

Military
www.globalfirepower.com
World military statistics and rankings

Nobel Prizes
nobelprize.org
The official website of the Nobel Foundation

Population, UK
www.statistics.gov.uk/hub/population
UK population figures

Religions
www.worldchristiandatabase.org
World religion data

Royalty
www.royal.gov.uk
The official site of the British Monarchy, with
histories

Rulers
rulers.org
A database of the world's rulers and political
leaders

US Presidents
www.whitehouse.gov/history/presidents
Biographies, facts and figures from the White
House

World Health Organization
www.who.int/en
World health information and advice

TOWN & COUNTRY

Bridges and tunnels
en.structurae.de
Facts and figures on the world's buildings,
tunnels and other structures

Buildings
www.emporis.com/en
The Emporis database of high-rise and other
buildings

Countries
www.theodora.com/wfb
Country data, rankings, etc.

Country and city populations
www.citypopulation.de
A searchable guide to the world's countries
and major cities

Country data
www.cia.gov/library/publications/the-world-
factbook
The CIA's acclaimed *World Factbook*

Country populations
www.un.org/esa/population/unpop
The UN's worldwide data on population issues

Development
www.worldbank.org
Development and other statistics from around
the world

Population
www.census.gov/ipc/www
International population statistics

Skyscrapers
skyscraperpage.com
Data and images of the world's skyscrapers

Tunnels
lotsberg.net
A database of the longest rail, road and canal
tunnels

CULTURE & LEARNING

The Art Newspaper
www.theartnewspaper.com
News and views on the art world

The British Library
www.bl.uk
Catalogues and exhibitions in the national
library

Education
www.dfes.gov.uk/statistics
Official statistics relating to education in the UK

Languages of the world
www.ethnologue.com
Online reference work on the world's 6,912
living languages

The Man Booker Prize
www.themanbookerprize.com
Britain's most prestigious literary prize

Museums and galleries
www.culture24.org.uk
A guide to exhibitions and events at the UK

Newspapers
www.wan-press.org
The World Association of Newspapers'
website

Oxford English Dictionary
www.oed.com
The online version of the *OED*, accessible via
most public libraries

Translations
databases.unesco.org/xtrans/stat/xTransStat.html
UNESCO's lists of the most translated books
and authors

UNESCO
www.unesco.org
Comparative international statistics on
education and culture

MUSIC

All Music Guide
www.allmusic.com
A comprehensive guide to all genres of music

Billboard
www.billboard.com
US music news and charts data

BRIT Awards
www.brits.co.uk
The official website for the popular music awards

The British Phonographic Industry Ltd
www.bpi.co.uk
Searchable database of gold discs and other certified awards

Grammy Awards
www.naras.org
The official site for the famous US music awards

Launch
new.uk.music.yahoo.com
UK music charts and news from Yahoo

MTV
www.mtv.co.uk
The online site for the MTV UK music channel

New Musical Express
www.nme.com
The online version of the popular music magazine

Official UK Charts
www.theofficialcharts.com
Weekly and historical music charts

VH1
www.vh1.com
Online UK music news

ENTERTAINMENT

Academy Awards
www.oscars.org
The official 'Oscars' website

BAFTAs
www.bafta.org
The home of the BAFTA Awards

BBC
www.bbc.co.uk
Gateway to BBC TV and radio, with a powerful Internet search engine

Film Distributors' Association
www.launchingfilms.com
Trade site for UK film releases and statistics

Golden Globe Awards
www.hfpa.org
Hollywood Foreign Press Association's Golden Globes site

Internet Movie Database
www.imdb.com
The best of the publicly accessible film websites; IMDbPro is available to subscribers

London Theatre Guide
www.londontheatre.co.uk
A comprehensive guide to West End theatre productions

Screen Daily
www.screendaily.com
Daily news from the film world at the website of UK weekly *Screen International*

Variety
www.variety.com
Extensive entertainment information (extra features available to subscribers)

Yahoo! Movies
uk.movies.yahoo.com
Charts plus features, trailers and links to the latest UK film releases

THE COMMERCIAL WORLD

The Economist
www.economist.com
Global economic and political news

Energy
www.bp.com
Online access to the *BP Statistical Review of World Energy*

Internet
www.internetworldstats.com
Internet World Stats

Organisation for Economic Co-operation and Development
www.oecd.org
World economic and social statistics

Post
www.upu.int
World post statistics from the Universal Postal Union

Rich lists
www.forbes.com
Forbes magazine's celebrated lists of the world's wealthiest people

Telecommunications
www.itu.int
Worldwide telecommunications statistics

UK Tourist attractions
www.alva.org.uk
Information and visitor statistics on the UK's top tourist attractions

The World Bank
www.worldbank.org
World development, trade and labour statistics

World Tourism Organization
www.world-tourism.org
The world's principal travel and tourism organization

ON THE MOVE

Air disasters
www.airdisaster.com
Reports on aviation disasters

Airports
www.airports.org
Airports Council International statistics on the world's airports

Air safety
aviation-safety.net
Data on air safety and accidents

Air speed records
www.fai.org/records
The website of the official air speed record governing body

Aviation pioneers
aviation.calderara.com
Links to data on early fliers

British waterways
www.britishwaterways.co.uk
British Waterways' information about canals and rivers

Car manufacture
www.oica.net
The International Organization of Motor Vehicle Manufacturers' website

Rail
www.uic.org
World rail statistics

Railways
www.railwaygazette.com
The world's railway business in depth from *Railway Gazette International*

Shipwrecks
www.shipwreckregistry.com
A huge database of the world's wrecked and lost ships

SPORT & LEISURE

Athletics
www.iaaf.org
The world governing body of athletics

Cricket
www.cricinfo.com
Cricinfo, launched in 1993, since merged with the online version of *Wisden*

Cycling
www.uci.ch
The Union Cycliste Internationale, the competitive cycling governing body

FIFA
www.fifa.com
The official website of FIFA, the world governing body of soccer

Football
www.football-league.co.uk
The official site of the Football League

Formula One
www.formula1.com
The official F1 website

Olympics
www.olympic.org/uk
The official Olympics website

Rugby
www.itsrugby.co.uk
Comprehensive rugby site

Skiing
www.fis-ski.com
Fédèration Internationale de Ski, the world governing body of skiing and snowboarding

Tennis
www.lta.org.uk
The official site of the British Lawn Tennis Association

Index

Acknowledgements

Special research: Ian Morrison (sport);
Dafydd Rees (music)

Academy of Motion Picture Arts and Sciences
– Oscar statuette is the registered trademark
and copyrighted property of the Academy of
Motion Picture Arts and Sciences
African Elephant Status Report 2007 (IUCN)
Airports Council International
Alexa
American Association of Port Authorities
American Film Institute
Amnesty International
Artnet
The Art Newspaper
Association of Leading Visitor Attractions
Association of Tennis Professionals
Audit Bureau of Circulations Ltd
BBC
Roland Bert
Billboard
Peter Bond
Box Office Mojo
BP Statistical Review of World Energy 2008
Richard Braddish
Breeders' Cup
Thomas Brinkhoff
The BRIT Awards
British Film Institute
British Library
British National Corpus
British Phonographic Industry
British Video Association
British Waterways
Cameron Mackintosh Ltd
Carbon Dioxide Information Analysis Center
Central Intelligence Agency, *World Factbook
2008*
Channel Swimming Association
Checkout
Christie's
Classic FM
Classical Music Magazine
Commonwealth War Graves Commission
Computer Industry Almanac
ComScore.com
Corruption Perceptions Index (Transparency
International)
Crime in England and Wales 2007/08
Death Penalty Information Center
*The Deloitte Annual Review of Football
Finance*
Department for Culture, Media and Sport
Department for Environment, Food and Rural
Affairs
Department for Transport
Department of Trade and Industry
EarthTrends
The Economist
Philip Eden
EM-DAT, CRED, University of Louvain
Emporis
Environmental Performance Index
Environmental Technology Center
Ethnologue
Euromonitor International
FA Premier League
Federal Bureau of Investigation

Fédération Internationale de Football
Association
Fédération Internationale de Motorcyclisme
Fédération Internationale de Ski
Film Database
Financial Times
Food and Agriculture Organization of the
United Nations
Christopher Forbes
Forbes magazine
Forestry Commission
Fortune
General Register Office for Scotland
Global Education Digest 2008 (UNESCO)
Global Forest Resources Assessment 2005
(FAO)
Global Powers of Retailing 2009 (Deloitte)
Global World Energy Council
Russell E. Gough
Robert Grant
Bob Gulden
Home Office
Human Development Report (United Nations)
Imperial War Museum
Index Translationum 1979–2008 (UNESCO)
Indianapolis Motor Speedway
International Air Transport Association
International Association of Athletics
Federations
International Atomic Energy Agency
International Commission on Large Dams
International Federation of Audit Bureaux of
Circulations
International Hydrographic Organization
The International Institute for Strategic
Studies, *The Military Balance 2009*
International Labour Organization
International Obesity Task Force
International Olympic Committee
International Organization of Motor Vehicle
Manufacturers
International Shark Attack File, Florida
Museum of Natural History
International Telecommunication Union
International Union for Conservation of
Nature and Natural Resources
Internet Movie Database
Internet World Stats
Inter-Parliamentary Union
Ladies Professional Golf Association
Man Booker Prize
Marketingcharts.com
Phil Matcham
Chris Mead
Ministry of Public Security (China)
Minova
MRIB
MTV
Music Information Database
National Academy of Recording Arts and
Sciences (Grammy Awards)
National Aeronautics and Space
Administration
National Basketball Association
National Center for Education Statistics
National Football League
National Statistics
National Trust

Natural History Museum, London
AC Nielsen
Nielsen Media Research
Nobel Foundation
NSS GEO2 Committee on Long and Deep
Caves
Official UK Charts
Online Computer Library Center
Organisation for Economic Co-operation and
Development
Organisation Internationale des Constructeurs
d'Automobiles
Roberto Ortiz de Zarate
People's Dispensary of Sick Animals
Periodical Publishers Association
Population Reference Bureau
Professional Golfers' Association
Railway Gazette International
RAJAR
River Systems of the World
Rolling Stone magazine
Royal Aeronautical Society
Royal Astronomical Society
Royal Opera House, Covent Garden
Screen Digest
Screen International
Robert Senior
Shakespeare Centre
Sotheby's
Statistics Denmark
Stockholm International Peace Research
Institute
Stores
Transparency International
The Tree Register of the British Isles
UIC Railisa Database
United Nations
United Nations Educational, Scientific and
Cultural Organization
United Nations Environment Programme
United Nations Population Division
United Nations Statistics Division
Universal Postal Union
US Census Bureau
US Census Bureau International Data Base
Lucy T. Verma
Ward's Motor Vehicle Facts & Figures 2008
World Association of Newspapers
World Atlas of Coral Reefs
World Bank
World Christian Database
World Conservation Monitoring Centre
World Development Indicators (World Bank)
World Health Organization
World Nuclear Association
World Population Data Sheet 2008
(Population Reference Bureau)
World Register of Large Dams
World Resources Institute
World Tennis Association
World Tourism Organization
The World's Mangroves 1980–2005 (FAO)
Jarosław Maciej Zawadzki, *1000
Najpopularniejszych Nazwisk w Polsce*
(2002)

Picture Credits

Corbis: 4b, 141 Juan Medina/Reuters; 5tl, 62-63 Kevin Dodge; 5tr, 108b Chen Wei/EyePress/epa; 5b, 199 G. Bowater; 12t, 95tl Roger Ressmeyer; 13tl Gianni Dagli Orti; 13bl Michael Jenner; 25 Francesc Muntada; 26 Michel Gounot/Godong; 27t, 91l Fridmar Damm/zefa; 29tr Winfried Wisniewski/zefa; 29tr (inset) Tim Davis; 30-31 Kimimasa Mayama/Reuters; 36l Tim Davis; 36r Martin B. Withers/Frank Lane Picture Agency; 38br Patrick Bennett; 40-41b Paul Souders; 45t Joe McDonald; 46bl Esther Beaton; 49tl Steven Vidler/Eurasia Press; 49tr Mak Remissa/epa; 55 Stringer/India/Reuters; 56l, 73b, 110, 124b, 136t, 140l, 148tr, 203b Bettmann; 56r Jose Mendez/epa; 57b Dani Cardona/Reuters; 59t Finbarr O'Reilly/Reuters; 68 Noah K. Murray/Star Ledger; 71b Lucas Dolega/epa; 74b, 75b Corbis; 76bl Pool/Reuters; 76br Altaf Qadri/epa; 79br Badri Media/epa; 80-81 Christian Schmidt/zefa; 83tl Amit Bhargava; 83tr Gavin Hellier/Robert Harding World Imagery; 86b Valdrin Xhemaj/epa; 88tl Qin Huai/Xinhua Press; 88tr The Francis Frith Collection; 91r Bruno Domingos/Reuters; 93t Arctic-Images; 94tl PoodlesRock; 94tc Chip East/Reuters; 94tr Jim Zuckerman; 95tr Ludovic Maisant/Hemis; 96l Ramin Talaie; 97r OMA/epa; 98 Chan Shu Kai; 98-99 Michael S. Lewis; 99tl Richard Cummins; 100tr, 105t, 181b Reuters; 101b Philippe Caron/Sygma; 107t Pallava Bagla; 109b Jason Hawkes; 111, 192-193 Blaine Harrington III; 113t Anders Wiklund/epa; 117br, 193b Atlantide Phototravel; 119t Andy Rain/epa; 121, 128 Mario Anzuoni/Reuters; 122 Michael Ochs Archives; 123 Rune Hellestad; 124tl Kalaene Jens/dpa; 125tr Neal Preston; 129l Stephane Cardinale/People Avenue; 129r Karoly Arvai/Reuters; 130tr Tobias Hase/epa; 130b Tobias Hase/dpa; 131b Jacek Bednarczyk/epa; 132 Kieran Doherty/Reuters; 133t Rick Nederstigt/epa; 133b Chip Somodevilla/Pool; 135t David Farrell/Lebrecht Music & Arts; 136b Underwood & Underwood; 136-137, 139b Hulton-Deutsch Collection; 137b Royal Mail/Handout/Reuters; 138 Joel Brodsky; 139t Steve Pope/epa; 145t, 149b Robbie Jack; 167 Ryan Pyle; 172 Keren Su; 175bl Ming Ming/Reuters; 177tl Matthew Cavanaugh/epa; 177bl Alessia Pierdomenico/Reuters; 177br CSPA/NewSport; 178bl ELTA/Reuters; 179b Lester Lefkowitz; 180tl Jose Fuste Raga; 181t Liba Taylor; 183b Michele Falzone/JAI; 185r Jean Michel Foujols/zefa; 187br Murat Taner/zefa; 189cr Jon Feingersh/zefa; 191t Peter M. Wilson; 193t Yuriko Nakao/Reuters; 197t Everett Kennedy Brown/epa; 201t Ludovic Maisant; 201b Shanghai Sanya/Redlink; 205t Thomas Frey/dpa; 209r, 214-215t Gero Breloer/epa; 210tr Liu Dawei/Xinhua Press; 211 Jiao Weiping/Xinhua Press; 213 Fei Maohua/Xinhua Press; 224t Eric Lalmand/epa; 227t Ben Radford; 228l Chris Williams/Icon SMI; 229c Leo Mason; 229b STR/epa; 230t Jochen Luebke/epa; 231t Andrew Gompert/epa; 232-233 George Tiedemann/GT Images; 233t How Hwee Young/epa; 233b Schlegelmilch; 236 Christophe Karaba/epa; 237 Rhona Wise/epa; 238 Tom Fox/Dallas Morning News; 239 Pascal Lauener/Reuters; 242b Bartomiej Zborowski/PAP; 244t Fred Prouser/Reuters.

Fotolia: 5cl, 182 pressmaster; 5cr, 228r, 229t sebastiankiek; 16t Kwest; 16b NatUlrich; 22-23b, 234-235 Sean Gladwell; 24 moodboard; 24tr Andy Mac; 27b Earl Robbins; 28t wildman; 28c Suto Norbert; 28b Gildas Douessin; 29b imageteam; 30l sparky; 30c Sebastian Kaulitzki; 30r Gudellaphoto; 31r grivelphoto; 33 Monty Chandler; 34-35b Eric Gevaert; 36-37t Nici Heuke; 37r, 42tr, 42-43b, 44t, 48cl, 48cr Eric Isséleer; 38t kristian sekulic; 38cl Makhnach; 38cr Papo; 42tl Perrush; 43tl Johanna Goodyear; 44b Cynthia Warner-Dobrowski; 45b Mirko Milutinovic; 46tl Patricia Elfreth; 47tr Jamie Wilson; 47br, 49b vnlit; 48t Alison Cornford-Matheson; 48c 'c'; 48b klikk; 50t Olga Lyubkina; 50cl momanuma; 50cr ann triling; 51t & cbr eyewave; 51ctl SergioPh; 51cbl Maciej Mamro; 51cbc arnowssr; 51cr Werg; 51-52b Kudryashka; 52t Alex; 52c zentilia; 58t Jose Manuel Gelpi; 58-59b (background) nra; 60tl Nikola Bilic; 60bl Tomislav Forgo; 60r angelo.gi; 61t, 150b Gino Santa Maria; 61b Hallgerd; 64 tl, second tl, ctl & second bl, 65ctr, cbr & br moonrun; 64bl KeepCoolBaby; 64cbl saschi79; 64-65 Antonio Nunes; 65tr chrisharvey; 66t Michael Drager; 66b, 155tl TimurD; 69b, 142b, 143b James Steidl; 70b ckalt; 70-71t Kasia Biel; 72bl, 189bcr Elena Elisseeva; 72br, 73tr, 75tr Victoria Martensson; 75tl Leo; 75tr Piter Pkruger; 76tl, 77tr sabri deniz kizil; 76tr Elnur; 77tl Cmon; 78bl Vladimir Mucibabic; 78br Pavlo Perets; 78-79t Jose Alves; 81tr objectsforall; 82t Anobis; 82b AlienCat; 83b bornholm; 85 iofoto; 90t Miqul; 90b broker; 92-93c RTimages; 94-95b iofoto; 103, 116-117 (insets) JChMedinger; 104l, 112r, 226t & r Andrzej Tokarski; 104tr RTimages; 104br janaka Dharmasena; 105b, 186tl ZTS; 106r Daniel Burch; 108t Volodymyr Kyrylyuk; 110-111 Renato Francia; 112-113 milosluz; 114l Palabra; 116tl, 117tl Michael Flippo; 116tr, 117tr Aleksey Bakaleev; 116b ZDM; 118t & b Igor Nikolayev; 118c clearviewstock; 118c (inset) ktsdesign; 119b Stephen Coburn; 124-125t foxygrl; 126-127t Julydfg; 130tl, 142tr DWP; 131t Yuri Arcurs; 134t waltart; 144t Laura Lévy; 144b sumnersgraphicsinc; 144-145b Sherri Camp; 145b Carolina K Smith MD; 148-149t Irochka; 152-153t Julian Addington-Barker; 152-153 Olga Mishyna; 154tr ville ahonen; 154br Dušan Zidar; 154-155 Vladimir Wrangel; 155bl Alexander Glagolev; 155bc marc hericher; 155br Victoria Short; 160-161t Tommroch; 162b Pavel Losevsky; 164t G.Light; 165b, 168t Michelle Robek; 168bl Freehand; 168br Ilja Mašík; 171 Franz Pfluegl; 176l Robert Ainsworth; 176r Vladyslav Danilin; 178 Nikos; 178tr Farouk Laboudi; 179tl Eray Haciosmanoglu; 179tr Anton Bryksin; 180tr Marko Plevnjak; 180b Artyshot; 184tl Denis Pepin; 184tr, 185tl & bl Harris Shiffman; 184bl Liv Friis-larsen; 186c Luminis; 186br davidjmorgan; 187l SWT; 187tr Matthew Bowden; 188tl Paul Binet; 188tr Fotolia VI; 188cl picamaniac; 188bl & bcr Maria.P.; 188bcl Markus Mohr; 188br Greg; 189tl broker; 189tr gunnar3000; 189bl & bc robynmac; 189br Graça Victoria; 190 Monika Adamczyk; 191b Okea; 192 Gabriel-Ciscardi; 196t Krom; 196cr awx; 196-197b Alvin Teo; 196-197b (background) Simon Pow; 202-203t mite; 204t enrique ayuso; 204c xiver; 204bl rimglow; 204bcl Jose Vazquez; 204bcr Yong Hian Lim; 204br Philophoto; 205bl Dmitry Rukhlenko; 205bcl & br steamroller; 205bc Olga Shelego; 205bcr, 245br Andres Rodriguez; 206-207 surpasspro; 209l, 220r Albo; 210 TFphotos; 210b Ramin Khojasteh; 212r Dariusz Kopestynski; 214-215b Accent ; 218 Peter Baxter; 218br Jean-Luc Cochonneau; 219t Nessquick; 219c Stacy Barnett; 220l Ana Vasileva; 222t Howard; 222c Christos Georghiou; 223t Sportlibrary; 224b sharply_done; 226-227b rotschwarzpdm; 230-231b TMAX; 240cl & cr, 241t davorr; 240b kathy libby; 240-241 Torsten Wenzler; 244b picsfive; 245tl 2windspa; 247 Aramanda.

Getty Images: 4t, 46-47b Colin Keates/Dorling Kindersley; 43tr Tim Flach; 46-47t Frank Greenaway; 57t Theo Westenberger; 67 Bhutan Government DIT; 69t Sven Creutzmann/Mambo Photo; 70t University Of Pennsylvania; 77b Scott Nelson; 78-79b VCL/Chris Ryan; 112l Mark Mainz; 114tr Manpreet Romana/AFP; 115t Khin Maung Win/AFP; 126tr Keystone; 127b, 137t Michael Ochs Archives; 134b Ethan Miller; 135b Serge Thomann/WireImage; 140r Maria R. Bastone/AFP; 148bl Gjon Mili/Time Life Pictures; 173t Tang Chhin Sothy/AFP; 173b Mitchell Kanashkevich; 174bl Robyn Beck/AFP; 174-175tc Philippe Huguen/AFP; 198 Melanie Stetson Freeman/The Christian Science Monitor; 217 Tom Shaw; 218bl Craig Hacker; 219b Bryn Lennon; 221 Ron Hoskins/NBAE; 222bl, 234 Toshifumi Kitamura/AFP; 223b John Shearer/WireImage for BWR Public Relations; 225b Andreas Solaro/AFP; 230c Andrew Yates/AFP; 235 Greg Wood/AFP; 240tl Brian Bahr; 241b Agence Zoom; 242t Phillip Ellsworth/WireImage; 243 Prakash Mathema/AFP.

iStockphoto: 6-7b Oleg Prikhodko; 20t linearcurves; 22tl, 31l jtgray; 58-59b Jill Fromer; 65bl blackred; 78-79c iStockphoto.com; 86-87 Valerie Loiseleux; 87r Albert Campbell; 88b Evgeniy Ivanov; 89b Mike Bentley; 92t Lachlan Currie; 92-93b Hugo Lacasse; 106l & 107bl Jonathan Werve; 106-107 Yasinguneysu; 108-109 Stock photo; 114-115 Don Bayley; 126bl Julie de Leseleuc; 126br Lise Gagne; 154tl Stephen Shockley; 166 Sergei Ivlev; 183t Andres Peiro Palmer; 184br juicybits; 189bcl Malcolm Romaine; 195 Stephen Strathdee; 225t Björn Kindler.

The Kobal Collection: 4cr, 156, 163, 169 Dreamworks; 142tl, 158t Warner Bros.; 143t Universal/Playtone; 147, 159l Walt Disney; 150t Warner Bros/DC Comics; 151 Danjaq/EON/UA; 152bl, 154bl, 165t MGM; 153br New Line Cinema/Vinet, Pierre; 155tr Columbia; 157 20th Century Fox; 158b Lucasfilm/Paramount Pictures; 159r Warner Bros./Bailey, Alex; 160b Walt Disney Pictures/Walden Media/Bray, Phil; 161t Dreamworks/Warner Bros./Morton, Merrick; 161b 20th Century Fox/Pera, Diyah; 162t 20th Century Fox/Wetcher, Barry.

NASA: 3, 13tr Jet Propulsion Laboratory; 4cl, 14-15 NASA; 9, 11 Space Telescope Science Institute; 12 Jet Propulsion Laboratory-Caltech; 14t, 15t Johnson Space Center; 4cl, 14-15 NASA; 31c Image courtesy of MODIS Rapid Response Project at NASA/GSFC.

PA Photos: 218t Niall Carson/PA Archive/PA Photos.

Peter Bull Art Studio: 27br (artwork).

Photolibrary: 17 J-C & D. Pratt; 18 Steve Vidier; 19, 107br Photolibrary; 20-21 Michael Snell; 22-23t Chad Ehlers; 35r David Paynter; 39 David B Fleetham; 41l Mark Jones; 41r Mike Hill; 52b Vladimir Medvedev; 53l Roberto Rinaldi; 53r Walter Choroszewski; 97l JTB Photo; 100-101t Yann Guichaoua; 109r Angelo Tondini; 115b Daniel Thierry; 200 Ken Gillham.

Rex Features: 5tc, 96r Sipa Press.

Science Photo Library: 34t Roger Harris.

TopFoto: 14b RIA Novosti; 73cr ullsteinbild; 149c Clive Barda/ArenaPAL; 202b Topfoto.

Publisher's Acknowledgements
Cover design by Grade Design Consultants
www.gradedesign.com

Packager's Acknowledgements
Palazzo Editions would like to thank Richard Constable and James Hollywell for their design contributions.